The Day Has Come!

Easter and Baptism in Zeno of Verona

Alcuin Club Collection Number 73

Gordon P. Jeanes

The Alcuin Club

THE LITURGICAL PRESS
Collegeville, Minnesota

Cover design by David Manahan, O.S.B.

Copyright © 1995 The Alcuin Club, Runcorn, Chesire, United Kingdom. Published by The Liturgical Press, Collegeville, Minnesota 56321. Printed in the United States of America.

1	2	3	4	5	6	7	8

Library of Congress Cataloging-in-Publication Data

Zeno, Saint, Bishop of Verona, d. 371.
   [Sermons. English. Selections]
   The day has come! : Easter and baptism in Zeno of Verona / compiled and edited by Gordon P. Jeanes.
      p.   cm. — (Alcuin Club collection ; no. 73)
   Includes bibliographical references.
   ISBN 0-8146-2341-7
   1. Easter—Sermons—Early works to 1800.   2. Sermons, Latin—Early works to 1800.   3. Sermons, Latin—Translations into English.   4. Baptism—Sermons—Early works to 1800. 5. Baptism—History—Early church, ca. 30–600.   6. Easter—History.   7. Paschal mystery—History of doctrines—Early church, ca. 30–600.   8. Liturgies, Early Christian—History.   9. Zeno, Saint, Bishop of Verona, d. 371.
I. Jeanes, Gordon P. II. Title. III. Series: Alcuin Club collections ; no. 73.
BX5141.A1A6   no. 73.
[BR65.Z462E5]
200 s—dc20   95-4792
[252′.014]   CIP

*To Arthur and Hilda
and to Mary-Jane*

CONTENTS

Preface . . . . *ix*

Abbreviations . . . . *xi*

Introduction 1

   I.   Zeno, Bishop of Verona 5
        1. Earlier Studies of Zeno 5
        2. Biographical Details 7
        3. The Cult of Zeno of Verona 17

  II.   The Sermons and the Manuscripts 20
        1. The Problem of the Sermon Collection 20
        2. The Arrangement of Sermons in the
           Manuscripts 22
           i.   The Paschal Groups of Sermons 23
           ii. The Non-Paschal Groups of
               Sermons 25
        3. The Relation of the Texts of the
          Sermons to the Sermons Preached 29
        4. A Critique of Löfstedt's Account 31
        5. Zeno's Sermons as Drafts Preserved
          Verbatim 43
        6. Some Details of the Manuscripts 49
           i.   The Place of the Fragmentary
               Sermons 49
           ii. The Titles of Sermons II.26; 28; 30 . . . 50
           iii. *Item* in the Titles of Sermons 51
        7. The Integrity of the Sermon Collection . . . 51

III.   Zeno of Verona: The Sermons
       Delivered at the Paschal Vigil 54

IV.   The Paschal Sermons 100
      1. The *Disciplina Arcani* 101
      2. The Sermons of the Paschal Vigil 105
         i.   The Paschal Proclamation
              (Praefatio Paschalis) 108
         ii. The Sermons on Genesis
              (De Genesi) 112
         iii. The Sermons on Exodus 12
              (De Exodo) 117
         iv. The Sermons on Exodus 14
              (De sequentia Exodi) 119
         v.   The Sermons on Isaiah *(De Esaia)* 121
              a. The Sermons on Isaiah 1 121
              b. The Sermons on Isaiah 5 123
         vi. The Sermons on Daniel
              (Tractatus Danielis) 127
         vii. The Invitation to the Font
              (Invitatio fontis) 128
         viii. The Post-Baptismal Sermons
              (Post traditum baptisma) 130
      3. The Lenten and Post-Easter
         Catechesis 137
         i.   Sermons from the Lenten Catechesis . . 137
         ii. Sermons from the Post-Easter
              Catechesis 140
      4. The Overall Vision of the Sermons 146

V.   The Paschal and Baptismal Liturgy 149
      1. A Summary of the Rite 149
      2. Sermons Describing the Whole Process
         of Initiation 152
         i.   An Allegory of the Seasons 152
         ii. An Allegory of Viticulture 153

iii. An Allegory of Wheat 154
iv. The Christian's 'Daily Pay' 155
3. The Rite in the Baptistery
Seen as a Whole 157
4. Preparatory Rites 165
5. Pre-Baptismal Anointing and
Renunciation 166
i. The Pre-Baptismal Anointing 167
ii. The Renunciations 171
iii. *Effeta/Apertio?* 173
6. From the Church to the Baptistery 174
7. The Blessing of the Font 177
8. Stripping 178
9. Immersion 178
10. The Post-Baptismal Anointing 179
11. The Sign of the Cross 182
12. The Denarius 182
13. A Possible Formula of Chrismation 186
14. The White Garments 188
15. Procession from the Font 188
16. The Paschal Eucharist 190
17. The Eucharistic Prayer in Verona 191
i. A Reference to Melchizedek 191
ii. A Reference to Abraham 194
18. Other Ceremonies at Easter 197
19. The Vigil in the Context of
Other Rites 198
i. The Use of Sermons Accompanying
the Readings 198
ii. The Selection of Readings in Various
Lectionaries 200
20. Zeno's Rite of Baptism in the Context
of Other Rites 206
i. Pre-Baptismal Anointings 208
ii. The Renunciations 210
iii. The Immersion 211

       iv. Post-Baptismal Anointing 211
       v.   A Simple or Magnificent Rite? 212
    21. Limitations and Insights 213
  VI. Zeno's Theology of Baptism 215
    1. Reading the Sermons 215
    2. The Attitudes and Reactions of
       Candidates During the Ceremonies 216
    3. The Communication of Initiation
       through Its Sensual Aspects 220
    4. The Theology of Easter Day 223
    5. Baptism as Entering into Divine
       History 226
    6. The Theme of *Imago/Veritas* 231
    7. The Devil and the Baptismal
       Liturgy 235
    8. The First Anointing—For
       Forgiveness 239
    9. Baptism and Martyrdom 241
    10. Guilt and Judgement 245
    11. Zeno's Treatment of the
       Theme of Water 247
    12. The Holy Spirit in Baptism 250
    13. Baptism as Regeneration 251
    14. Images of Unity 252
    15. Two Theologies of Baptism? 255

Conclusion 259

Appendix 261
Table of Sermons in Their Various Groups
Showing Their Role and Content

Bibliography 265

Index of Proper Names 272

Index of Sermons 279

PREFACE

Nearly fourteen years have passed from when I began this study of the sermons of Zeno of Verona until its preparation for publication, a far longer time (according to my own calculations at least) than that of Zeno's own episcopate. As I complete the study I am aware not only of the immense effort it involved but above all of the support, encouragement, help, and toleration given me by so many people. First and foremost my thanks must go to Fr. Edward Yarnold, S.J., who initiated me first to the study of liturgy and then to the sermons of Zeno himself. What is more, he freely gave much time, encouragement, and advice, and virtually every page of this work owes something to him through his knowledgeable insights and critical questions. Campion Hall became a familiar haunt (more so even than in my undergraduate days) and I owe a debt of thanks to Father Yarnold and the Society for their kind hospitality and friendship over the years.

Among others' support I must mention especially the Warden of Keble College and the trustees of the Liddon Theological Studentships, who kindly set me on my way with a grant for the purchase of books, and to my own Merton College and to the Convent of the Sisters of the Church at Ham Common who by their hospitality enabled me to make solid progress in my research away from the pressures of parish life. But I would never have had the confidence to carry on without the unfailing support of my bishops, fellow clergy, and congregations. Kenneth Stevenson who examined the thesis on which this is based has made many helpful comments;

I am grateful to him and to Bryan Spinks, Donald Gray, and Michael Perham for their help in preparing the work for publication. To Mary-Jane, who has perhaps heard more of Zeno than she would care to, and shown great patience throughout the enterprise, I owe particular thanks.

ABBREVIATIONS

AIR	E. Yarnold, *Awe-Inspiring Rites of Initiation.* Slough, 1972.
Ap. Trad.	Hippolytus, *The Apostolic Tradition.* Ed. B. Botte, *La Tradition Apostolique de Saint Hippolyte.* Münster Westfalen, 1963.
BA	L. L. Mitchell, *Baptismal Anointing.* London, 1966.
CCL	Corpus Christianorum Latinorum. Turnholt, 1954ff.
CSEL	Corpus Scriptorum Ecclesiasticorum Latinorum. Vienna, 1866ff.
DBL	E. C. Whitaker, *Documents of the Baptismal Liturgy,* 2nd ed. London, 1970.
De myst.	Ambrose, *De mysteriis.* Ed. B. Botte (Sources Chrétiennes 25 bis). Paris, 1960.
De sac.	Ambrose, *De sacramentis.* Ed. B. Botte (Sources Chrétiennes 25 bis). Paris, 1960.
HBS	Henry Bradshaw Society. London, 1891ff.
Löfstedt	B. Löfstedt, *Zenonis Veronensis tractatus.* Corpus Christianorum Latinorum 22. Turnholt, 1971.
PG	Patrologia Graeca. Ed. J.-P. Migne. Paris, 1857ff.
PL	Patrologia Latina. Ed. J.-P. Migne. Paris, 1844ff.
SC	Sources Chrétiennes. Paris, 1942ff.
SL	*The Study of Liturgy.* Ed. C. Jones and others. London, 1992.
Truzzi	Truzzi, C., *Zeno, Gaudenzio e Cromazio.* Brescia, 1985.

INTRODUCTION

Zeno was a revered bishop of Verona when Ambrose was a prominent civil servant, Jerome was a young man experimenting with asceticism, and Augustine was a boy in his teens. When we look for details of Church life and thought in the late Roman Empire we might easily turn to these three famous writers, and with profit. Behind them lies the background of a Latin Christianity that was confident but still small, where the older generation had lived through the reigns of emperors who were pagan, Christian (Catholic or Arian), or apostate; where Church festivals were few and far between, and concentrated on the Sunday Eucharist, the feasts of martyrs, anniversaries, and above all Easter Day. There was no Holy Week as the next generation would understand it. Christmas, or Epiphany, and Pentecost would be known to many. But for the small, conservative congregations scattered throughout Italy, the concept of a Christian year meant above all the one Day of the Resurrection, the first of days. Of this Church Zeno is our best witness.

The sermons of Zeno of Verona are the oldest surviving collection of Latin sermons. What makes them even more important is that they are among the comparatively few documents portraying for us the Church in the West, the poor cousin, as it were, of the Greek East with its flourishing life and fierce disputes, and the parent of the later Western Church shaped by Augustine, Ambrose, Jerome, and their generation who would dominate the later Empire and Western Christendom. Zeno exemplifies the confidence of the Church as it grew in numbers and influence under the fragile protection of emperors. He presents to us a portrait of the life of the North Italian congregation and of the bishop presiding over it at its festivals.

Central to this study is a translation of the sermons preached by Zeno at the Easter Vigil, the first time that they have all been translated into English. (There remain some thirty other sermons, many much longer, untranslated.) Recent studies of Zeno have worked with the suspicion that many of the sermons were reworked by later hands. Here however we set out with full confidence in the integrity of the text as preserving for us more than sixty sermons preached at the paschal Vigil by Zeno over some eight years. In the light of this approach a full and detailed examination of the liturgical practices gives us new and important insights into the paschal and baptismal rites. Most importantly, we have by far the earliest description of the paschal Vigil and its lectionary of readings in the Western Church. Next we have many references to the baptismal rites. Zeno has a curious style of speaking which is both concrete in its imagery and allusive—and elusive—in its references. It will be seen that understanding precisely what he is referring to is often no easy matter, but the task has been undertaken and, in the context of other approximately contemporary rites, the baptismal rite of Verona is explored, described, and takes its proper place in the history of liturgy. That proper place is one of great importance, for Zeno is our only source in the West for the period immediately before Ambrose. Also Zeno's sermons have a different setting from those of Ambrose. The latter describe events in detail after they have occurred and expound the liturgical formulae. The former give us a kind of running commentary as the ceremonies happen. We rarely learn the formulae, but we have a unique and precious insight into the rites as they are presented to the candidates for baptism. Occasionally we can identify a liturgical phrase, and it is indeed fortunate that we can find in Zeno the earliest reference that we can date with confidence to the Latin tradition of the Eucharistic Prayer as we find it in the Roman Canon.

Zeno's own theological understanding of Easter and baptism has never been properly investigated. Here we shall follow his thoughts as they are presented in the sermons, filled as they are with images and symbolism rather than with abstract concepts. Zeno is allowed to speak for himself, as it were, and he speaks about salvation with a language that is both familiar and strange. Just as the liturgy in his day was developing, so also was the theological understanding of baptism. New emphases were coming to the fore and blending themselves with traditional insights. In baptism the Church was defining its new position in the post-Constantinian world and we see Zeno sharing in the search for a new meaning.

There is no way in which Zeno can be presented as equal in importance to Ambrose, Jerome, or Augustine. He was far inferior intellectually, he was no giant on the stage then for his contemporaries and he cannot be now for historians. But to acknowledge this is by no means to underestimate his importance. As a witness to the liturgical and theological norms of his day it is his very unimportance and his ordinariness that represent his historical value. As a theologian and a preacher, in both respects with his own unique style and his own distinctive use of Scripture, only in recent years has he been better appreciated. This study hopefully goes some way in furthering that appreciation.

Chapter One
ZENO, BISHOP OF VERONA

1. EARLIER STUDIES OF ZENO

Zeno's life, the origin of the manuscript tradition of his sermons, and his own fame will be discussed below. At this stage a summary of previously printed editions of his sermons and scholarly studies will be of use. Zeno was greatly admired by the humanists for his style, and was dubbed the 'Christian Cicero'.[1] The first printed edition was made in 1508 in Venice by P. A. Castellanus and J. de Leuco. Another edition was made by R. Bagata and B. Peretti in Verona in 1586, and this was used in subsequent collections. The edition in 1739 by the Ballerini brothers was used in Migne's *Patrologia Latina,* volume 11, and so has been the text best known to scholars in recent years. In this edition the sermons were arranged according to subject matter rather than their order in the manuscripts, and were accompanied by introductory material and a commentary, all reprinted in Migne along with other material. A modern critical edition has been made by B. Löfstedt, who has presented the sermons in their original manuscript order.[2] It is this edition which will be used in this

[1]L. Palanca, *The Prose Rhythm and Gorgianic Figures in the Sermons of St Zeno of Verona* (Ph.D. dissertation, Washington, D.C., 1970) 9.

[2]B. Löfstedt, ed., *Zenonis Veronensis tractatus,* CCL 22 (Turnholt, 1971). Löfstedt includes a summary of all the previous editions (p. 3) and a critique of them (pp. 46*ff.). For a critique of Löfstedt's edition, see F. Dolbeau, 'Zenoniana: Recherches sur le texte et sur la tradition de Zénon de Vérone,' *Recherches Augustiniennes* 20 (1985) 3–34 (also summarising previous articles).

study unless mention is made to the contrary, and the translation of the Vigil sermons are presented in Löfstedt's order and numbering.

Among the studies made, particular mention may be made of several. Most recently, Carlo Truzzi has made a most useful study of Zeno along with Gaudentius of Brescia and Chromatius of Aquileia.[3] This work presents us with both a comprehensive portrait of the three writers and, in extensive footnotes, a survey of the work of previous scholars. For the purposes of this study, the following works are most pertinent and will be referred to frequently in detail.

The Ballerini, as has been mentioned above, accompanied their text with a commentary and with introductory material which, still for us three centuries later, contains a wealth of useful information and many important insights. For Zeno's date and biographical details, A. Grazioli presents us with a wealth of detail,[4] and A. Bigelmair has been most important in his studies, including a refinement of the Ballerini's study of the dating.[5]

The sermons themselves have been subject to considerable study in recent years, both for their content and for their unique form, since some two-thirds are extremely short and are set in a paschal context. The most recent scholarly opinion is set out by Löfstedt and followed by Truzzi, namely that the shorter sermons as we possess them today were reworked for liturgical purposes. (It will be seen below that I believe that they are all from the pen of Zeno and that they represent his *ipsissima verba*.) Palanca's study demonstrates the consistently competent, indeed elegant, style which supports the theory of a single author's work untouched by later editorial hands.[6]

[3]Carlo Truzzi, *Zeno, Gaudenzio e Cromazio* (Brescia, 1985).

[4]A. Grazioli, 'San Zenone di Verona', *La scuola Cattolica* 68 (1940) 174–99.

[5]A. Bigelmair, *Zeno von Verona* (Münster Westfalen, 1904); *Des heiligen Bischofs Zeno von Verona Traktate* (Munich, 1934).

[6]Palanca, 'Prose Rhythm'.

The liturgical customs referred to by Zeno have been examined by various writers, as we can see in Truzzi's survey. But all of these have been brief, even B. Pesci's study, 'De Christianarum antiquitatum institutionibus in S. Zenonis Veronensis Episcopi sermonibus'.[7] This present study attempts to examine the sermons in detail and to establish as far as possible the liturgical details of the paschal and baptismal rites, and to set them in the context of the rites described by other Western writers.

Zeno's theology has been the subject of a very brief survey by G. de Paoli.[8] Here again a much more detailed examination will be made, which presents a very full portrait of Zeno's theological method and his use of conventional baptismal themes in a highly personal manner.

It has been necessary for reasons of clarity and space to ignore much of great interest in the sermons. Zeno's place in the doctrinal conflicts of the fourth century is not studied here; his imaginative use of Scripture is noted occasionally but would be a study in its own right. We must perforce limit ourselves to an examination of his paschal sermons, to unravelling the liturgical detail and bringing to life the thoughts and mannerisms of a bishop in a period of which we know little, but which is so important for our understanding of the Church in the late Roman Empire.

2. BIOGRAPHICAL DETAILS

Of Zeno himself we know virtually nothing. In his sermons his character and outlook come across clearly. But before we begin our study of the sermons, we must pause to review what little we know of his biographical details.

---

[7]B. Pesci, *Antonianum* 23 (1948) 33–42.

[8]G. de Paoli, 'L'iniziazione cristiana nei Sermoni di S. Zeno di Verona', *Rivista liturgica* 54 (1967) 407–17. De Paoli has also examined the liturgy of Zeno in an unpublished thesis, for which I have had to rely on Truzzi's comments.

First it is important to know precisely when Zeno was bishop of Verona, so that we are able to assess his true role and importance in the history of the Western Church. Conditions and customs were changing quickly in the second half of the fourth century, and it is obviously an advantage to be as precise as possible. There is no firm evidence of dates, but all that we do have, each piece of evidence being somewhat vague in itself, points consistently to a date around A.D. 370. External evidence and internal evidence concur in this, and will be treated together.[9]

For establishing the dates when Zeno was bishop of Verona, we can most conveniently start with the lists of bishops of Verona in the *Velo di Classe* and the *Versus de Verona*.[10] Although these documents date from around the second half of the eighth and the first half of the ninth centuries, their lists are held to be historically accurate. Both give the same list of bishops: Euprepius (the first bishop of Verona), Dimidrianus, Simplicius, Proculus, Saturninus, Lucilius, Gricinus, Zeno, Agapitus, Lucius, Siagrius.

Zeno's predecessor but one, Lucilius (or Lucillus) was present at the Council of Sardica in 345, and his name is mentioned by Athanasius among those still alive at the time of his writing—ca. 353-56.[11] This date must be the absolute *terminus post quem* for the beginning of Zeno's episcopate in Verona, and we must still allow for his immediate predecessor, Gricinus. For the date of his death, there is a *terminus post quem* in that Zeno quotes from Hilary of Poitiers's *Commentary on the Psalms,* which was written around 364-67.[12] However he does not quote any later writer, even Ambrose, whose literary activity began around 377, so it would seem that he

[9]There has never been any suggestion that the sermons are wrongly ascribed to Zeno. Truzzi (50-52) in his review of the evidence affirms that the ascription of the sermons is correct.

[10]C. Cipolla, 'Il Velo di Classe', in *Le gallerie nazionali Italiane,* vol. 3 (Rome, 1897) 195-249. G. B. Pighi, *Versus de Verona* (Bologna, 1960).

[11]Athanasius, *Apol. ad Constantium* 3. Truzzi, 52.

[12]Truzzi, 52.

may not have lived long after the former date.

It has been held by some writers that Zeno referred in a sermon to the battle of Adrianople of 378. However the references in question are not relevant to Adrianople or to any other military disaster but reflect stock literary types.[13] Therefore the battle cannot be used as a *terminus post quem.*

We do have a *terminus ante quem* for Zeno's death in Ambrose's letter to his successor but two, Siagrius. He refers to Zeno as having consecrated a virgin who now after many years (*post tot annos*) is the victim of various accusations. Zeno himself is dead, being described as 'of holy memory' (*sanctae memoriae*). This letter is traditionally dated 380 but is placed by many writers towards the end of Ambrose's episcopate in 397.[14] We must remember that Siagrius was the third bishop after Zeno, and Ambrose is looking back over *tot annos,* so that, unless Agapitus and Lucius had very short reigns indeed, we would be prudent to suggest an early date for Zeno's own episcopate. If the earlier date for Ambrose's letter is correct, we must assume an early date for Zeno and/or two exceedingly short episcopates after him.

Zeno must have been bishop for at least eight Easters since, as we shall see, we have that number of paschal sermons.

All the dates and details given so far are consistent in giving the following approximate chronology:

Lucilius	*floruit* ca. 353–56
Gricinus	
Zeno	*floruit* post 364–67
Agapitus	
Lucius	
Siagrius	*floruit* ante 397

[13]See G. P. Jeanes, 'The Paschal and Baptismal Sermons of Zeno of Verona' (B.D. Thesis, Oxford 1989) 14–19.

[14]Letter 1.5.1. For the earlier date cf. A. di Berardino, *Patrology* vol. 4, trans. P. Solari, O.S.B. (Westminster, Md.: 1991) 127. For the later date see H. Dudden, *The Life and Times of Saint Ambrose,* vol. 1 (Oxford, 1935) 154. Cf. Sister Mary Melchior Beyenka, Fathers of the Church 26 (New York, 1954) 152, note 1 to the letter. Truzzi, 48, n. 5.

The date for Zeno based on Hilary's *Commentary* fits well with the dates of the other bishops. We do not have the dates for the bishop before Zeno, or for the two following him, but the law of averages would suggest a shorter period between Lucilius and Zeno than between Zeno and Siagrius. The most reasonable approximate date on the basis of this evidence would be that Zeno was bishop in the 360s and died circa 370.

The Ballerini dated the beginning of Zeno's episcopate more closely on the basis of the traditional day of his consecration as bishop, which is given as 8 December. Since, they reasoned, that day would have been a Sunday, the consecration would have been in 356, 362, or 373. Of these the first is most probably too early to fit Gricinus in the sequence, and 373 is too late to allow for Agapitus and Lucius. (The Ballerini were working on the basis of the traditional date of Ambrose's letter as ca. 380, so this later date for Zeno's consecration is not quite as unlikely as it seemed then.) They concluded that Zeno's episcopate began on 8 December 362.[15] Truzzi describes this theory as 'un'ingegnosa ipotesi', leaving us wondering whether he really approves. But he is willing to describe as 'un'ipotesi non sufficiamente fondata' the theory by Bigelmair that the length of Zeno's episcopate can be accurately calculated from the number of Easter sermons preached as having been eight or nine years, and therefore that he died in 371 or 372.[16] The date of Zeno's death is well known from the liturgical calendars as 12 April.

Bigelmair's suggestion about the length of the episcopate cannot be taken as a claim of certain accuracy. Quite apart from the possibility (albeit unlikely) that some sermons were never preached, there is no way of knowing whether all of the Easter ceremonies at which Zeno presided are represented in the surviving collection of sermons, or indeed how many sets of sermons we are dealing with beyond a minimum of eight. If in fact Bigelmair is correct, Zeno was bishop from 8 December 362 to 12 April 370/371.

[15]PL 11: col. 78C–81B.
[16]Bigelmair, *Zeno von Verona*, 53. Truzzi, 53.

The traditional date of Zeno's consecration as bishop, used by the Ballerini in their theory, has come under some discussion. It was suggested by V. Fainelli that 8 December was in fact the date of the reconsecration of the Church of Saint Zeno between 803 and 810, for such is the description in the old Veronese calendars. This, Fainelli believed, was then confused with the consecration of the bishop.[17] However G. Phillippart has discovered two calendars that predate the Carolingian restoration and that record a feast of Zeno on this day. Furthermore Phillippart notes a possible reference to the season of Advent in the sermon (discussed below) of Petronius of Bologna *In natale s. Zenonis* of the fifth century, though he concedes that the origins of Advent are uncertain. But this again would fit with the traditional date of the consecration of the bishop, often called the *dies natalis*. Phillippart agrees that the Carolingian church seems to have been dedicated on this day, but suggests that the confusion arises simply because the dedication was held on the consecration day of the saint.[18]

Even though the evidence for a *dies natalis* of Zeno on 8 December does seem to predate the restoration in the early ninth century it is difficult to assess how trustworthy it might be for the fourth century. In the light of this kind of uncertainty perhaps Truzzi's cautious appreciation of the ingenuity of the Ballerini's hypothesis is to be followed rather than any confidence in its correctness. This and the theory of Bigelmair, along with my own calculations, even if they are all correct, fit in with what we have reason to believe rather than extend what we know, namely that Zeno was bishop of Verona for some eight years or more, and died circa 370.[19]

[17]V. Fainelli, *Codice diplomatice Veronese,* vol. 1 (Venice, 1940) 92–93; reviewed in *Analecta Bollandiana* 62 (1944) 268–70.

[18]G. Phillippart, 'La Fête de S. Zénon de Vérone le 8 Décembre', *Analecta Bollandiana* 92 (1974) 347–48.

[19]In II.7.5. Zeno while attacking second marriage quotes 1 Corinthians 7:29-31, and says that it was written four hundred years or more ago ('ante annos ferme quadringentos vel eo amplius'). This curious dating would

It might be useful to place Zeno's dates in the context of those of other writers. He would have died only a few years after Hilary of Poitiers (d. 367), the famous defender of orthodoxy against the Arians and one whose books Zeno himself read. It is probable that throughout his episcopacy his metropolitan bishop in Milan was the Arian Auxentius (bishop 355–74), and that Zeno died before the accession of Ambrose. In Rome, Damasus was Pope from 364 to 384. In northern Italy the Church was still small and trying to establish itself in a pagan environment, and Zeno belongs to the generation before Gaudentius of Brescia (ca. 390–410) and Chromatius of Aquileia (ca. 390–408) when the Christian presence was far stronger in numbers and more secure under the government.[20] In Zeno's own time the more notable emperors were Julian (361–63), the would-be restorer of paganism, and Valentinian I (364–75), a Nicene Christian. In 362 a bishop of Verona would have had an Arian metropolitan and a pagan emperor. By 375 both would be Nicene Christians. Zeno lived at the point when much must have seemed in the balance and he would have died before the scales descended in favour of the Nicene party. He also belonged to the last generation be-

---

seem to require either a much later date for Zeno or an hypothesis of textual corruption. However neither is likely. The Ballerini (PL 11: 41–4) quote many parallels for a tendency to round dates upwards. Of these, Philaster of Brescia is especially notable for our purposes, as coming from almost exactly the same time and place as Zeno and presenting a very similar problem. Writing in the period 383–91, Philaster dates the time of our Lord as being 430 years before his own (*Diversarum haereseon liber*, 112 (84), 20). H. J. Lehmann speculates that this number results not so much from exaggeration as from a chronological error, and that Zeno's dating may be linked to Philaster's, depending on the contemporary notions of the world lasting seven thousand years and that Christ was born around the year 5,500. Now, four hundred years or more later, the second coming was imminent, heralding the millennium of the Sabbath rest (H. J. Lehmann, *On Some Round Numbers in Some Patristic Texts* [Aarhus, 1974], 8–9, 13–15).

Obviously this text is of little use for our purposes here of dating Zeno, and the Ballerini and other writers have been right to discount it as evidence while respecting the integrity of the text.

[20]Cf. Truzzi, 321.

fore the great liturgical developments instigated in Jerusalem swept through the West. Cyril of Jerusalem (bishop ca. 349–86) was a contemporary, but one of whom Zeno seems to have been ignorant, and whose liturgical influence is not to be seen in Verona. Egeria, travelling in the East in the 380s, could still treat of the Jerusalem liturgy as a novelty to her sisters in France or Spain, and perhaps, some ten years after Zeno, it would have been a novelty in Verona.

It is typical of the age that Ambrose mentions Zeno in the context of the consecration of a virgin. Athanasius, who had met one of Zeno's predecessors, had helped to make the ascetic life popular in the West. Hilary of Poitiers, whose books Zeno read, was an early pioneer. A contemporary, Eusebius of Vercelli, lived under a common rule with his clergy. In Aquileia the young Chromatius was experimenting with the ascetic life with, among others, the young Jerome. Zeno may have regarded this area as the great new dimension of faith given to his generation, and the paschal ceremonies, for all of his evident care and enthusiasm, may have had the feeling of weighty tradition rather than exciting novelty. For, although Zeno's sermons are the earliest from the Western Church which survive to this day, they obviously represent an ancient and flourishing tradition as well as reflecting the particular needs and issues of the late fourth century. We are extremely fortunate in possessing this rare glimpse, indeed a rich portrait, of a modest but exuberant Church life, in the last years before the stage is crowded by the heroes, Ambrose, Augustine, Jerome, Leo, and the rest, magnificent in the riches of establishment, supported by Catholic emperors in Milan and Constantinople, and learning a new liturgical richness from Jerusalem.

While the dates of Zeno's episcopacy are reasonably clear, other details of his life are almost totally absent, and we can only reconstruct hypotheses from hints in his own writings and the references of other writers and the dubious claims of hagiographers. Of course we might normally have assumed that Zeno was a native Veronese, but hints of foreign origin are sufficient for us to look more closely for influences on his career and his sermons.[21]

There are a number of early writers from whom we learn details (true or false) about Zeno. We have already seen Ambrose's mention of Zeno *sanctae memoriae,* which may assure us that Zeno was, as far as Ambrose was concerned, both a revered bishop and dead. Next we have the sermon of a certain Petronius (discussed below with regard to the cult of the saint) who adds little to what we know from Ambrose.

Writing around 800, Coronatus portrayed Zeno as living a life of humble monasticism in Verona, without any hint of foreign origins.[22] However, there has been constant speculation that Zeno came originally from Africa because of frequent links in his sermons with the Christian culture of that province, and that he may have passed some time in Syria because of a reference to that province in the *Versus de Verona,* the list of bishops already discussed above. The *Versus,* also dated around 800, gives a description of the Veronese saint.

> The eighth is the pastor and Confessor, Zeno the famous martyr, who by his preaching brought back Verona to baptism. He healed the daughter of Gallienus of an evil spirit, he brought back from the sea oxen drowning with a man. And indeed he delivered many from a pestilential enemy. He brought back to life a dead person taken from a river. By his constant fasts he destroyed many idols. I cannot describe the many deeds of this saint, the marvels which almighty God showed through him by his coming from Syria to Italy.[23]

---

[21]G. I. Dionisi (*Le opere de S Zeno volgarizzate,* XLX [Verona, 1784] quoted by Grazioli, 'San Zenone', 177) denied a tradition that he was Greek (no doubt because of his name) and affirmed that he was of Veronese origin. Grazioli also rejects the idea that any conclusions can be drawn from Zeno having a Greek name. Greek names were to be found throughout the Western Mediterranean at this period.

[22]PL 11: col. 199–204. The story is also quoted by Grazioli, 'San Zanone', 193–95, from another MS.

[23]'Octavus Pastor et Confessor Zeno Martyr inclytus,
Qui Veronam praedicando reduxit ad baptismum,

This document raises several problems, and in itself seems to be a very unreliable authority for any details about Zeno's life. Quite apart from the problem of the historicity of the miracles, we have here the idea that Zeno was contemporary with Emperor Gallienus (253–68). (Coronatus makes the same mistake. The two documents narrate closely connected traditions.) Grazioli however rationalises the account: Zeno was held to be responsible for the conversion of Verona to Christianity. The exorcism of the emperor's daughter was a symbol of this freeing of the city from the devil, and she was identified with Gallienus on account of a mention of that emperor in an inscription recorded over one of the gates of the city. In effect, the woman represents the city. Further deliverances are in the same tradition, and the story of the rescues from the river are reminiscent of the story told by Pope Gregory the Great of the river Adige not entering the Church of San Zeno during a flood.[24] Thus the whole account, while seemingly late and fanciful in its form, is held to be based on authentic traditions about the saint.[25]

This leaves the question of the mention of Syria: 'a Syria veniendo usque in Italiam'. Grazioli however believes that this is an idea with little foundation. He holds, with many others, that Africa is a much more likely place of origin for Zeno, on the basis of internal evidence in the sermons. Perhaps Zeno travelled to Syria, but his home was Africa.[26] Wherever Zeno came from originally, there is nothing extraor-

---

A malo spiritu sanavit Gallieni filiam,
Boves cum homine mergentes reduxit a pelago
Et quidem multos liberavit ab hoste pestifero
Mortuum resuscitavit ereptum e fluvio
Multa Idola destruxit per crebra jejunia
Non queo multa narrare hujus Sancti opera.
Quae a Syria veniendo usque in Italiam
Per ipsum omnipotens Deus ostendit mirabilia'.
[24]Gregory the Great, *Dialogues* 3.19, quoted in PL 11: col. 225 A-C.
[25]Grazioli, 'San Zenone', 195–99.
[26]Ibid., 177.

dinary about his arrival in Verona to be bishop 'a Syria'. Antioch was a major city of the Empire, and travel was a thing of relative ease and security. Jerome, Rufinus, and Egeria, to name only a few, travelled in Syria and Palestine. Gaudentius of Brescia was elected bishop while on his travels somewhere in the East, though Zeno, if described accurately as being 'a Syria', would more probably have arrived in Verona as a newcomer, whereas Gaudentius was known to the people of Brescia and summoned back from his travels.[27]

Zeno's own writings show clear links with Africa. Most explicit is the sermon on the martyrdom of Archadius in Caesarea Mauretaniae (Sermon I.39). The sermon has extremely close links with the *Passio,* so that there is evidently a literary dependence of one on the other. The style of the *Passio* is close enough to that of the sermons for scholars to conclude that it was either based on Zeno's sermon or was itself written by him.[28]

Zeno shows the influence of Tertullian and Cyprian in his sermons again and again. Löfstedt lists over twenty places where Zeno depends on a wide range of Tertullian's works, and also over sixty references to Cyprian. Of these about half are to the *Testimonia,* but Löfstedt cites ten other books of Cyprian as well.[29] Even among a very wide selection of ancient authors, both Christian and pagan, the influence of these two Africans is strong. In addition Grazioli notes the influence of two other Africans: Lactantius with regard to certain material, and Apuleius of Madaura with regard to Zeno's rhe-

---

[27]"When, on the death of Philaster, the see of Brescia fell vacant, and the citizens bound themselves by an oath that they would have no other for their bishop than a certain Gaudentius, who was absent on pilgrimage in the East, Ambrose and the Western prelates not only wrote in the most urgent terms to Gaudentius himself, but seem even to have requested the bishops of the East to exclude him from communion unless he should consent to receive consecration." H. Dudden, *Life and Times of Saint Ambrose,* 1:72.

[28]Grazioli, 'San Zenone', 178–79.

[29]Löfstedt 217–26. Grazioli, 'San Zenone', 180–81.

torical style.[30] Finally Zeno's scriptural quotations reveal that in this respect also he is within the same tradition as Tertullian and Cyprian, and so that he seems to be using an African translation of the Scriptures.[31]

Such are, in summary, hints within Zeno of an African origin. They have generally been influential, though F. E. Vokes has cast considerable doubt on how much may be concluded from these connections with Africa in an age in which religious, cultural, theological, and literary influences spread far and wide.[32] It remains that an African origin for Zeno remains a distinct possibility, but by no means a certainty.[33]

3. THE CULT OF ZENO OF VERONA

The later fame and cult of Zeno was limited largely to the area around Verona. Ambrose, the metropolitan bishop of Milan with authority over Verona, speaks of him as *sanctae memoriae,* but without any evidence that he knew him other than by repute. Zeno escapes mention by other great contemporaries. Jerome never mentions him, let alone includes him in his *De viris illustribus,* nor does Gennadius of Marseilles in his continuation of Jerome's work. But in Verona itself he was obviously remembered and loved. The beginnings of a cult of Zeno as a saint are clearly seen in the sermon of a bishop, Petronius, from the fifth century. Described as bishop of Verona by the MSS, but identified by G. Morin as

[30]Grazioli, 'San Zenone', 181–82.

[31]Ibid.; Truzzi, 50 n. 16.

[32]F. E. Vokes, 'Zeno of Verona, Apuleius and Africa', *Studia Patristica* 8/2 (1966) (Texte und Untersuchengen 93) 130–34. Vokes is sceptical of the sharpness of the distinction made between the Italian and the African *Vetus Latinum.* The works of writers and their influence were widespread, and the cult of various saints had already spread beyond their native cities— Saints Perpetua and Felicity were venerated in Rome, and Lawrence in Hippo. In effect, says Vokes, we do not have a clear enough portrait of the ancient world to reconstruct biographies from such literary evidence.

[33]Cf. di Berardino, *Patrology* 4: 127–28.

Petronius of Bologna, the preacher (who does not seem to be resident in Verona) is commemorating the feastday of Saint Zeno: *natale sancti Zenonis.* He describes Zeno as 'a most holy confessor' and 'an outstanding priest of Christ'. He mentions the building that contains the tomb of the bishop, and which is the centre of Zeno's fame and evidently the place where miracles are worked. Perhaps Petronius knew something of Zeno personally, for we can recognise the saint in his description, 'From the perpetual fountain of his holiness a delightful stream pours forth, cleansing sinners and multiplying the joys of salvation'. But it is the miracles that attract the preacher's attention, continuing at the tomb what Zeno had performed in his lifetime.[34]

It is the miraculous that leads Gregory the Great to mention Zeno: not a continuity of the healings described by Petronius, but the story of the river Adige in flood not coming into the Church of Saint Zeno.[35] Gregory describes Zeno as *martyr,* a vagueness of title which only much later gives rise to ideas that he died for the faith,[36] but does not reveal any further knowledge of the man or his writings.

The fact that Zeno was comparatively little known or read outside Verona gives us a particular interest in studying his sermons. Since we can be reasonably confident in assuming that Augustine and Ambrose never read his sermons, practices, ideas, and literary themes that we find in Zeno and in the writings of these great men are more probably the current and common ideas of the time than literary borrowings between a few individuals. Thus, for example, we find both in Zeno and in Augustine the candidates for baptism likened to bread, and a very similar allegory of the parable of the good Samaritan. We might therefore suppose that these were common themes in the sermons of contemporary bishops.

[34] G. Morin, 'Deux petits discours d'un evêque Petronius', *Revue Bénédictine* 14 (1897) 3–8. Truzzi, 95–97.

[35] Gregory the Great, *Dialogues* 3.19; quoted in PL 11: col. 225.

[36] The idea that Zeno was a martyr is discussed by Grazioli, 'San Zenone', 290–96.

There is evidence that some people read and were influenced by the sermons. The *Coena Cypriani* is of the same genre as Zeno's sermon I.24 and, as we shall see, may well have been based on it. There is other evidence which seems to link this work with the area of Brescia and Verona, and so the idea of a literary link would fit with what we know of a strong local tradition for the bishop.[37] It is possible that Chromatius of Aquileia and Peter Chrysologus of Ravenna (both close geographically) quote him.[38] The literary influence of Zeno did spread even further; traces of some of his sermons are to be found in Eusebius Gallicanus,[39] and there is obvious borrowing of his sermons II.22 and II.26 in two prayers in the Bangor Antiphonary. It is not necessary to suppose that his sermons were known in Ireland by the end of the seventh century when the antiphonary was composed. A. Galli suspects that the passages found their way in some intermediary form such as some Gallican liturgical pieces.[40]

Grazioli gives an account of the geographical spread of the cult outside Verona. In 552 a church was dedicated to Zeno in Ravenna, and others are recorded throughout northern Italy, as far from Verona as Pavia, Pisa, and Aquileia. In particular Pistoia had a particular devotion to Zeno and the cathedral there is dedicated to him. The cult spread into southern Germany in Carolingian times.[41] Meanwhile in Verona itself the Church of Saint Zeno was successively enlarged and embellished and boasts a medieval statue of the saint who, unusually for the sanctified, has a broad grin.

[37]Cf. di Berardino, *Patrology* 4:315.

[38]Possible quotations are listed by the editors, CCL 9; 24, 24A, 24B. Some are more convincing than others.

[39]CCL 101: viii–ix, 1082–83.

[40]A. Galli, 'Zénon de Vérone dans l'Antiphonaire de Bangor', *Revue Bénédictine* 93 (1983) 293–301. Dolbeau's recent review of the manuscript tradition (see n. 2 above) shows it to have been more widely disseminated than was previously supposed.

[41]Grazioli, 'San Zenone', 296–301.

Chapter Two

THE SERMONS AND THE MANUSCRIPTS

1. THE PROBLEM OF THE SERMON COLLECTION

Before we look at the liturgy witnessed to by Zeno, it is necessary to establish the authenticity of the sermons, with regard not so much to authorship as to their integrity as being the sermons which were, to all intents and purposes, those actually preached by Zeno when he presided as bishop over the paschal rites. It is necessary to do this because, as we shall see, recent scholars have suggested that in the period between the delivery of the sermons and the gathering together of the texts into a single collection, they underwent considerable change through being preserved, copied, and plagiarised for liturgical purposes. Löfstedt himself, the editor, emphasises the distance between the sermons as preached by Zeno and those which we possess today.

The rest of this study presents nothing that should make one doubt the consistency of style and content of the material which has come down to us under the name of Zeno. The work of secondary hands nowhere shows any evidence or influence. In this chapter the integrity of the sermons will be demonstrated and the contrary thesis rejected. Much of the discussion will necessarily be extremely detailed, but the overall picture is consistent and clear, namely that we have here the sermons in their integrity as composed by Zeno.

We shall begin with a survey of the sermons as we find them arranged in all the MSS. It is immediately apparent even from a perusal of the index of sermons that there is a certain order. It is not complete and perfect, but it is substantial. Sermons preached at the paschal Vigil, that is, one preached at the beginning of the ceremonies, one in the baptistery and one in the church after returning from the baptistery, together with sermons on the readings of the Vigil, are found together in groups, often in the order in which they would have been preached, so that each group represents an individual celebration of Easter. These groups I call 'paschal groups'. There are also 'non-paschal groups', containing sermons on various subjects, including some sermons belonging to the paschal Vigil but which have evidently been detached from the paschal groups. The non-paschal groups, unlike the paschal groups, usually have a form of standardised heading for each sermon.

Despite this order, the disorder present strongly suggests that the compiler of the single collection was not responsible for the arrangement of the sermons, but that the prime and probably only motive in making the collection was to preserve all that remained of the bishop's writings.

In order to establish the history of the individual texts of the sermons before they were collected together, we will have to establish their relation to the sermons as actually preached. Were they preparatory drafts written by the bishop, or stenographers' copies, or later versions drawn up either by Zeno for publication or by later liturgists using Zeno's material? The last theory is the one supported by recent scholars, but it will be seen that the evidence is inadequate, and it is almost certain that in effect we possess the preparatory drafts composed by Zeno himself. This is established not only from the evidence of the MSS and the texts of the sermons but from a survey of contemporary rhetorical practices and an examination of Zeno's own style and methods.

The alternative theory of the history of the texts, that the sermons were preserved, worked over, and collected by liturgists, is discounted. We must therefore trace an alternative history of the texts from their having been preached to their being gathered into the single collection. We envisage that the collection contains all the bishop's writings available, even meaningless scraps. The paschal groups of sermons were most probably copied as found, in their original liturgical order as used by Zeno, with minimal interference in the meantime. The non-paschal groups show some signs of selection and arrangement, possibly by more than one person, but this was probably a private and informal activity, which was taken over by the collector.

A number of details of the text will be noted in support of this theory of the history of the sermons. It will be seen that certain features fit in with the idea that the final single collection was made from sermons on individual sheets of paper. The fragments of sermons were probably preserved through being on the same sheets as other sermons.

2. THE ARRANGEMENT OF SERMONS IN THE MANUSCRIPTS

There is no need here to give all the details of the manuscript tradition. Löfstedt gives a full description of the MSS he uses in his introduction, and Dolbeau describes some additional MSS. Suffice it here to say that the MSS fall into two 'families', α and β, which will be mentioned from time to time in this study. The α family includes the more ancient MSS; Löfstedt was inclined still to give considerable credence to the readings in the β family and is chided for this by Dolbeau; it is likely that this family shows more evidence of late editorial revision than of original readings.[1]

The sermons of Zeno are divided into two books in the original MSS. This order is reproduced by Löfstedt in his edition.[2] The two books are unequally divided, with sixty-three sermons in the first[3] and thirty sermons in the second. This un-

[1]Dolbeau, 'Zenoniana', 33–34.

[2]The Ballerini edition, used in PL 11, has a revised order but the original MS order is described in col. 235–36.

[3]One is omitted from the index in the α MSS which lists sixty-two sermons, and so we have the numbering I.46A, 46B in the text of Löfstedt.

equal division does not bear any connection to the length of the individual sermons. In addition, Löfstedt divides a sermon in the first book into two, namely 10A and 10B, making a total of sixty-four sermons in the first book.[4]

The sermons can be divided into several distinct types. At the beginning of books I and II (and scattered elsewhere) are a number of sermons on moral and doctrinal points.[5] There are a number of sermons on passages and events from the Old Testament.[6] There are two sermons for special occasions, namely the consecration of a church and an account of the martyrdom of Archadius in Caesarea Mauretaniae.[7] There are three mere fragments of sermons.[8] These fragments make very little sense and it is hard to see any reason for their inclusion except that the person responsible for the collection wished to include all that could be found of the bishop's writings.

(i) The Paschal Groups of Sermons[9]

The various types of sermons will be considered in their turn. First we must examine the largest genre of all: sixty-two sermons are closely connected with the liturgy of the paschal Vigil and the baptismal rites, being composed either as sermons on the feast, or for before or after the baptisms, or as commentaries on the biblical passages that were read at the Vigil service, namely Genesis 1; Exodus 12; Exodus 14; Isaiah 1 (or Isaiah 5); and Daniel 3.

---

[4]Also Truzzi, 57 divides I.34 into two, the first being paragraphs 1-4, and the second, paragraphs 5-9. But this is of course not represented in Löfstedt's edition, and we shall continue here with his numbering of sixty-four sermons in the first book.

[5]I.1; 2; 3; 4; 5; 14; 36; 54; II.1; 2; 3; 4; 5; 7; 8; 9.

[6]I.13; 15; 25; 34; 35; 37; 40; 43; 59; 62.

[7]II.6; I.39.

[8]I.21; 60; II.18.

[9]A table of the sermons in their MS order but divided into groups can be seen in the Appendix.

That these sermons were composed for successive celebrations of the same liturgy can be seen in two ways: first, in their content and subject matter which identify their place and role in the liturgy; and secondly, in their relative positions in the MSS, which correspond to the order in which the sermons were delivered. The content of the sermons is discussed below. Here we shall concentrate on the MS order.

These sermons are arranged in the MSS in groups, roughly in the order in which one would expect them to have been delivered. Thus the order generally begins with the paschal proclamation, followed by the sermons on the Vigil readings. Afterwards comes the sermon preceding, and then that following, the baptism.

Nowhere is there a complete and perfect correspondence between the MS order and the liturgical use. There are several gaps in series of sermons, interpolations of sermons that do not belong to the context, and other sermons that belong to the series but are in the wrong order. The group of sermons II.10-17 is in complete disarray. Other Easter sermons are found outside any such grouping. Nevertheless, as can be seen from even a perusal of the order in the index, there is still a remarkable correspondence, notably in the groups I.16-24; I.26-32; and I.44-49.

On the basis of the order that can be perceived, it is possible to identify a number of groups of paschal sermons. The lack of tidiness in the groups shows that this order, whatever its origin, was not the intention of the editor who made the present arrangement of sermons in the MSS, for if that were the case it would only have taken a few minutes' work to complete the order. But the sermons as they are to be found in their groups, or outside them, can be arranged as shown in chart 2.1.

As has been said above, the sermons can be identified by their content as well as their position relative to one another as belonging to the paschal Vigil. The similarity of content means that the sermons can be compared one with another, and each type of sermon treated as a mini-genre in its own

Chart 2.1	Pasch. Proc.	On Gen. 1	On Exod. 12	On Exod. 14	On Isa. 1/5	On Dan. 3	Invit. to the font	Post Bapt.
	Prae. Pasc.	*De Gen*	*De Ex.i.*	*De Ex.ii*	*De Isa.*	*De Dan.*	*Invit. fontis*	*Post traditum*
Book I	6	7	8	9	10A*10B*	11	12	
	16	17	19	18	20	22	23	24
	26	27	28	29	30	31	32	
	33							38
								41
								42
	44	45	46A	46B	47	48	49	
		50	51	52		53	55	
		56						
	57							
	58				61			
Book II	13	12	17	16	11*	15	14	10
	19		20		21	22	23	24
		30	25	26		27	28	29

* denotes sermons on Isaiah 5 rather than Isaiah 1. See pp. 121–7.

right. They will be discussed in this way below. The similarity of content also helps us to identify with reasonable confidence the paschal sermons that are separated from their group. The main exception to this is I.61, which may well have been preached on some other occasion. The problem of this and other individual sermons will be discussed in the context of the others of the same subject matter.

(ii) The Non-Paschal Groups of Sermons[10]

Apart from the series of paschal sermons which are still, at least approximately, in their original order, a perusal of the index shows us that the other sermons preached on different

[10] A table of the sermons in their MS order but divided into their groups can be seen in the Appendix.

occasions are by no means scattered through the MSS but are brought together into a few groups. These we call the 'non-paschal groups'.

Like the paschal groups, the collection of this material is incomplete and, while it may reflect earlier attempts to sort the sermons into some order, it cannot be said to be the work of the person who copied up the sermons into the final collection. Otherwise, again like the paschal groups, only a few minutes' work would have completed the ordering.

The non-paschal groups can be identified as follows, listing their titles:

A) I.1–5. moral and doctrinal sermons
   1. On chastity: *De pudicitia*
   2. On the resurrection: *De resurrectione*
   3. On circumcision: *De circumcisione*
   4. On patience: *De patientia*
   5. On greed: *De avaritia*

B) I.13–15. one moral and two typological sermons
   13. Sermon on Judah: *Tractatus de Iuda*
   14. Sermon on avarice: *Tractatus de avaritia*
   15. Sermon on Job: *Tractatus de Iob*

C) I.33–43. Sermons on various subjects, including a proclamation and some post-baptismal sermons detached from the paschal groups.
   33. Again a sermon on the Lord's Day: *Item tractatus diei dominici* (a paschal proclamation)
   34. Sermon on the prophet Jonah: *Tractatus Ionae prophetae*
   35. Sermon on Psalm 100: *Tractatus psalmi centesimi*
   36. Sermon on faith, hope, and love: *Tractatus de spe, fide, et caritate*
   37. Sermon on Jacob's dream: *Tractatus de somnio Iacob*
   38. Sermon on the zodiac to the neophytes: *Tractatus de xii signis ad neophytos* (a post-baptismal sermon)
   39. Sermon on the martyr Archadius: *Tractatus de Archadio martyre*

40. Sermon on Susanna: *Tractatus de Susanna*

41. Sermon on the Lord's Day on a comparison with wheat: *Tractatus diei dominici de comparatione tritici* (a post-baptismal sermon)

42. Sermon to the neophytes on another day of the Pasch: *Tractatus ad neophytos alio die paschae* (a post-baptismal sermon)

43. Sermon on the patriarch Abraham: *Tractatus de Abraham patriarcha*

D) I.56–62. A collection mainly of stray sermons from the paschal groups; two sermons on Abraham.

56. Sermon on faith: *Tractatus fidei* (a sermon on Genesis)

57. Sermon on the Pasch: *Tractatus paschae* (a proclamation)

58. Again a sermon on the Pasch: *Item Tractatus paschae* (another proclamation)

59. On Abraham: *De Abraham*

60. On Isaiah: *De Esaia* (a mere fragment)

61. Again on Isaiah: *Item de Esaia* (a paschal sermon?)

62. Again on Abraham: *Item de Abraham*

E) II.1–9. A collection of moral and doctrinal sermons and one for the consecration of a church.

1. On justice: *De iustitia*

2. On fear: *De timore*

3. Sermon on faith: *Tractatus fidei*

4. On the spirit and the body: *De spiritu et corpore*

5. On the scripture: 'When he hands over the kingdom to God the Father': *De eo quod scriptum est: Cum tradiderit regnum deo et patri*

6. On the building of the house of God by Solomon: *De aedificatione domus dei a Salomone*

7. On continence: *De continentia*

8. On the birth of the Lord: *De nativitate domini*

9. On humility: *De humilitate*

Inevitably there are a few stray non-paschal sermons to be found among the paschal groups:

I.25. Again a sermon: *Item tractatus;* a sermon on the 'sacrifice of praise'.

I.54. On the birth of Christ: *De nativitate Christi*

I.21. On greed: *De avaritia*

II.18. Sermon on Daniel for the Pasch: *Tractatus Danielis in pascha*

The last two sermons are incomplete fragments. It will be suggested below that they are scraps of writing found on the paper Zeno was using for another sermon. The title of II.18 is wrong, and the β MSS suggest an alternative, *pro fidei veritate* ('for the truth of the faith'). I.21 is found within a group of paschal sermons. II.18 lies between two such groups.

The groups show some signs of editing, both by their subject matter and their titles. Groups A and E, which stand at the beginning of books I and II respectively, are collections of sermons on moral and doctrinal subjects, with the exception of II.6, on the consecration of a church, and II.3, which is said by Truzzi and others to be a letter rather than a sermon. The sermons in these two groups, except for II.3, bear titles of the form *De . . .* (e.g., *De pudicitia*).

Group B, consisting of three sermons and therefore hardly a group in its own right, could be seen as a detached part of group C. Its form of titles would fit that group.

Group C is a collection of sermons very different from groups A and E. In the index, though not in the headings in the text in all the MSS, they are defined by the form of title *Tractatus de . . .* or *Tractatus (+ genitive) . . .* (e.g., *Tractatus de somnio Iacob; Tractatus Psalmi centesimi*). In subject matter the collection is highly varied, with doctrinal and typological material, the *Passio* of Archadius, and also several post-baptismal sermons which seem to have been detached from their paschal groups in order to be included in this collection. These sermons (I.38; 41; 42) are all examples of Zeno's most imaginative and even eccentric style, which would lead us to suppose that whoever put this collection together found them highly attractive. But I.24, perhaps the most eccentric of all of Zeno's sermons and possibly the model on which the *Coena*

Cypriani was based,[11] is omitted. Was it too much for the collector? We may wonder whether this collector had access to the sermons of book II, or on what grounds II.11, the allegory of viticulture, was omitted from this collection.

Group D is a varied group, both in material and in the titles given to the sermons. It is our opinion that this is merely a collection of stray sermons. The titles of the three paschal sermons in this group, all *Tractatus Paschae* or *Tractatus fidei,* show affinity with the many sermons in book II of that kind of title. This, and corresponding gaps in the paschal groups, suggests that this collection may be of sermons which really belong with those in book II.

Such is the arrangement of the sermons as we find them in the extant MSS. There is clearly some order, but it is limited and imperfect. Before we can explore the problem of the inclusion of the sermons into the present collection, we must examine the nature of the sermons in themselves. We have the texts of sermons. But sermons of course are delivered orally, and so there is not an exact identity of the written text with the sermon as actually preached. What relation the text has to the sermon as preached is important for our understanding of the texts as we have received them.

3. THE RELATION OF THE TEXTS OF THE SERMONS TO THE SERMONS PREACHED

There are four basic possibilities as to this relationship:

1. that Zeno read the sermons from the page;
2. that the texts are based on stenographers' copies of the preached sermons;
3. that the sermons, or at least some of them, were the polished versions written up after they had been preached, perhaps with publication in mind;

[11]Cf. di Berardino, *Patrology* 4:315; Ballerini PL 11: col. 484 n. 6; Truzzi, 63.

4. that the texts are preliminary drafts of the preached sermons, written by the preacher in advance and either used as a rough basis for what was preached or memorised *verbatim*.

To take the four possibilities in turn, the first, that Zeno read the sermon directly from the page, must be discounted as highly unlikely because, in a culture that set a high value on rhetoric, reading from a prepared text was disapproved of. Quintilian, the model for the teaching of rhetoric, would allow the use of brief memoranda for an unwritten speech, but strongly disapproved of any paper or aid used for a text which had been fully written out. 'We should not write anything,' he says, 'which we do not intend to commit to memory.'[12] Preachers could hold and quote from books, particularly of the Scriptures, but this liberty would not extend to one's own prepared text.[13]

The second and third possibilities, that we have in our text the evidence of stenographers' copies and/or Zeno's rough drafts and polished copies of the same sermons, are used by Löfstedt to explain the chaotic order of the MSS and the sermons which are plainly based one on another. Löfstedt thinks that at some stage after Zeno's death the sermons were collected together for liturgical purposes. In this process, he suggests, the more polished versions were collected and preserved along with the rough drafts, both being either from Zeno's hand or from the drafts and finished copies made by stenographers. As an example of such influence Löfstedt cites how Jerome complains of alterations made by secretaries and stenographers.[14]

[12]Quintilian, *Institutio Oratoria* 10.7.31–32; ed. and trans H. E. Butler, vol. 4 (London and New York: Loeb Classical Library, 1922) 150–51.

[13]Cf. A. Olivar, 'Preparacion e improvisacion en la predicacion patristica', in *Kyriakon,* ed. P. Granfield and J. A. Jungmann (Aschendorff, 1970) 2:736–67, 749.

[14]Löfstedt, 9*–10*.

Such is Löfstedt's hypothesis, from which he draws three conclusions. First, the number of extant sermons (and/or drafts) cannot be depended on as corresponding to the years of Zeno's episcopacy in Verona. Secondly, the *ipsissima verba* of Zeno himself are lost to us. We have in effect a collection of secretaries' and/or liturgists' notes. Thirdly, this explains the historical picture that we have of Zeno's insignificance outside Verona for some years. His sermons were at first left unpublished, and were later copied only for local liturgical use.[15]

4. A CRITIQUE OF LÖFSTEDT'S ACCOUNT

Löfstedt's theory has proved extremely popular and has been followed by subsequent published studies and articles. Since this study takes a different view, it is incumbent on us to present a full criticism of the now traditional view and a defence of our own. First Löfstedt's theory will be discussed under eight points.

1. *Are the sermons appropriate for publication?*

The possibility that we are dealing with polished versions of sermons is attractive at first sight. Sermons were often prepared for publication subsequent to delivery. However, we have no evidence (apart from the verbal parallels between sermons, which will be discussed below) that any of the sermons have been revised later by Zeno himself with publication or any other purpose in mind. It is possible, though no more than possible, that some of the longer sermons are literary productions, but these are not the ones which have multiple versions in the manuscripts and it would be hard to imagine what kind of public would wish to read the short and repetitious paschal Vigil sermons.

[15]Löfstedt 11*.

2. *If later hands were believed to be at work, we might expect to find the style of more than one writer.*

Are all the sermons in the MSS to be ascribed directly to Zeno, or could some perhaps have been composed by another hand? Löfstedt suggests that later plagiarists had liturgical purposes in mind, which would at least explain why the parallel sermons are to be found in their proper liturgical place. But Löfstedt himself acknowledges the distinctive style of Zeno which militates strongly against the likelihood of any considerable interference by other hands.[16]

Palanca's thesis on the style of Zeno's sermons bears witness to the evident care that he exercised in composition. In Renaissance times, indeed, he was known as the 'Christian Cicero'.[17] Palanca's study compares Zeno's style in terms of quantitative metrical forms with those of Cicero, Pliny, and Hilary; in cursus types with Hilary, Symmachus, and Jerome; and in Gorgianic and associated prose figures with Hilary.[18] In much of this, the purpose of the study is to trace the changing nature of Latin from the quantitative to the accentual system. But at the same time Palanca declares that Zeno ranks with the great orators in refinement of prose rhythm, excelling even Cicero and Pliny and approaching the great master Hilary in the use of the five preferred metrical forms. He also heeded the dangers of repetitious employment of these clausulae, using a remarkably wide range of less common ones. Zeno's accentual rhythm is even more remarkable: he is quite clearly aiming for cursus and employing great range and refinement. The Gorgianic figures exceed the use of Hilary who sought a moderate style. Zeno sought attention and stimulated interest by a sustained grandeur, while avoiding monotony by using a profusion of stylistic devices.[19]

---

[16]Löfstedt 6*.

[17]Palanca, *Prose Rhythm*, 9.

[18]The Gorgianic figures:

homoioteleuton (or paramoion):	aquam de petra bibisti
	manna de coelo gustasti

Palanca follows the traditional understanding of the Easter sermons as introductions or cursorily treated themes from which sermons could be easily improvised. However he states that the rhetoric of these short, repetitious sermons is as remarkable as that of more elaborate ones.[20] And it is an Easter sermon, II.16, that he chooses (because of its convenient shortness) for analysis as an example of Zeno's style. In it he finds every kind of figure and refinement.[21]

The present writer has no expertise in this field and can only repeat the conclusions of others. But given Palanca's

---

antithesis: non necessitate sed merito
parison—even balance in the members of a sentence
  columna nubis
    te deduxit per di*em*
    ut ostenderet caec*um*
  ignis columna
    per noct*em*
    ut significaret arsur*um*
(NB homoioteleuton with ABAB pattern: -em, -um, -em, -um)

the stylistic devices:
isocolon—where order of words is same in two clauses—example given above under homoioteleuton.

chiasmus—where the order of words in one clause is inverted in a second clause—see example under parison, columna nubis / ignis columna.
parallelism—passim in the other forms.

The five favourite metrical clausulae:
cretic spondee: $-\cup-$ $--$ double spondee: $--$ $--$
diachoree: $-\cup-\cup$ double cretic: $-\cup-$ $-\cup-$
cretic tribrach: $-\cup-$ $\cup\cup\cup$

Cursus types of accentual rhythm:
planus: $\acute{-} - - \acute{-} -$ velox: $\acute{-} - - - - \acute{-} -$
tardus: $\acute{-} - - \acute{-} - -$ trispondaicus: $\acute{-} - - - \acute{-} -$

[19]Palanca, 'Prose Rhythm', 200–206.
[20]Ibid., 7.
[21]Ibid., 196–97.

choice of a paschal sermon for his analysis, it might be useful to ask whether all these sermons show similar evidence of a studied composition, the same as or even more than in the longer sermons. If this were the case, it might be taken as evidence that the short sermons were not designed for expansion, but were considered to be complete in their own right; also it would lead us to consider from the stylistic point of view the possibility that these pieces may owe more to the genres of the *praefatio* of the Eucharistic Prayer or of the *praeconium paschale* than of the sermon.

3. *If stenographers or revisers were believed to be at work,*
    we might expect to see obvious changes, insertions, or
    incongruities in proportion to their work.

On the question of later hands at work in the sermons, there is one passage that has been interpreted as a later interpolation: 'But since this command of the apostles has been operative for some four hundred years or even more than that'. . . .[22] The reading, 'or even more than that', which gives a totally unacceptable date for Zeno, has been understood as a later interpolation by Bigelmair.[23] However, as we have already seen above, this is not at all likely, and we probably have an authentic reading as intended by Zeno. Even if Bigelmair were right and this were a later interpolation, it would still be an isolated instance of scribal interference, and certainly does not impugn the general authenticity of the sermons.

We must also consider, and confidently discount, a further feature which may be seen as evidence for stenographers. One may sometimes find in the stenographers' texts hints of the impromptu asides that a preacher may include even when his sermon is carefully prepared. For example, Jerome says, 'There are many things to be said, but we are prevented by

[22]'At cum ante annos ferme quadringentos vel eo amplius apostolicum hoc operetur edictum.' II.7.5.
[23]Bigelmair, *Zeno von Verona*, 34.

the time'.[24] More drastically, Augustine hesitates in his speaking, 'Please wait . . . I am sorry I said, wait. Indeed there is no reason to wait'.[25] So the hand of the stenographer might be deduced in the recording of Zeno's comment, 'Time does not permit me, brothers, to give the truth for the image'.[26] However this sermon is one of those which have a parallel and here too Zeno says, 'Time does not permit me to give the truth for the image'.[27] Both cannot be impromptu asides. Such comments can be composed in advance. It must be allowed, therefore, that in the above case of Zeno's admission of the lack of time, we do not have a stenographer's recording of an impromptu aside but, at least in one case and therefore quite probably in both, Zeno foreseeing the pressure of time and preparing his sermon accordingly. Zeno is not making an apology for going wrong in his sermon in the same way as Augustine does above, which must be taken as clear evidence of the stenographer rather than the preacher foreseeing the situation. Cases such as Zeno's are extremely doubtful evidence for the stenographer.

4. *Is the presence of a stenographer even possible on some occasions?*

The work of a stenographer is also somewhat unlikely in the case of the sermons delivered in the baptistery. Are we to imagine a secretary following after the procession into the baptistery to record the few words of episcopal exhortation uttered there?

5. *The number of sermons copied* verbatim *from one another is very small and does not affect our picture of the overall work.*

---

[24]'Multa sunt quae dicantur, sed hora excludimur, Jerome, *Tr. de Ps xiiii*, 5; quoted by Olivar, 'Preparacion', 750.

[25]'Rogo, appende . . . Poenitet me dixisse: Appende. Prorsus non est quod appendere'. Augustine, *Sermo* 302, 5. Olivar, 'Preparacion', 749.

[26]'Tempus non sinit, fratres, imagini reddere veritatem'. I.9.

[27]'Tempus non sinit imagini reddere veritatem'. II.16.

The fact that some sermons were quite clearly copied from others is a major factor in Löfstedt's hypothesis. The similarity between particular sermons on the same subject can be quite striking, and on occasion sermons can be virtually identical; thus I.9 and II.16; I.27 and II.30; and I.17 and I.56 are all parallels. In each case one sermon has quite evidently been copied from the other. (There is no need to hypothesise a third, common source.) In other instances a sermon may be seen as a combination of two or three others. Thus, I.42 is a combination of parts of three sermons, II.10; 24; and 29.[28] I.57 uses material from I.44 and 58.[29] Even a brief perusal of any of these will enable one to see how the writer made only minimal changes. Even when moving from one source to another he would not add any connecting material but would, as it were, simply stick together fragments from different sermons.

But these are the only cases of direct copying *verbatim*. They are all to be found in the paschal sermons, and involve only thirteen of these more than ninety sermons. As we shall see below, other paschal sermons may still be strongly reminiscent of one another even though the imitation is more free. This is particularly the case with the shorter sermons and can be exemplified by the Exodus passages, where the same themes run through the addresses but there is little word-for-word copying. Thus, with regard to the institution of the Passover, various things are pointed to as evidence of God's rejection of the Jewish ritual: the ruin of the Temple, the end of the priesthood, Christ as the true Lamb rejected by the Jews, etc. The wording in the sermons on Exodus 12 varies considerably, but these and other themes recur regularly. The sermons on Isaiah and Daniel, other proclamations and the invitations have parallel content which is less than that in the Exodus sermons, but still considerable.

---

[28]In Löfstedt's text, I.42, lines 1–5 = II.29, ll.1–5; lines 5–11 = II.10, ll.12–18; lines 11–26 = II.24, ll.14–20, 22–29.

[29]I.57, lines 7–10 = I.58 ll. 6–9; lines 1–7, 11–14 = I.44. ll. 1–7, 7–13.

But the copying of Zeno's sermons need not be blamed on later writers or on Zeno redrafting the same sermon for publication, for it can be seen how Zeno is by no means averse to copying another writer in his sermons. For example, while he does not copy Hilary of Poitiers quite as closely as he sometimes does his own sermons, a synopsis is possible.[30]

Hilary *In ps.* 130.32 (CSEL 22; 658, ll. 12–17)	Zeno II.9.7, ll. 63–69
David enim, et propheta et rex,	David quippe
erat humilis antea et	humilis,
abiectus	abiectus
neque convivio patris sui dignus;	ignobilis sui iacebat in patris oves semper pascendo propemodum peregrinus. Innocens cum innocentibus deputatus
sed deo conplacuit,	hic placuit deo.
unctus in regem est,	Unctus in regem,
adspiratus in prophetam.	spiratus in vatem,
Non insolescit in regno,	non insolescit in regno, obumbrat neminem prophetae terrore. Iniurias suas non exsequitur regia potestate;
non odiis conmovetur:	odientes se diligit;
persequentes se amat,	
inimicorum mortes honorat,	inimicis parcit;
incestuosis et	
parricidalibus	parricidalibus
filiis parcit.	filiis ignoscit.

In conclusion, the number of sermons containing verbal parallels is small. If they were all considered to be successive drafts or the work of stenographers or later liturgists, they

---

[30]Cf. Bigelmair, *Zeno von Verona*, 68ff., who sets out many other borrowings from Tertullian, Cyprian, Lactantius, Hilary, et al.

would be insufficient in number to affect our view of the vast majority of the sermons. But there is every reason to suppose that the copyist is Zeno himself, freely using his own material on subsequent occasions.

Points one to five have concerned the content of the sermons, and it would be useful to interject some kind of conclusion here before we move on to points six and seven which examine the evidence of the order of the sermons in the manuscripts and our final point eight. The nature and content of many of the sermons do not lead us to expect them to be suitable for publication. The supreme elegance of the style, even in the case of the shorter sermons which have often been dismissed by critics as fragments, the absence of other writers' styles or evidence of their interference all lead us to suppose that there is no need to hypothesise either revision for publication or the baleful influence of stenographers or editors. The number of *verbatim* duplications is small, and we have seen that Zeno was happy to copy other writers' work and was no doubt happy to plagiarise his own. The simplest thesis is that we have here, as far as we have them for any ancient writer, the *ipsissima verba* of Zeno of Verona.

But now let us proceed to the manuscript order of the sermons, and see if it supports the theories for revision for either publishing or liturgical purposes.

6. *Does the order of the manuscripts reflect copying or revision for publication?*[31]

On the question of the position of sermons with parallel material in them, if it were simply a matter of successive drafts of the same sermon, one might expect them to be found together in the MSS. In fact, this is not normally the case; the

---

[31]Löfstedt would not see the necessity for the evidence of order in the MS if his thesis is correct that the order was subsequently changed for liturgical needs. But it will be seen that this thesis cannot be maintained, and so the requirement of some evidence from the position of the sermons comes to the fore again.

parallel sermons are more likely to be found within their respective liturgical groups. The parallel I.9 and II.16 are both in their groups. Of the parallel I.27 and II.30, the former is certainly within a group; the latter could be said to have been tacked on to the end of the MS, as it were, but it is most likely that it belongs to the group II.25-29. II.10; 24; and 29, the sources for I.42, are all in their respective groups, rather than close to I.42.

There are two exceptions to this. I.57 has one of its sources close to it, namely I.58. (The other source, I.44, is still in its group.) This exception would seem to be a possible instance of successive drafts for a sermon, with I.58 being written first and rejected, then I.57 being written as an improved version, drawing also on I.44. I shall suggest below that I.58 may have found its way into the MS through being written on the same piece of paper as I.57. The other exception is the two closely connected Isaiah sermons I.10A and I.10B. When these are discussed it will be seen that one of them is probably a rejected draft. In fact neither of these has verbal parallels either with each other or with other sermons. These two pairs of sermons are best explained as drafts, and the proximity of each sermon to its double in the MS is the main reason for explaining them as such. But the exceptions prove the rule. In other cases the proximity does not exist, and parallel sermons are far apart from each other, usually to be found in their respective liturgical groups, as if the writer were simply concerned to keep each year's sermons together.

What can be deduced from this? In the case of the parallels I.9/II.16 and probably of I.27/II.30, the only case for copying would seem to be in order to preach approximately the same sermon on a subsequent year. *A fortiori* the same reason for copying may be reasonably applied to the other parallels, even when they are not found within a paschal group (e.g., I.42; 56; 57/58). Sermons with verbal parallels suffer the same disordering in the MS order as do sermons without parallels. For example, I.42 is to be found together with I.38 and I.41 in what would seem to have been an attempt at some kind of collecting or editing of the sermons, but there is no reason to suppose that that involved an interference with the content of I.42 any more than with that of I.38 or I.41.

7. *Does the present arrangement of the sermons in the MSS support Löfstedt's theory of reordering for liturgical purposes?*

We have already described something of the order—and disorder—of the sermons in the MSS, and will consider it in further detail below. The differing views can be summarised here: while Löfstedt believes that the collector of the sermons played a major part in determining the arrangement of the sermons according to his liturgical needs, my own view is the opposite, namely that the liturgical order reflects the original state of the sermons as composed by the bishop. These underwent a certain reordering and confusion, but the person responsible for collecting them into one document did not attempt to amend this but simply preserved what he found.

Löfstedt thinks that at some stage after Zeno's death the sermons were collected together for liturgical purposes.[32] He cites the instances of two a family MSS of the sermons, R and $P,$ which with their common ancestor were used liturgically. All our extant MSS of Zeno have the same contents and order of sermons, pointing, argues Löfstedt, to there having been one original, perhaps official act of collecting and editing. And so the collector or other hands after Zeno may have been responsible for some of the repetitions and parallels, using his sermons for their own liturgical needs.

How far can this be borne out by the MSS? That R and P were used liturgically is relevant only to those MSS and their time. In fact the liturgical notes in R and P do not reflect the formation of the MS tradition but rather are imposed artificially upon it. The origin of the order of sermons in the MSS reflects the paschal Vigil service and the readings. The liturgical glosses in P point to chosen sermons being read at Sexagesima, Quinquagesima, and Quadragesima.[33] In R there

[32]Löfstedt, 9* ff. (followed also by Truzzi, 54 n. 34).
[33]Ibid., 23*.

is a wider selection of sermons made for reading out at various ceremonies during the year. Thus the proclamations I.6; 16; 26; and 44 are read in the weekdays of Easter Week.[34] The proclamation I.33 is read at the beginning of the ceremonies on Easter Day, but it is evident that this is because of its suitability of content rather than because this proclamation rather than the others was read by Zeno on Easter Day. There are sixteen sermons with a liturgical gloss up to I.44, and then no more. Evidently this was taken to provide enough sermons. The MS *R* is destroyed, but a reference to the Church of *S. Stephanus ad martyres* in the gloss of I.38 would date this liturgical material to after the founding of this church in 770. A dedicatory inscription by Hincmar gives his date of death (882) as a *terminus ante quem*.[35]

Of course this does not mean that the MS was not first collated with liturgical purposes in mind; only that *R* and *P* represent liturgical practices different from Zeno's time, indeed a state of affairs some four hundred years later, and that their particular liturgical practices are not those of the MSS as originally compiled.

Might the compilation have been made with the paschal Vigil in mind? But, as we have already seen, the considerable liturgical disorder in the series of paschal sermons makes it unlikely that the compiler had liturgical practices uppermost in his mind. The chaotic order and the inclusion even of fragments point to his having been concerned above all to preserve whatever could be found of the bishop's writings.

In points one to five we have discussed the content of the sermons, and their arrangement in the manuscripts in points six and seven. Finally let us combine the issues of content and context:

---

[34]e.g., I.6 has the gloss: 'To be read in the monastery to the brothers on the third day of the Pasch in the presence of the bishop before the Assembly'. ('Tertia feria Paschae in conventu fratribus coram pontifice recitanda ante stationem'.)

[35]Löfstedt, 20*.

8. *Is there any significant incongruity between the contents of the sermons and their ostensible liturgical roles which might lead one to suppose that their context has been changed?*

If we were to believe, as we shall see Truzzi does, that some of the sermons on Genesis were originally composed for a feast of Christmas, then there is good reason to hypothesise their removal to the context of the paschal Vigil. Likewise, T. M. Finn takes the idea of the sermons being fragments to extreme and somewhat improbable lengths when he suggests that the 'invitations to the font' were all part of one complete homily, which must have been a very curious piece indeed.[36] But when the sermons for the paschal Vigil are discussed below it will be seen that there is no discrepancy between the content and context. They fit the occasion so well that they could have been composed especially for it! The sermons on Genesis fit the Vigil as well as any Christmas feast that may have been celebrated in Verona; indeed their concern for the incarnation within the context of the Pasch is congruent with a rather traditional Church of the mid to late fourth century. The computations had been made that identified the incarnation with the Pasch and the spring equinox, and therefore the birth with the winter solstice. But if Christmas was celebrated as a feast it had a comparatively low profile. Zeno shows great concern for the incarnation, but provides no concrete evidence for the feast of Christmas.

It is unnecessary to presuppose another feast and then to suggest that sermons are moved from it when in fact they fit their present context perfectly well. Likewise it is unnecessary to hypothesise larger sermons out of which the literary gems that we possess might have been taken. As this study proceeds I hope the reader will be impressed by the unity of thought evident in the sermons and the richness of theology based entirely on the paschal celebration and, with the pres-

---

[36]T. M. Finn, *Early Christian Baptism and the Catechumenate: Italy, North Africa, and Egypt*, 'Message of the Fathers of the Church' 6 (Collegeville, Minn., 1992) 55.

ent writer, be assured that we have a unique and immediate vista on the liturgy and theology of a fourth-century bishop.

5. ZENO'S SERMONS AS DRAFTS PRESERVED *VERBATIM*

We are directed, therefore, to consider the fourth possibility outlined at the beginning of this discussion, namely that Zeno composed the texts as preparatory drafts for his sermons.

Comparisons with contemporary Christian writers and with the tradition of classical rhetoric show that this was a most natural situation. Quintilian speaks of three forms of composition: writing the speech out in advance and memorising it, pre-meditation (*cogitatio*), and improvisation or extempore speaking. All have their role. Quintilian regards the last as the crowning achievement of rhetoric and also is adamant that it is absolutely necessary. Every lawyer or public speaker, if he is to be of service to his friends, his clients, or the state, must be equal to the sudden emergency or unexpected turn of events. But Quintilian also recognises the difficulty of extempore speaking. He acknowledges that many will not prefer it and, if anything, he warns people against rashly assuming it. He simply requires that the speaker be ready for it should the need arise. Pre-meditation is necessary also for when there is little time to prepare a speech, for example in marshalling answers to an opponent's points in debate.[37] But, for his pupils at any rate, Quintilian talks most about speeches being prepared by writing. The pen, he says, gives the greatest precision of speech. He teaches careful writing for the time when the lawyer will need to write quickly under pressure of time.[38] The speeches are then memorised. The master gives various methods of helping the memory, but most commonly expects his pupils to memorise a written passage *verbatim*.[39] Memoris-

[37]Quintilian, *Institutio Oratoria* 10.6–7; Butler, 126–34.
[38]Ibid., 10.3.3, 10; Butler, 96.
[39]Ibid., 11.2; Butler, 210f.

ing the sense only is a second best for a dull memory under
pressure of time. 'For the loss of even a single word that we
have chosen is always a matter for regret, and it is hard to
supply a substitute when we are searching for the word that
we had written.'[40] But a good speaker, according to Quintilian, should always be open to the inspiration of the
moment.[41]

In practice the great masters like Cicero often only wrote
out the beginnings of their speeches and trusted to *cogitatio*
or improvisation for the rest.[42] But this would only have been
for the great, since the expected standards were very high,
and the transition from prepared to improvised speech should
be imperceptible.

In Zeno's time, the same practices and stands applied.
G. Iulius Victor, a leading rhetorician of the fourth century,
is distrustful of clever aids to memorising speeches, and recom-
mends only the exercise of memorising of passages *ad verbum*,
no doubt with the aim of doing the same in real life situations.[43]

Alexander Olivar traces the various practices of leading
preachers in the preparation or improvisation of their speeches.
Augustine in his youth put in preparation, but he was a bril-
liant extempore speaker both when he chose to speak thus and
in responding to unexpected situations, for example when the
reader read the wrong lesson. Most of his sermons are
preserved for us by stenographers. Likewise Jerome was an
improviser, though his style was very simple in contrast to
Augustine's rhetorical flair. Ambrose on the other hand preferred to write his sermons in advance. These he would then
memorise and deliver, and he would normally rework the
stenographers' notes for publication. Ambrose was quite capable of improvisation, as once when the opponents in a debate failed to appear and he turned his material into a one-off

[40]Ibid., 11.2.49; Butler, 241.
[41]Ibid., 10.6.5; Butler, 130–31.
[42]Ibid., 10.7.30–31; Butler, 150.
[43]G. Iulius Victor, *Ars rhetorica,* ed. R. Giomini and M. S. Celentano
(Leipzig, 1980) 95–96.

speech. But this would simply be fulfilling Quintilian's standards for a public speaker, and Ambrose's preferences were for thorough written preparation.[44]

Maximus of Turin and Peter Chrysologus carefully memorised their written drafts. The former, like Zeno, was in the habit of borrowing from his own and other people's writings.[45] Peter was open to small improvisations, and would allow them in his published versions even if they were appeals for silence or comments on the reaction of the audience.

Leo the Great was a consummate artist of the memorised sermon. Olivar comments that his sermons were perfect in form and could almost have been sung like a preface.[46]

It would seem most likely then that Zeno should be placed among those who wrote a draft of the sermon in advance and learnt the draft verbatim. We today possess the copies of the drafts, and what improvisation he made in the actual delivery we cannot say. But in all probability the improvisation was very limited. The brevity of the sermons would not really admit much new material, and the small differences Zeno introduces both in sermons he copies and in, for example, those on the end of Jewish ritual (I.19; 28), where variation is very limited, leads one to suppose that he is already being very careful in his choice of words.

This would also explain why Zeno copied down sermons again rather than reuse old sermons. The act of copying was in itself an aid to memorising the text. As Quintilian says, 'Thus it results that after writing for several days, with a view to acquiring by heart what we have written, we find that our mental effort has of itself imprinted it on our memory.'[47]

[44]Olivar, 'Preparacion', 754.

[45]C. E. Chaffin thinks that he kept and copied from his own drafts: 'Maximus of Turin and the Church in North Italy' (unpublished thesis, Oxford, 1970) 188.

[46]Olivar, 'Preparacion', 747ff.

[47]'quae per plures dies scribimus ediscendi causa, cogitatione contineamus', Quintilian, *Institutio Oratoria* 11.2.10; Butler, 216–17.

Zeno's habit of copying sermons, both his own and other people's, can be seen as evidence in favour of this theory. The copying is so close that it would be impossible to be impromptu memory. At the same time, unless he were writing for the sake of memorising, it is hard to see why he should write such close copies out a second or even third time rather than simply reread old drafts.

We may also see here a possible solution to a problem about the collection of sermons, that there are very few indeed that are not involved with the Easter celebrations. Apart from the sermons for the Vigil and baptisms, there are, besides a number of fragments, the sermons on doctrines, virtues and vices, and the only two sermons for major occasions outside the paschal season, namely the *Passio* of Archadius and the sermon for the consecration of a church. It would be extraordinary if such a distribution were representative of Zeno's preaching career. We could suppose that the survival of mainly paschal sermons was by chance, and that others for the rest of the year have perished. Or it may be that the bishop was in fact inclined to improvise most of his sermons through the year, using notes at most which have not survived, and that for the Easter celebrations and for special occasions, when a more polished rhetoric was in keeping, he took the trouble of writing a full draft. In this context we might bear in mind Palanca's findings about Zeno's style.

Just as we discussed Löfstedt's theory by proceeding from the content of the sermons to their arrangement in the MSS, so now, having suggested that the sermons are essentially Zeno's own drafts, we must consider how their order can best be explained.

The signs of some order among the Easter sermons leads us to speculate what their fate was between their being preached and the time of their incorporation into a single MS, and what the reasons were for their publication. Some things are clear. The widespread confusion and the multiplicity of short, repetitious sermons preclude any idea that Zeno intended to publish them in anything like their present form.

As a literary collection, whatever the merits of individual pieces, this is highly unsatisfactory. As liturgical source material (after the pattern of the much later Leonine sacramentary) it would be quite anachronistic.

There is no way of knowing when the sermons were collected or by whom. It is quite likely that it would have happened after Zeno's death, but there could have been a gap of weeks, years, or even decades. The fact that the sermons have been consistently and, as far as we can tell, correctly ascribed to Zeno in the absence of any explicit internal evidence would suggest that the collection was made within the span of a generation when the sermons could still have been recognised as his, perhaps by handwriting or being among his personal effects.[48]

Before being collected together, it is evident that the sermons existed on a very large number of separate pieces of paper. Otherwise the collection could not have been so confused.[49] But the partial order of the collection is as interest-

[48]Dates suggested by various writers range from the years immediately after the bishop's death (so the Ballerini, PL 11:22A) to the sixth or seventh century (so G. B. Pighi, 'Scrittori latini di Verona Romana', in *Verona e il suo territorio,* vol. 1 (Verona, 1960) 353. Cf. Truzzi, 54 n. 36.

[49]The whole investigation of the material used by Zeno has so far been based exclusively on the evidence of his sermons as they are preserved in the manuscripts. It would be an advantage if we had some examples of the use of individual slips of paper from other writers, and these we find described by R. P. Evaristo Arns (*La technique du livre d'après Saint Jérôme* [Paris, 1953]). He describes the use of draft papers (*schedae*) and slips of paper (*chartulae*). He points out how Jerome uses the term *brevis* to emphasise the smallness of the *chartula*, and also quotes him for its use: 'I want to write some nonsense on my slips of paper, commenting on scripture'. ('Volo in chartulis meis quaslibet ineptias scribere, commentari de scripturis', *Ep. ad Pam.* 57.4; ibid., 15–19).

All this is discussed by Arns under the heading of 'Papyrus', but it would seem that there was no particular prestige in parchment that would prevent it from being used for such notes. Indeed, in letter-writing, papyrus was preferable to parchment which 'faisait pauvre' (ibid., 27). Parchment notebooks of a private nature seem to have been used from at least the first century A.D. (see C. H. Roberts and T. C. Skeat, *The Birth of the Codex*

ing as its confusion. It is hard to believe that the order is the
result of work by the editor. If that were the case, only a few
minutes' effort would be needed to put the sermons into a
much better order, either of each series according to its original
liturgical order, or in some other pattern as, for example, the
Ballerini have done in their revised order of the sermons, plac-
ing sermons of the same subject matter together.

It is interesting that, even when sermons are copied, they
do not necessarily lose their original context. It has been seen
above that the most natural explanation for the earlier sermons being still in their proper places must be that Zeno was
himself responsible for copying them for use on subsequent
Easter celebrations, and replaced sermons after using them.
In effect, he was careful in filing his old sermons for later use!
Groups of paschal sermons were kept distinct from one another. The confusion in their internal order might point to
a limit on Zeno's organisational ability (e.g., the state of the
group II.10–17 might suggest that he was not necessarily in-
terested in keeping the individual group in liturgical order),
and/or to the sermons being put out of order by some other
person. We may well imagine the papers being rummaged
through by various curious persons, perhaps if they were found
after the bishop's death, before they were written up together.

The only proper conclusion is that such order as exists in
the paschal groups is derived from their original composition
by Zeno, and that later rearranging contributed only to the
evident disorder of the groups.

The non-paschal groups represent a slightly different case,
where sermons of different types have been sorted into groups
reflecting particular interests on the part of the selector and
with each group marked by a common form of title. Some
sermons have been removed from the paschal groups. However, the selection process was extremely limited. The non-
paschal groups were evidently not separated from the gen-

[London, 1987] 15–23). Therefore we may suppose that either material
may have been used by Zeno.

eral collection of papers, since they were written up with the rest. The way in which paschal and non-paschal groups are mixed together in the MSS suggests that the collector found them all together and in the same condition. The non-paschal groups may therefore represent an early attempt to sort out a selection of the bishop's writings before it was decided to preserve them all. Perhaps this was seen as a temporary measure to preserve the sermons until someone could prepare a proper edition. But such is the way with temporary measures.

6. SOME DETAILS OF THE MANUSCRIPTS

The collection of the sermons has a number of peculiar characteristics which require some kind of explanation, and which we see as being simply explained by the hypothesis described above for the origin of the MSS.

(i) The Place of the Fragmentary Sermons

It has already been noted how the sermons include mere fragments (e.g., I.60) whether or not the material makes sense. The collector's only concern was to preserve for posterity the contents of the pile of papers. However, it might be asked how the fragments found their way into the collection in the first place.

As a suggested answer to this problem we can describe a number of the sermons in the collection as *recto* or *verso*. Pairs of sermons may have been written on the same piece of paper before they were included in the collected single manuscript. In some cases it will appear that the sermons were actually written on the *recto* and *verso* of the piece of paper. In other cases the precise relation of the pair to one another is not clear, beyond the fact that there is evidence for their being physically linked. For convenience, with a minimal sacrifice of strict accuracy, all these pairs are denoted as *rectos* and *versos*.

The fragmentary sermons I.21 and II.18 have several points in common. Both are the beginnings of sermons, one on avarice and the other on Christ's use of miracles. They are mere introductions, nothing more. But a curious factor, which would also explain their preservation and position in the MSS, is that both are very similar in length to neighbouring sermons. The text of I.21 is 72 words long; I.20 is 79 words long, and I.22 85 words long. II.18 has 109 words. Next to it, II.19 has 104 words. It would therefore seem very likely indeed that both fragmentary texts, whether they had previously been preached or were rejected drafts, were on the reverse side of the Vigil sermons and were preserved with them and copied up at the same time.

It is quite likely that the scrap of a sermon represented by I.60 was preserved in much the same way. The preservation in the MSS of rejected drafts in the case of I.58 and I.10A/B is quite probably because they were on the same piece of paper as were the final versions. This is the best explanation of why I.10A and I.10B are found together, being two sermons on Isaiah in a group where there should only be one, and why I.57 and I.58 should be together and result in there being nine proclamations when there is evidence only of eight of any other type of paschal Vigil sermon.

(ii) The Titles of Sermons II.26; 28; 30

The last six sermons in book II also display a curiosity which could perhaps be explained by the arrangement of the sermons on sheets of paper. Alternate sermons (26; 28; 30) have in their titles the same phrase, *cuius supra,* translated in the text as 'as above'. This curious phrase seems to be roughly equivalent in meaning to *eiusdem.*[50] This could refer to the

---

[50]Cf. Löfstedt, 92–94*. Löfstedt understands *cuius supra* as referring to the author, namely, *sancti Zenonis,* the purpose being to differentiate the last sermon of Zeno (II.30) from those of Hilary, Potamius, and Rufinus which follow in the MSS. This would make good sense in itself, but fails

previous sermon and its title, and sermons 25; 27; 29 all make it clear in their titles that the context is the Pasch. Thus, for example, II.27 is titled *Tractatus Danielis in Pascha,* and II.28 has *Invitatio fontis cuius supra.* That this peculiar note should occur in alternate sermons suggests that we are dealing with the sermons coming in pairs, presumably on one piece of paper.

(iii) *Item* in the Titles of Sermons

There is one piece of evidence in the index titles for the work of the final collector. A curious feature of the index is the use of the word *Item* in some of the titles. In many cases (I.29; 58; 61; 62) it means, as we might expect, that the sermon follows another of the same title (I.28; 57; 59; 60). However in I.6; 16; 25; 26; 33 this is not the case. There are no such preceding sermons. But these sermons are the first ones of groups I, II, III, C, and the stray I.25. In these cases, *Item* would seem to refer not to a second sermon but to another pile of papers, as it were. Like almost every other feature of the editing of these sermons, this is not followed through systematically in the first sermon of every group. But it does show that the person who wrote up the index was aware of the sermons being in groups, and therefore he could have been the original editor who gathered them together as one collection.[51]

7. THE INTEGRITY OF THE SERMON COLLECTION

This lengthy but very necessary study of the text allows us not only to affirm the integrity and authenticity of the sermons as being those preached by Zeno, but also gives us a

---

to explain why the phrase should occur in the heading not only of the very last sermon but of two others as well.

[51]See the Appendix where this use of *Item* is demonstrated.

detailed knowledge of the steps by which the collection was drawn up.

First, the texts themselves were composed by the bishop with very great care in preparation for the paschal ceremonies. On many occasions he might have trusted in preparing by *cogitatio*, working out in advance what he was to say without writing it all out; at most he might have made a few notes. He may even have preached extempore according to his confidence and inspiration. But on important occasions, and for the great feast of Easter, he composed even the briefest pieces with care over every word, employing all his considerable skills of rhetoric. Sometimes he would use previous years' sermons, but every time he would refashion the material in some way or other, however slightly. He wrote out the sermon on pieces of paper as an aid to memorising, and he stored the papers each year so that he could consult them as required. Sometimes the paper he used already had drafts and fragments of sermons written on them, but for his purposes that would not matter. Each Easter's sermons were kept as a set, the several sheets of paper bundled up together. Sermons from other occasions would easily find themselves together with the paschal groups.

Zeno died, revered by the Christians of Verona. At some point, probably not long after his death, his sermons were examined and a number of them were sorted out into separate bundles reflecting various interests. They were each given headings explaining their contents, but not interfered with beyond that. In the event it was decided to preserve everything, whether on a permanent basis or as a temporary measure. All the material was included in the collection, even scraps which can have made little or no sense. The editor wrote up the various bundles of sermons as he found them; perhaps titles were added to any sermons that still lacked them. An index was made up at the same time, based on the titles of the sermons. At first this was done very carefully, and the editor even noted the transition to each new bundle of papers. But the procedure became less careful, and one sermon title was omitted altogether. The collection filled more than one book. At some point some sermons of Hilary, Potamius, and Rufinus were added to the second book.

Thus was the manuscript collection preserved by the Church in Verona, copied, and passed down to posterity. Throughout this period there is no reason to believe that the contents of the sermons were interfered with in any way. Such corruption in the texts as may have occurred would have been in the normal course of copying, with the hazards entailed by that process.

The text that we possess is therefore shown to be as authentic a copy of the sermons of Zeno of Verona as we can possibly hope to possess.

Chapter Three
ZENO OF VERONA:
THE SERMONS DELIVERED
AT THE PASCHAL VIGIL[1]

I.6: HERE BEGINS A PROCLAMATION

On its laborious path, proceeding through the daily apportion-
ments of its worldly task on its circuitous route and returning
by its own tracks from itself to itself, ever new in its life-giving
death, the day of salvation has come, lavish with every kind
of gifts for all who attend on the Lord's mystery. For it grants
pay to loyal priests, to subordinate ministers the advancement
of promotion, the fruit of immortality for the baptised [*fideles*],
healing for penitents, the way of light for catechumens, for
the *competentes* the remission of all their sins, and thus it gathers
all into the one grace of the body of Christ and leads them
to the heavenly realms through our Lord and saviour Jesus
Christ, who is blessed for ever and ever.

I.7: ON GENESIS

1. No one can ever enjoy his goods in security unless he resists
the enemy who attacks him. For there are many who try to
assert that in the beginning was chaos, that is, a formless and

---

[1]The text translated is that of Löfstedt, except for a few places where,
as is signified, we have followed the suggested emendations of Dolbeau
('Zenoniana') or L. Håkanson ('Textkritisches zu Zeno Veronensis', *Classica
et Mediaevalia* 31 [1970] 223–38).

shapeless mass of blank nature remaining by itself and in itself in some heap of its own bulk; but that afterwards God
resolved this and from it made and adorned the world.[2] So
then if, as they want to say, God did not make the material
which he used, but it is eternal as he is, then there are two
beginnings which in fact are contrary to one another.[3] **2.** In
such a case we have to ask, which is the mightier of the two:
that which has or that which lacks consciousness? Who can
doubt that the mightier is the one which is conscious, which
has knowledge and thought, which can move and be moved,
which by its wonderful providence could make even chaos to
be no longer chaos, which separated out its parts and set them
in order, adorned it with colours, set the extent of its bound-
aries, and taught it to be useful in due service? And so the
beginning is not the one which grows old, which is the result
of another's activity, which is not endowed of its own power,
which is removed from its original nature, which is changed,
which is moved by another's agency, which cannot at any time
be conscious of its present, past, or future states.

3. So God alone is the beginning, God who himself gave from
himself to himself the beginning; alone before all things and
after all things, since all things are in his hand. His being is
of himself. He alone is conscious of himself, of his eminence
and nature. He alone is perfect, since he cannot in any way
be added to or diminished. He alone is all-powerful, since
he made all things out of nothing, he rules them by his power
and protects them by his majesty. He alone is unchangeable
and always the same, since there is no ageing in him. He alone
is eternal, since he is the Lord of immortality. **4.** This is our
God, who poured himself into God. This is our Father who,
while remaining in the integrity of his being, mirrored himself in the Son, lest he should deprive himself of anything.
In short each rejoices in the other in the fullness of the Holy
Spirit, reflecting one original coeternity. If one may say it,

[2]Cf. Lactantius, *Divine Institutes* 2.8.8; Ovid, *Metamorphoses* 1.7ff.
[3]Cf. Lactantius, *Divine Institutes* 2.8.31.

it is like two seas that flow into one another, connected by a strait which brings the alternating currents together. Although they are distinct in their signification, place and terminology, yet in the threefold deep there is one essence, one substance, one nature of the liquid, neither can the incomprehensible common mass of water be divided as it flows, copiously passing from one to the other. It belongs to both and is exclusive to neither. For indeed those who deny what one receives from the other in the common current suffer the loss of richness and grace.

I.8: SERMON ON EXODUS

1. A person suckles the riches of the divine Law, brothers, when he understands it spiritually. For indeed the Jews, since they have a carnal belief and so look for a lamb who combines a double nature in their herds of animals, have lost the true Lamb whom they had found. For they did not understand that by 'from the goats' is meant a human flesh burdened with its sins, and by 'from the sheep' the spirit of majesty (Exod 12:5). These from either nature have been brought together in Christ and produced the lamb prescribed by the Law. **2.** This is the lamb, brothers, of which the Law says, 'It is the Pasch of the Lord' (Exod 12:11). Also the apostle Paul says, 'Christ our Pasch has been sacrificed for us' (1 Cor 5:7). John the Baptist proclaimed beforehand the reason why he allowed himself to be sacrificed, in these words, 'Behold the Lamb of God, behold him who takes away the sin of the world' (John 1:29). And so he is called 'firstborn' (Exod 13:12) because he alone knows the lifespan of the Father; he is 'fully grown' (cf. Exod 12:5) because after him there is no other; he is 'eternal' (Isa 40:28) because he was killed and has been found to be alive; he is 'without blemish' (Exod 12:5) because he alone is without sin; he is 'saving' (Ps 64:6) because through him we overcome death; he is 'male' (Exod 12:5) because he is the power of God; he, I say, is the 'perfect' (Heb 7:28)

Lamb, because in him that great priest, who was made one with his victim in a holy mystery, has today made to be God the human being whom he has offered.

I.9: AGAIN A SERMON ON THE CONTINUATION OF EXODUS

Time does not permit me, brothers, to give the truth for the image. However why, O Jew, do you rejoice in the records of your crime? You served for a long time in Egypt, not by the foreigner's lot but by just deserts. You were delivered from there; you did not escape by your own power. The pillar of cloud led you by day, to show you are blind; the pillar of fire by night, to warn you that you will burn. An angel went before your camp as a guide, so that you should prove yourself to be ungrateful even in the presence of God. You walked through the sea on foot so that you should suffer shipwreck on land. In the desert you drank water from the rock and tasted manna from heaven for this purpose, that when you were later turned out to poverty you should be the more sharply tortured by remembrance of the former good things.

I.10A: SERMON ON ISAIAH

As the tone of the reading shows, brothers, the Jewish people is accused of impiety, but the Christian people equally is warned against a similar fate. So one is terrified so that the other should fear God; one is afflicted for the profit of the other. O nation which enjoys the advantage of happiness, learn from the other's peril what you must avoid. So, brothers, I must show concern rather than eloquence in such a matter. Hear me in a few words: whoever wishes to escape the wrath of God whose threats hang over all must serve him blamelessly.

I.10B

1. Discussion of the vineyard in the story, dearly beloved brothers, has ramifications which spread far and wide, and the pressure of the mysteries to come does not permit me to go through them with an adequate sermon. But lest due observance should be totally neglected, learn a little of it in a brief sermon.

2. The first vineyard of God was the synagogue. It was worthless with dense shoots of wandering branches; it spread its luxuriant leaves widely through sensuous and wicked places and so brought forth thorns instead of fruit and wild grapes instead of grapes. In his indignation over the matter the Lord abandoned it and of his own will planted another one for himself, that is mother Church. He cultivated it with the priestly offices, fertilized it with divine watering and trained it to bear a rich harvest hanging from the fertile wood. **3.** So it is that today some of your number have been brought as new vines to the cross-bar and to the joy of all have filled the Lord's wine cellar, aglow with the sweet stream of flowing new wine. God the Father almighty will grant that this comes to you also as your faith matures, through our Lord Jesus Christ who is blessed with the Holy Spirit for ever and ever.

I.11: SERMON ON DANIEL

It is part of martyrdom, dearly beloved brothers, not to tremble at the execution of the martyrs. Truly just as mournful consideration of the many forms of cruelty holds one back from the crown, so the noble and perfect faith of the one being tortured multiplies his offering. Certainly in their sacred contest the three children placed before their eyes God and not the flames, the reward of the world to come and not the punishment. And so as they triumphed among the dreadful surge of balls of fire over the barbarian king, all his threats and the execution itself, they showed that fire is weaker than holy

people, through our Lord Jesus Christ who is blessed for ever
and ever.

I.12: SERMON AFTER PSALM 41

Come, brothers, parched by the longed-for craving of blessed
thirst. The sweet murmur of the stream of nectar invites you:
hasten without delay to the milky water of the life-giving font
and drink deeply, while you may. Immerse yourselves with
all haste in the wave, let its stream run over you, and with
all ardour and zeal fill your vessels so that the water may satisfy
you for ever; and know this before everything else, that this
water must not be wasted nor be drunk a second time.

I.16: PASCHAL PROCLAMATION

1. In travelling round its swift course of the entire year to
the fullness of the twice sixfold change of horses, in one and
the same circuit, which is itself but not itself, the great day
has come, ever new in itself from its own sunset [*occasus*]. It
follows what it has been before; it goes before what it will be.
It is ever new and ever old. At every moment it changes not
in nature but in number. It is the son of the hours and the
father of all the ages. **2.** This is the day, brothers, on which
the whole world was redeemed by our Lord, when a new
people—our own[4]—was quickened by the heavenly seed. This,
I say, is the day which shows to us the figure of the resurrection. Indeed by its very nature we are more happy, because
he died in order to live for ever, and the baptised [*fidelis*] who
rises after the death [*occasus*] of the second birth will never
be seized by the horror of darkness.

I.17: ON GENESIS

1. The beginning, dearly beloved brothers, is indeed our Lord
Christ, embraced before all ages by the Father in the hidden

---

[4]Reading with Dolbeau: 'novellus id est noster populus.'

unsearchable depths of his sacred mind and his consciousness
known only to himself, not without love for his Son but without showing him forth. And so that ineffable and incomprehensible wisdom generates wisdom, and omnipotence
generates omnipotence. **2.** From God, God is born, from the
unbegotten the only begotten, alone from the alone, whole
from the whole, true from the true, perfect from the perfect,[5]
having everything that is the Father's yet taking nothing from
the Father. He who was in the Father before he was born proceeds to birth. He is equal in all things, since the Father begat in him another self, that is, of his substance which is
beyond birth. Remaining in this being, happy for ever, he
procreated his Son who has equally everything which he has;
who is God, blessed for ever and ever.

I.18: ON EXODUS

1. In that the Jews think themselves to be happy, they recognise that they are wretched. For I think it is more bearable
for one who is wretched and remains all the time in his
wretched state than for one who has been happy and then
reduced to utter misery. For they proclaim that their fore-
bears destroyed the Egyptian people by fleeing, that God led
their ancestors and went before them on the road, but they
do not understand from this that he had removed them from
his face and cast them behind his back along with those who
would come after them. Also the Red Sea had split down the
middle into twin banks, and on the right hand and left the
piles of water had been heaped up in line, and while the water
of the deep remained, its amazed dried nature hung supported
upon itself. A path on the ground sparkled among the waves,
announcing not the merit of a heavenly people but the fate
of dispersion throughout the world which would befall an
earthly race. **2.** And so he led them into the desert and en-
joined the healing of the wounds of their detestable minds by

[5]Cf. Hilary, *De Trinitate* 3.8.

the provision of milk and honey; for the infirm and weak he provided the soft dew of manna. For they were not ready or worthy to enjoy the sound solidity of the heavenly bread. The rock gushed out for them into a fountain that they might afterwards drink filthy water, as they deserved, from broken cisterns, as the Lord says, 'They have abandoned me, the fountain of living water and dug for themselves broken cisterns which cannot hold water' (Jer 2:13). Ultimately what can the wretches hope for from the image when they have not deserved to recognise its truth, our Lord Jesus Christ?

I.19: AGAIN A CONTINUATION OF EXODUS

1. How the Pharisee can celebrate a Pasch according to the Law, I cannot see. That distinguished and renowned Temple of his lies buried in its own dust, level with the fields in a wretched devastation. The priestly 'seat of pestilence' (Ps 1:1) has been abolished because of the sacrilege of his rites. The empty oil horn no longer exhales its perfume. **2.** The prophets testify that his feast days have been turned to mourning and his songs to lamentation. We have understood that the bulls, rams, goats, and lambs have often been rejected by the Lord. What more is there? He cannot celebrate any mystery, brothers, when you see that his sacrifice has been condemned by divine judgement through our Lord Jesus Christ, who with the Holy Spirit is blessed for ever and ever.

I.20: ON ISAIAH

It is deeply moving, brothers, when one who can very easily revenge oneself complains of injuries suffered. But, among the wise and noble, disgrace over some infamy is worse than death, and so God puts the Jewish people to shame with a public rebuke that they have been corrupted by basking in luxury.[6] He calls heaven and earth as witnesses to emphasise

---

[6]Reading with Dolbeau: 'luxurie aestuante' for 'luxuriae aestu exuberante'.

the crime. He calls them sons to frighten them with being disowned, he says he raised them up in order to scare them with their fall, he accuses them of rejecting him to show their treachery. Brothers, it is a wretched guilt which finds no room for any kind of excuse. Certainly it is a hateful son whom a kind father condemns against his will.

I.22: HERE BEGINS A SERMON ON DANIEL

1. Whoever can believe in the martyrdom of the three children without terror can himself also obtain martyrdom. For such was the might of the contest that even the very fire trembled at it. For in the barbarian king's most cruel decision for the three children the fire of the furnace was piled up with straw seven times more than usual. **2.** I believe also that by divine providence their spiritual number accorded with the mystery of the Trinity. Certainly they obtained the grace of the dewy oven of baptism. Oh what a wondrous fire! What a spectacle truly worthy of God! Those who hear are struck with fear. Those who would burn the children are themselves burnt. Those who are cast in the flames proceed from the oven sanctified and unharmed, through our Lord Jesus Christ.

I.23: AFTER PSALM 41

Hurry, hurry for a good wash, brothers! The water, living with the Holy Spirit and warmed with the sweetest fire now invites you with its soft murmur. Now the bath attendant is girded up and waiting for you, ready to provide the necessary anointing and washing, and also a golden denarius signed with the union of the triple seal. So rejoice! You will indeed go down naked into the font, but soon you will rise from there robed in white, dressed in heavenly vesture. Whoever does not defile it will possess the heavenly kingdoms, through our Lord Jesus Christ.

I.24: AFTER THE ADMINISTRATION OF BAPTISM

1. After the chaste fast of holy expiation has been most devoutly accomplished, after the sweet vigils of a night dazzling with its own sun, after your souls grew to the hope of immortality by the life-giving bath of the milky font from which you who differed in age and race have come up suddenly as full brothers, suddenly as infants all born together, I urge you to celebrate the feast of such a great birth with a joyful banquet. But this is not one in which the belly is overwhelmed with different rich courses competing to the utmost in the allure of the flavour of seasoning, and heaves with the vomiting of undigested and acid food, or in which the worldly sweetness of your new wine is ruined by the breathing out of the foulness of the previous day's wine; this is a heavenly feast, honourable, pure, wholesome, and eternal. Receive it avidly, so that you can be full and happy for ever. **2.** From his table the father of the household lavishes upon you precious bread and wine from his store. The three children of one mind lead, bringing vegetables on which they sprinkle the salt of wisdom to bring out their flavour. Christ pours on oil. Moses has quickly prepared for you a first-born and fully grown lamb, Abraham has faithfully prepared rich veal marinaded. Isaac innocently brings a jar[7] and wood. Jacob patiently presents his various herds. Joseph who has been given charge over the distribution pays out to everyone their allowance. **3.** Indeed if anyone lacks anything, Noah the captain of the ark who has stored everything will not withold it from him. Peter the fisherman sets before you the abundance of his catch fresh from the sea, and his miraculous fish. Tobias the traveller carefully prepares and roasts the entrails of his

---

[7]MSS: *oleum*. The repetition of *oleum* (already poured on by Christ) and its inappropriateness to Isaac suggests that the MSS are incorrect here. Löfstedt replaces *oleum* with *ollam*, a jar for carrying the fire. This is a curious emendation. *Ignem,* though a difficult emendation, is surely better (cf. Vulg. Gen 22.7: 'Ecce ignis et ligna. Ubi est victima holocausti?') or perhaps *ovem,* although this should for the story's sake be *arietem.*

fish from the river. John in his camel hair runs devoutly from
the wilderness with honey and locusts. Let no one eye his
neighbour as he eats: so warns Paul who invites you. David
the royal shepherd serves at every moment silvery milk and
cheese. **4.** Zacchaeus without delay hands out presents four-
fold to the guests. Our Lord and God Jesus Christ the son
of God, as the one who first ate this banquet before us,[8] says,
'How sweet are your words to my taste, sweeter than honey
and the honey comb to my mouth!' (Ps 119:103) My brothers,
if anyone freely believes this, he will find yet more lavish food,
and if he is a good steward of it he will fill himself and others
with all good things through our Lord Jesus Christ.

I.26: HERE BEGINS A PROCLAMATION

Turning on the splendid circuit, the sacred day is borne on
the four-horsed chariot of the seasons in its daily apportion-
ment of worldly work, rich in its twelvefold exchange of horses
on its entire course of the months, content with no resting
place, because its course is immortality. Whether it proceeds
or recedes is unclear since its former position remains so that
it may return. What marvellous logic! The various periods
of the innumerable ages renew the cycles of time by wearing
them down, and yet their circuit is always one. This bids us,
brothers, to celebrate the saving mysteries of our Lord's passion and resurrection with one mind and heart, through our
Lord and defender Jesus Christ.

I.27: ON GENESIS

1. Nothing, dearly beloved brothers, is so necessary and useful above all else for a person who fears God than that he

---

[8]The translation omits from this clause the word *dulcia,* which makes
no good sense and is possibly a duplication from the first word of the following quotation.

should know himself. For it is madness itself to investigate an understanding of the secret of one's nature, since the substance of one's nature cannot be understood at all by human conjecture. No one knows it except the one who made it.

2. And so, what especially applies to our task, let us see what it is that God says: 'Let us make humanity in our image and likeness' (and it says, 'God made humanity in the image and likeness of God') (Gen 1:26), and in another place it says, 'I am who I am and I do not change' (Mal 3:6). Since this is so, how can a human being bear the image of God when his face is subject to suffering, liable to every change and at every moment altered by labour, age, weakness, anger, joy, sadness, and there are as many faces as there are moods, and there is not a single day when it seems fixed in one likeness? **3.** Since this is how things are, do we then not have the image of God? Of course we do and indeed this is clear from the very fact that it is not seen by us who bear it. For the image of the incomprehensible God must be invisible, so it is not to be seen by fleshly eyes. For when it enters our body and when it leaves the body, it cannot be detected by anyone, and it has such power that, when it is enclosed within the walls of its dwelling place, it shows forth at every moment whatever it wills. So we must believe that the image of God is not this fleshly dwelling place, but the spiritual image of the heavenly person which of his abundance the Lord lavishes on those who believe in him when they are renewed in the heavenly birth from the sacred font through our Lord Jesus Christ.

I.28: HERE BEGINS A SERMON ON EXODUS

1. The Jew claims that he is conducting a Pasch according to the Law, when nothing remains of the old mystery other than a tale woven with empty sighs. In short that royal Temple lies level with the fields. They have profaned the altars of God which he has turned over with his own hand and which lie scattered in the dust with their sacrifices to themselves. The priestly 'seat of pestilence' (Ps 1:1) has been abolished by its own reputation. **2.** The saving Lamb which is chosen 'from the sheep and goats' (Exod 12:5) cannot be found among the herds. In accordance with the voice of God his feast days and songs have become wailing and mourning to him. That proud city is in slavery. Indeed he kills unnumbered herds of sheep which he consumes in bitterness. Who cannot understand, brothers, that that is no Pasch but the wintery feast of a blood-thirsty bandit? Through Jesus Christ our Lord.

I.29: HERE BEGINS THE SECOND SERMON ON EXODUS

1. What a marvellous account, dearly beloved brothers, of sacred history which has been read! When the people of Israel were being crushed by king Pharaoh under the monstrous yoke of captivity and were being killed by the harsh conditions in Egypt, in the mercy of God they were ordered to set out under the leadership of Moses. By day they had not the disc of the sun but a pillar of cloud; it was not the white moon but a pillar of fire that lit the road by night. When they came between the two elements they feared there their fate with death looming over them. On the one side they were hard pressed by the thick swords of the pursuing Egyptians, on the other they were blocked and hemmed in by the great barrier of the sea. **2.** They had no ships, no resources for getting across, when suddenly by divine providence the sea is split open, the waters are heaped up[9] on the right hand and the left, restrained in an icy stupor into glassy walls and providing a way across for the people of God, while for the pursuers the waters were the sea. Ungrateful Israel were led on the path in which they could not fear either swords or the waves. What a marvel! Dusty in the midst of the deep, they

[9] Reading with Dolbeau: 'digeruntur' for 'diriguntur'.

rejoice and happily see around them perishing in shipwreck those who would triumph over them. The Jew proclaims this, my brothers, and yet madly still does not believe in God, who is blessed for ever and ever.

I.30: SERMON ON ISAIAH

As the reading of blessed Isaiah shows, God is angry at the Jewish people and puts it to shame with a public reproof in case it should repent. By human standards it is worse to be discarded than to be punished. So he calls them sons to frighten them with being disowned, he says he raised them up so that their fall might terrify them, he accuses them of rejecting him that they may recognise the dreadful punishment that hangs over them. They are an example for us, brothers: avoid following it with all your might and at the same time rejoice that it is by another's punishment that you learn the discipline of God through Jesus Christ.

I.31: HERE BEGINS A SERMON ON DANIEL

A great punishment sometimes is followed by an even greater glory, especially in things of religion, in which the blessed rely on their devotion and preserve their faith rather than their safety. And so when I hear of the three children being commited to the flames, first I shudder dreadfully. But then I would wish to be one among them, when I realise that in the midst of the flames they are safe, covered in dew and singing a hymn to God. For such is the strength and power of faith which compels even the very elements to change their nature and to wait upon the servants of God. And so, brothers, do not let consideration of this most dreadful matter terrify you, for no punishment is now to be feared when the one who survives being cast in the flames taunts the fires with his survival.

I.32: INVITATION TO THE FONT

Rejoice, brothers in Christ, hasten with all desire and receive
the heavenly gifts. Now the saving warmth of the everlasting
font invites you, now our mother adopts you so that she may
give birth to you, but not in the manner in which your mothers
bore you when they brought you into the world, themselves
groaning with birth pains and you wailing, filthy, done up
in filthy swaddling clothes and surrendered to this world, but
with joy and gladness⟨   ⟩ [10] and freed from all your sins,
and she feeds you not in a stinking cradle but with delight
from the sweet-smelling rails of the holy altar, through our
Lord Jesus Christ.

I. 33: HERE BEGINS A SERMON ON THE LORD'S DAY

1. The heir and father[11] of the ages, advancing and retreating on its swift course, returning on itself round the solemn
mile posts and bringing forth its own beginning from its end
and infinite numbers of birthday gifts from its death, the eternal day has dawned. Now winter has lifted and its sadness
is shaken off, and with the new Zephyr's caress everywhere
the meadows are sprouting and carry the sweet perfume of
flowers different in kind and colour and scent, scattered in
a single birth. The new but rich summer rejoices as it happily pounds the crowning ears of corn into various piles of
grain. Fittingly autumn follows, abounding in new wine, so
that the delight of the grace of bread and of wine must be
joined together.

2. Who cannot recognise that these things conform to
heavenly mysteries? For sluggish, filthy, and sad winter refers
to those who are devoted to idolatry and are shackled by

---

[10]Omitting 'caelestis ⟨ . . . ⟩ libera'.
[11]Reading with Håkanson: 'heres et pater pernici.'

worldly desires; they apply themselves to their lusts and their gullet. Because they love the works of darkness God has destined them to the long night, that is to eternal death. Spring we must understand as the sacred font, from whose rich vessel our infants are brought forth, the dazzling sweet flowers of the Church which are engendered not by the Zephyr wind but by the Holy Spirit and which in their blessed faith exhale the divine perfume of various gifts but the one birth. **3.** Summer is the faithful people, angelic and pure, which boldly bears the palm of its profession and, cleared of the chaff of sins, desires to bring itself, the precious grain, into the divine barns. Although it bears fruit by its own fountain, yet it always burns with thirst for righteous works. And autumn is the place of martyrdom, in which it is not the vine's blood but the confessor's[12] that is shed so that a blessed life may be procured by the vintage of a precious death. **4.** And the day refers to the mystery of the resurrection of our Lord Jesus Christ, who is 'all in all' (1 Cor 15:28). He is truly the eternal day without any night. The twelve hours serve him in the apostles; the twelve months in the prophets. The four saving seasons of the gospels proclaim him. There is not a yearly but a daily yield of fruit as the nations who believe in God sing their hymn, they who have been brought forth for ever by the seed of immortality. As we walk in the light of this day let us exult in our faith and rejoice in good conduct so that we may be counted worthy to obtain eternal life through our Lord Jesus Christ.

I.38: SERMON ON THE ZODIAC TO THE NEOPHYTES

1. Rejoice, heavenly peoples, new children in Christ, and guard with perpetual care against staining in any way the whiteness of your flowering spiritual birth today. What is given

[12]Reading with Håkanson and Dolbeau: 'confessoris' for 'fossoris'.

cannot be repeated. Behold, you who were children, teenagers, young adults, and old people of either sex, guilty and filthy by your worldly birth, now are free of all guilt and pure babes and, what is most wonderful and pleasing, suddenly you who were of different ages are in a moment all the same age. **2.** But I am well aware of your curiosity. With the taking away of your old life, which henceforth is forbidden you, perhaps you would like to know from us under which constellation and which sign your mother bore you together, so varied, so many, and so different, in a single birth. I shall do this as with children and in only a few words explain the secrets of the divine horoscope.

3. Brothers, your birth is of the following kind. First it was not Aries but the Lamb who received you; he rejects no one who believes in him. He has clothed your nakedness with the shining white of his wool and tenderly poured his own blessed milk into your lips which were wide open with crying. You are admonished not by Taurus with his massive neck, menacing face and threatening horns, but by the delightful, gentle, tame, and mild Calf, so that you will not seek after divination by any means but, taking on his yoke without malice and making the ground of your flesh fruitful by subduing it, you may bring into the heavenly barns a rich harvest of divine seed. **4.** And he admonishes you with the following Gemini, that is, the twin Testaments which proclaim salvation, that above all you may shun idolatry, indecency, and greed. This is the incurable Cancer. But our Leo, as Genesis bears witness, is a 'lion's cub' whose gracious mysteries we celebrate. He 'lay down and slept' (Gen 49:9) in order to conquer death and he kept vigil in order to confer upon us the gift of the immortality of his blessed resurrection. **5.** He is followed straightway by Virgo who foreshadows Libra, that we might know that equity and justice have been brought to birth by the Son of God, incarnate and born of a virgin. Whoever steadfastly observes these virtues and faithfully carries them out will tread with unharmed feet—I shall not say on Scor-

pio but, as the Lord said in the gospel—on all serpents. **6.**
Nor will he ever fear even the devil himself, who indeed is
the sharp-stinging Sagittarius armed with all kinds of fiery
arrows and wounding at every moment the hearts of the whole
human race. Because of this the apostle Paul says, 'Put on
the whole armour of God, that you may be able to stand
against the wiles of the devil, taking the shield of faith with
which you can quench all the darts of the evil one, which are
full of fire' (Eph 6:11, 16). For with these calamities in due
course he sends Capricorn with his misshapen face, whose
horn protrudes out, whose pale lips foam with bubbling poi-
sons, who rages through all the limbs of his captive—the poor
wretch—with shuddering ruin. He drives some mad, other
frenzied, others to be murderers, or adulterers, or enemies
of religion, or blind with greed. **7.** It is a long business to
narrate each instance. He has innumerable 'tricks for making mischief', but our Aquarius is used to wiping all these
out without great effort, pouring out his saving stream. Of
necessity the two Pisces follow in one sign, that is, the two
peoples from Jews and Gentiles who live by the water of baptism, sealed by one sign into the people of Christ.

I.41: SERMON ON THE LORD'S DAY ON A COMPARISON WITH WHEAT

1. Let us rejoice, brothers in Christ, and give thanks and
praise to God the Father almighty because we have been en-
riched by the yield of such a great crop. He has changed tares,
darnel, burs, and thistles into rich corn which has been win-
nowed with great care, joyfully ground by the gracious weight
of the millstones, thoroughly sifted and, with all the bran removed, it is now white flour and gleams with a marvellous
brightness. Unadulterated with any yeast it is moistened and
kneaded. Salt is added to it. It is leavened with oil,[13] blended
with suitable care and made into loaves of unleavened bread.

---

[13]Oil: 'Oleo gremiali'.

2. Those whom you see with the delightful smell of this excellent baking have been cooked not in an oven but a font, not with human but with divine fire. No draught has ruined them, no bitter smoke has blighted them, no cold has spoiled them. What is more, they have been leavened without yeast. Indeed they are not sooty or stale or burnt or undercooked or mouldy. Their colour is milky, their taste is milky.

3. But perhaps something is felt to be wrong with the baker, since some of them seem to be smaller than others. That makes no difference to me, brothers. For I may be poor but I can hold my head high and I know my good faith. Indeed let the workers who are with me say if they know of anything wrong. I rejoice in the profit but, to be sure, I confess it without having any conscience of theft. But then you retain the old weights, you have the balance. Make the measurement in whatever way you like. Weigh each one and you will find that not one of them is short. All that are used at the table are three pounds' weight, and signed with the one measure of the sacred stamp.

I.42: SERMON TO THE NEOPHYTES
ON ANOTHER PASCH

1. Rejoice, my brothers in Christ! Guard carefully, strictly, and faithfully the royal favour of mercy which you have received. For every action for which you are liable has been cancelled. Rejoice freely! Now you owe nothing to the world. Until now, my brothers, you were indeed in great guilt. But you have been examined strictly and you have prayed well for yourselves in vigil in order to receive mercy. You have been most favourably heard. It is a new kind of judgement, in which the guilty person, if he denies the crime, is condemned, but if he confesses, he is forgiven. What logic, what power, what graciousness has our judge! Sinners of every kind rush to be punished by him so that they may live happy. What marvellous logic! Indeed what a marvellous mystery! The guilty person remains whole, but the guilt is punished in the guilty; in the person who is safe and sound, guilt dies the death that the person deserved. **2.** So it is that our confession has no need of torture. The guilty person confesses his crimes, not by the grim sweat of the torturer, but spontaneously so that he may become innocent. Brothers, what a precious thing it is which provides honour and reward. What deep loving wisdom of our deliverer! What unparalleled excellence! What sweet sentence! What necessary condemnation! The person in himself is killed so that he may live. The executioner and the executioner's sword are not seen. The victim's wound does not open, no blood flows; the dying person's body does not convulse, his colour does not pale. He is the same and yet he is not the same. The old dwelling place remains, but a new inhabitant rejoices in the change in his way of life and will prove to the unbelieving the dignity of his birth by virtues of every kind.

I.44: PASCHAL PROCLAMATION

1. Crowned with many forms of grace and 'treading its steps with swift feet'[14] in solemn ceremony through the circuitous routes of the seasons, the stable runner, the day of salvation has come. The same as its predecessor and as its successor, ever new in its long old age, the parent of the year and the year's offspring, it precedes the seasons which it follows and sows the unending ages. **2.** It gives birth to its own beginning from its end, and today it will also grant this to our *competentes* whom now the happy sunset *[occasus]* invites so that, immersed in the milky depth of the sacred ocean, and rising from there, new with the new day, and, radiant with their own light, they may come with us in a safe course on the heavenly path of immortality to the time of promise where one rises for ever.

---

[14]Cf. Virgil, *Aeneid* 11.718.

I.45: HERE BEGINS A SERMON ON GENESIS

1. Those of a carnal mind, dearly beloved brothers, endure it as a scandal, not in order to harm the truth but to frustrate it, whenever God the Son of God and the greatest glory of the Father is proclaimed by Catholics as equal to the Father. So it is that in their crafty reasoning they scorn the foundations of the Law, they leave out mention of God proceeding from God, and they hurry on to the ordinary human meanings of 'father' and 'son' which can be attacked by their arguments. They do not understand that in the beginning of the sacred Scripture God is said to be equal to God both in divinity and name, which precludes all the conjectures of human thinking. For it says, 'Let us make humanity in our image and likeness' (Gen 1:26). It does not say, 'You make it in yours', but 'Let us make it in ours', lest the Son who will take on a human being should seem to suffer any inferiority. **2.** Do you see, dearly beloved brothers, that no one explicitly orders the other to do this, but no one is idle in the deed? What holy equality of the divinity, most worthy of himself alone! A single person is made in the image and likeness of the two, and yet nothing is found which can be ascribed to one rather than the other. If, then, the equality of the Godhead cannot be distinguished in its external working, how can God possibly be inferior to himself in another person? For when you withhold anything from one of the two who are like one another in everything without distinction, you do not know from whom you have withheld it.

3. One might say, 'But the one who receives the command is the inferior'. What, is he not proved to be of equal status by the fact that he accomplishes the will of the Father's heart from which he proceeds? For it is no less a matter to do great things than it is to say them. However nothing that is said or can be said by the Father is without the Son, since the Son is the Word. And nothing that is done or can be done by the Son is without the Father's blessing, because the Son is not without the Father, as he himself says, 'If I do not do my

Father's deeds, do not believe in me; but if you do not wish to believe in me, believe in the deeds and recognise that the Father is in me and I in him' (John 10:37ff.). It is clear, then, that it is equal status that he takes along with the Holy Spirit.

I.46A: HERE BEGINS A SERMON ON EXODUS

1. The Pharisees claim that they are conducting a Pasch according to the Law even when they have lost the high priesthood along with the chief Temple, as it was imagined to be. They have been deprived of the horn of royal anointing. Circumcision, the proof of an impure mind, even now by the infliction of the wound which marks them out threatens the punishment which hangs over them. Every kind of beast is condemned along with their sacrifice to him. Their fasts, feast days and every solemnity are an abomination to God. **2.** In these circumstances, by whom, how, and with what is their Pasch celebrated? Add to this the fact that they have lost the lamb prescribed by the Law, whom they had found: the one whom Scripture pointed out 'from among the sheep and goats' (Exod 12:5); 'from the goats' clearly because of the dress of sinful flesh, 'from the sheep' because of the spirit of majesty. It is said to be 'firstborn' (Exod 13:12) because no one was before him except the Father; 'fully grown' (cf. Exod 12:5) because he is eternal, 'perfect' (Heb 7:28) because he is the power of God and the wisdom of God, 'without blemish' (Exod 12:5), because he alone is without sin, 'saving' (Ps 64:6) because he changed death into life; for us he who was killed and lives, who was buried and rose, was reckoned as a human being and was found to be God, glorious for ever and ever.

I.46B: CONTINUATION OF EXODUS

1. If the Jews can glory in the remembrance of the empty image, how much more can the Christian, in whom is not the figure but the truth! Recognise and acknowledge the truth

from the events themselves. The Jews proclaim that their ancestors were oppressed by the heavy yoke of slavery to Pharaoh and his army and that they were freed from Egypt. It
is not just our ancestors who are freed from the madness of
the devil and the violent horde of idols but every Christian
offspring from the true Egypt, that is, from this world, always at every moment. 2. Moses provided leadership for
them; our leader is Christ the Lord. A pillar of cloud and fire
showed them the way; for us the brightly shining oracles of
the Old and New Testaments proclaim the way, the true Lord
Christ who says, 'I am the way and the truth' (John 14:16).
Their fugitive people crossed the Red Sea dry foot with amazed
rocks of waves to right and left. But our sea receives people
of their own accord, it makes them happily shipwrecked and,
destroying every kind of sin, submerges them in the life-giving
wave, that they may be made heavenly and not know how
to desire the earth. 3. Finally after the sea they came to the
desert, but we after baptism come to Paradise. When they
were hungry manna was bedewed upon them, but we cannot hunger since we carry with us the everlasting supplies of
the heavenly bread. When they were thirsty the rock flowed
into a cup, but whoever drinks at the font of Christ does not
know thirst ever again. They were provided with the sweetness of milk and honey in the desert, but we are granted far
more, the blessing of eternal life in the kingdom of God, which
is sweeter than honey and whiter than milk.

I.47: SERMON ON ISAIAH

Mortal speech fails at the wickedness of the Jewish people who
overcame the patience of God with the impatience of their
obstinate hearts. Their crime was no trifle simply because God
complains about them even though he could as soon punish
them. But since, among those who do not believe in the world
to come, death is counted as being spared punishment, and
in effect what is unreported is regarded not to have happened,

God decided to accuse them before heaven and earth as witnesses so that they had no excuse for their crime and were subject to appropriate judgement. All this was fulfilled in our Lord's passion: heaven lost its daylight at midday, the earth lost its stability in a huge earthquake. From this one may guess what has been laid up for those because of whom nature bore the dreadful punishment of the grief of Christ's death.

I.48: SERMON ON DANIEL

Dearly beloved brothers, the sacred history has produced for us a marvellous contest of fire and faith which is delightful to God. For the two conflicting natures have come together in agreement in devotion for their Lord. For faith did not fear to be punished in the three children. When they were thrown into the oven the raging fire supported them when it sensed that they were of one fortitude. So the fire burnt those who threw them into the flames and not the ones who were thrown in. What marvellous dealings! What inestimable glory of God! The nature of such a powerful element is subdued by the mystery of the Trinity. Those who were thought to be destroyed by fire emerge more blessed from their burning.

I.49: INVITATION TO THE FONT

Now, brothers, more quickly than I can say it, enter the heavenly gates and plunge into the life-giving vessel of the everlasting waters, and do not reckon that here there is any favour for particular individuals. You are your own judge in your birth. Know this: the more one believes, the more noble one will prove oneself to be. So steadfastly and faithfully throw off that old self of yours with his filthy garments; soon you will come forth all new, all robed in white, all rich with the gift of the Holy Spirit.

I.50: ON GENESIS

As sacred Scripture bears witness, there existed before all things one and the same, another of himself to himself, God, who alone is aware of his own secret nature. From his mouth came forth his only begotten Son so that the universe which did not yet exist might be made. He was the inhabitant of his noble heart and of necessity was made visible so that he could create the world and visit the human race, but in all other respects was equal to the Father. For whatever the Father commanded to be done, the Son, as 'the power of God and the wisdom of God' (1 Cor 1:24), completed everything in a marvellous working as he spoke. The curious try to violate this person with their vain conjectures; the wretches do not understand how curiosity makes one guilty, not learned.

I.51: HERE BEGINS A SERMON ON EXODUS

The Jews cannot celebrate a Pasch according to the Law: hear why, O Christian, in a few words. Solomon's Temple lies buried in its own ruins, overthrown by enemy destruction: where do they sacrifice? They now have no priests: who sacrifices for their salvation? The Lord abhors the bulls, goats, rams, and lambs: with what do they sacrifice? They have abandoned God, they have turned over his altars: to whom do they sacrifice? Indeed this alone remains to them, that they increase their vile imaginings more and more and baptise themselves in ever viler washings every time, forever ungrateful to God.

I.52: CONTINUATION OF EXODUS

Why does the vain Pharisee puff himself up with delight at the disappeared shadow of a moment in time? He rejoices that he increased in Egypt, yet he decreased in his native soil; that he was released from the bonds of captivity, but to this day he is bound in the customs of barbarian frenzy. God provided him with leadership, afterwards he cast him off from before his face! He obtained a kingdom, so that after enjoying the royal dignity he might serve the Roman Empire for ever with all the more shame. Perhaps you wish to know the sum total of this holiness? A people the sea could carry all together the earth cannot bear now it is dispersed.

I.53: SERMON ON DANIEL

1. Christian, give ear with a believing heart to the marvellous affair which is reported as an example of fortitude to all: the three Hebrew children, with constancy greater than that of old men, with fortitude stronger than that of young men, equalled only by themselves, fortified by the mystery of the Trinity, strong in the one faith of the Unity, equal in the same fortitude, glorying in the victory of their suffering! The barbarian king ordered them to be burnt, because they scorned adoration of his statue. **2.** When they were thrown into the furnace of blazing fire, the eager fire received them with reverence, the fawning flames lick at them, covered in dew. It is a marvellous thing: there is shade within and flames outside. Within, a hymn is sung; outside, wailing is heard. O what great power of God! Those who threw them into the flames are burnt up by the fire. Those who are thrown in survive the fire and proceed in triumph out of the furnace, by the gift of our Lord Jesus Christ.

I.55: TO THE NEOPHYTES

Why do you stand there, different in race, age, sex, and rank, who soon will be one? Hasten to the fountain of the sweet womb of your ever-virgin mother and there know in your nobility and faith that, as one believes, so one will possess blessedness. Oh what a marvellous and truly divine, most blessed honour, in which she who gives birth does not groan, and the one born never cries! This is renewal, this is resurrection, this is eternal life, this is the mother of all, who has united us, brought us together from every race and nation and straightway made us one body.

I.56: SERMON ON FAITH

1. The beginning, brothers, is indeed our Lord Christ, hidden somehow in the consciousness of God in the undivided fullness of the Spirit, not without love for his Son but without distinction, and embraced before all ages by the Father of them both as yet within himself, the God of blessed eternity. But in order to construct the created order which he had devised, that ineffable power and that incomprehensible wisdom 'pours forth the Word' (Ps 44:2) from within his heart, and omnipotence gives birth to itself. From God, God is born, having everything that is the Father's, yet taking nothing from the Father. One shines in the other; the glory of either is the honour of both, for what is the Son's is the Father's, and what is the Father's is of both. The Father rejoices in the other self whom he begat from himself. **2.** But it is madness to conjecture how the one who proceeded was generated. For the Son constrains himself for the sake of the universe, lest the weakness of the world should not be able to sustain the Lord of unrestrained majesty. When the Father orders the world to be made, the deed is completed by the Son even as it is spoken. But no one orders and no one asks how, how great, or of what kind it was to be made. It would be to the Father's wrong if the Son had need of such a requirement, since he who existed in the bosom of the Father did not learn the perfection of his will, but possessed it.

3. And so when the world was completed, last of all a human being is made from the dust of the earth by the finger and hand of God. It is made as an empty automaton totally unconscious of itself and, to make it the image of God, it is breathed into by God to render it a 'living soul' (Gen 2:7). It received a spirit such that it does not know, cannot see when it enters and cannot prevent from leaving. And a person reckons that he knows the secret nature of God, when he is ignorant of what is hidden in his own body? And so, brothers, for our creation and birth let us fear, love, and honour the God whom we have found. Indeed those who do not have him with them seek him still.

I.57: SERMON ON THE PASCH

Crowned with many forms of grace and stepping solemnly on its stable course through the circuitous routes of the seasons, the day of salvation has come. The same as its predecessor and as its successor, ever new in its long old age, the parent of the year and the year's offspring, it precedes and follows the seasons and the unending ages. It gives birth to its own beginning from its end and yet it is as near as ever to the cradle of its birth. Indeed it bears the image of the mystery of the Lord, for it announces the passion by its setting *[occasus]* and the resurrection by its rising *[ortus]* to new life, and thus it promises to us as well the gift of future blessedness, and it will also grant this to our *competentes* whom now the happy sunset *[occasus]* invites so that, immersed in the milky depth of the sacred ocean and rising from there, new with the new day, they may come with us to the glory of immortality.

I.58: AGAIN A SERMON ON THE PASCH

Living by its death, quickened in the nest of the tomb, traversing the innumerable mile posts of the seasons in its passage through the years, in one and the same circuit, the great day has come, opening months into seasons, seasons into years, years into ages. Without faltering it grows to old age and yet it is as near as ever to the cradle of its birth. Indeed it bears the image of the mystery of the Lord, for it announces the passion by its setting *[occasus]* and the resurrection by its rising *[ortus]* to new life, and thus it promises to us as well the resurrection of future blessedness.

I.61: AGAIN ON ISAIAH

1. 'Hear, O heaven, and give ear, O earth, for the Lord has spoken. I have begotten sons and raised them up, but they have rejected me' (Isa 1:2). The opening words of this book speak of the great offence of the Jewish nation and show the fierce anger of divine displeasure. This is a warning to other people—us—though the word of God should rather be heard by them. For it is no small crime that, while the word of God should always be applied to them, now it seems to have been transferred to others. Hence the rejection of the Jews is the election of other people because, when it is said to others that they should hear the word of God, Israel is thus found to be false and, when the prophet cries out, 'Hear, O heaven and earth', he means that the Jews have despised hearing him.

2. He says, 'Hear, O heaven, and give ear, O earth'. The prophet must have borne witness about heaven and earth or complained about something else, as it were, since he says, 'Hear, O heaven and earth', though neither the heaven nor the earth has ever been able to hear, since heaven and earth are obedient to the command of God: heaven does not withhold its rain nor earth its fruit. But this prophecy was to be fulfilled in the end times at the coming of our Lord and Saviour, who would not be heard by the people of the Jews, foretelling that the apostles and people from the Gentiles would hear him, and so it is that he says, 'Hear, O heaven and earth'. **3.** Now by the clear testimony of the truth he affirms that the heavens are the apostles, for he says, 'And I shall see the heavens, the works of your fingers' (Ps 8:4). Clearly he is not here speaking about the actual heavens which he had always seen, but about the apostles whom he hoped to see. And again: 'His power covered the heavens' (Hab 3:3), in that the Holy Spirit overshadowed and covered the apostles for the working of miracles. And again he says, 'The heavens recount the glory of God' (Ps 18:2), and here clearly he is not just speaking of the heavens which no one has ever heard talking but he is pointing to the apostles by whose preaching the glory of the Lord has been proclaimed throughout the whole wide world. **4.** The constant assertion of the prophets has shown that 'earth' should be understood as 'people'. 'Rejoice, all the earth' (Ps 65:1), he says, and elsewhere, 'Hear, O earth, the words of my mouth' (Deut 32:1). No doubt in this term he includes the Gentiles in whom up to now were the works of the earth. This then is the meaning of his saying, 'Hear, O heaven and earth', that Christ the Lord, while the Jews would not hear him, would be heard by the apostles and Gentiles.

5. He says, 'I have begotten sons and raised them up'. This is the voice of the Lord by which he was already reproaching the unbelieving Jews through the prophets and warning them of what was to be before it happened. For it is in God's ability to understand what has already happened and to know what is to come. He says, 'I have begotten sons and raised them up'. By their boundless faithlessness the Jews have earned the hatred of our Lord; great as is the grace of God's love, so will be the coming punishment for their offence against it. For it is certain that there is great punishment for that son after he has abandoned the father who loved him with the utmost affection. And just as the father showed goodness to his beloved son who returned the love, so when spurned he demands vengeance. When the beloved son does not respond to his father, he receives his proper sentence when he is disinherited. **6.** And when his ingratitude does not return parental love with an equal affection, it is a sin not to have loved a human parent, and an unspeakable crime not to have loved the Lord our father. So the Jews are miserable and wretched to have rejected God their father by whom they were begotten. They were forgetful of their great honour and ignorant of their great privilege. For what can be more blessed than if God bestows on humans the honour of his fatherhood, and if he who is in the highest heaven should hold insignificant humans as dear and beloved? **7.** He says, 'I have begotten sons'. How sweet it is that the Lord says this about human beings! How base to have offended such a father! 'I have begotten sons and raised them up'. Indeed the Lord begat sons when he chose Abraham from whom they were born. He begat them in Egypt, into which a small number entered and from which proceeded a multitude without number, and the Lord led them into the desert 'with a mighty hand and an outstretched arm' (Ps 135:12). Israel was raised on high when for three days darkness and cloud enveloped the whole of Egypt. Israel was raised on high when he alone feared and felt nothing of all the dreadful plagues of the Egyptians. **8.** What of the time when God led Israel on dry ground through the middle of the sea? What of the daily food from heaven in the desert,[15] and drink from the rock? What of the bitter water made sweet by the rod: the water which we would drink when our Gentile bitterness has been purged by the wood of the cross? The sons of Israel were raised up when he came in safety from Horeb to the Jordan. What of the daily conversations with God? 'But they have rejected me', for they led him to the cross, the same cross by which they had escaped Pharoah. But again, 'the daughter of Zion will be abandoned' (Isa 1:8). . . .

II.10: HERE BEGINS A SERMON ON BAPTISM

1. Rightly did the most blessed David say, 'Happy are those whose iniquities are forgiven and whose sins are covered' (Ps 34:1), since, my brothers, the person who remains in his first birth cannot be happy. He is burned at every moment by the flaming torch of scorching sins, he carries round with him the stench of the prison, he detects the executioner before he can see him, he is in terror of mention of the judge, from a

---

[15]Reading with Håkanson, 'Quid cibus de caelo cotidianum in eremo' for 'Quid [quibus] de caelo cotidianum manna in eremo'.

whisper he supposes that he is being sought, that he is found out. He has no prospect of security: perhaps there is no one to accuse him, but there is always one who knows and can bear witness—himself. For conscience, more fierce than any torture, never leaves the sinner. **2.** Until now, my brothers, you were in this guilty state. But you have been examined strictly. You have prayed well for yourselves in vigil in order to receive mercy, and you have been most favourably heard. It is a new kind of judgement, in which the guilty person, if he denies the crime, is condemned, but if he confesses, he is forgiven. Oh what power, what wisdom, what graciousness has our judge! Sinners of every kind rush to be punished by him so that they may live happy. The gracious sword descends into the sinner's entrails, and in one and the same blow, the physical body remaining unharmed, kills the old self, and creates a new one, and buries it in the element of the sacred stream. And while it is the nature of all water to take living people into its depths and to cast them up dead, our water receives the dead and casts them up alive, from natural beings made into true human beings, and ones who will proceed from humans into angels, if the advance of years does not disfigure their infancy.

II.11: HERE BEGINS A SERMON ON ISAIAH

1. The wording of the title of the psalm recited makes it clear that what the prophet demanded of the old vineyard, founded by the Lord in Egypt, looked for its effect to the time of the new one. For it reads thus: 'To the end, for those who will be changed' (Ps 79:1). And the people of the Jews, which is called the first vineyard of God, indeed flourished but its flowers were infertile and shed, and it could bear no fruit. So it brought forth thorns instead of fruit and wild grapes instead of grapes. In his horror at its sterility the Lord of his own will planted for himself another vineyard into which all the fruit spoken of by the prophet devolved, that is our people.

Here, most reverend farmers, forgive me, a mere bumpkin, if my inability detracts in any way from your expertise as I give a true understanding of the vineyard.

2. As you do often and so well, the vine branch is by careful measure cut to size as a shoot, it is placed in the trench so that when it shoots it is fed by the liquid substance of the life-giving water which is always present. It is essential to tie it to the supporting stake so that it grows up in its protection and defence. When it has developed into a mature vine and come to the cross-rail, all its luxuriant shoots are cut off with a pruning hook, the pruned vine is laid along the horizontals and fastened on tight lest it somehow be torn away from the wood on which it is carried and by whose support and guidance it is drawn further along to produce a rich vintage. **3.** Then, solemnly weeping, it is softly bedewed with its own rain-drops and with its happy tears announces the rising sap of the new grape juice. At once the buds open *[oculis ruptis]* and the leaves spread out wide; underneath them and putting themselves in their care, smile the ensuing fruit. The heat of the sun, the wind, and the rain bring it on with their discipline and ripen it. But when vintage time comes, the beauty is scattered, the grapes are ripped away and trodden under the workmen's feet in the winepress, crushed in the press and forcefully squeezed by the twin beams until all the sweet juice hidden within is extracted. So the precious liquid is drunk by the wine treaders and is brought into the owner's wine cellar to mature with age.

4. According to the spiritual interpretation I give in my poor ability, the shoot which is cut to measure is understood as the *competens* who is examined by the lawful reckoning of the examination. We must take the trench to be the holy font which receives the true twigs, dead people, and by the heavenly water soon instils the Spirit and makes them alive. The assisting stake on which the vine is stretched up and carried symbolises the Lord's cross, without which the Christian cannot live and achieve immortality at all. It is placed on the horizon-

tals to show how exalted are the path and life of heaven.
5. It is tied on with bands, while the one who renounces the
world by his bond is spiritually bound by the sacred questions. The luxuriant shoots are cut off with a pruning hook;
that is, all the sins are removed altogether by baptism and
the activity of the Holy Spirit. The vine weeps happily when
it is pruned; from the one who is washed drip the divine currents of heavenly teaching, the buds being opened, that is the
eyes spiritually opened. The ensuing fruit sits under the care
of the leaves which sprout first; likewise the Christian is similarly defended and nourished by complying with the guiding
pronouncements of the divine commands, in which is the fruit
of eternal life. **6.** He comes to the crossbar when, having first
dispensed of all his property to the poor, carrying his own
cross and having fulfilled all righteousness he follows Christ
without any encumbrance. The fruit is brought to maturity
by the violence of the weather, sun and rain, and the just person is brought to his crown by many frequent and various
temptations. When the time of vintage has come, that is the
day of persecution, the grapes are torn away, that is violent
hands are laid roughly on the holy. They are carried to the
winepress, that is they are led off to the place of execution.
There they are trampled by the workmen, in other words they
are made sport of by their persecutors with abuse and violence and are slaughtered. **7.** The grapejuice is squeezed out
by the twin bars of the winepress using all the weights; likewise on the Day of Judgement the blood of the confessors is
avenged by Christ according to the twin tablets of the Law
and payment demanded to the last penny. The wine treaders
drink from the juice they have trodden, and the persecutors
who often come to believe in Christ taste, and some even
drink, the precious cup which shortly beforehand they have
trodden and poured out. The new wine is stored in the owner's
cellar to be made precious by fermentation, and the martyr
is taken to the safety of the Lord's dwelling, there to be trans-
formed from a human being into an angel and to glory in
the blessing of eternal life.

II.12: ON THE BIRTH OF THE LORD
AND HIS MAJESTY

1. According to God's promise through his prophets that at
the proper time he would send to the human race his Son as
saviour, in the fullness of time, laying aside the dignity of his
Godhead though not his sovereign power, he comes down from
heaven as the foretold measurer of the Temple[16] and as a
chaste guest he enters the sanctuary of the virgin's shrine.
There he devises his being according to his will; no, rather
he works to fulfil what he devised long ago. For he rests with
joy in the blossoming home of chastity and within the body
of the holy virgin he prepares for himself a body to be born
according to his own discretion. God is conformed to a human
being and encompassed in the covering of flesh, and he who
manifests eternity to time takes on himself human life in time.
2. What a marvel! Mary conceives of the one whom she bears;
her womb swells up with majesty, not with the seed; a girl
contains what the world and the fulness of the world cannot
contain. Meanwhile the limbs move their maker and creation clothes in its form the creator. Mary gives birth not in
sorrow but in joy; a boy is born without a father, but does
not belong totally to the mother, since he was responsible for
his own conception and was a gift to his mother in his birth.
She marvels above all that such a son has come to her; he
would not have been believed to have been born of her if she
had not remained after the birth as she had been before: a
pure virgin even after she had conceived. **3.** What novel logic!
Reduced to infancy by love for his image, God cries. He who
had come to free the debts of the whole world allows himself
to be bound in swaddling bands. He who attests that he is
the shepherd and sustenance of the nations is placed in the
manger in a stable. He whose eternity knows no passing years
submits to the ages of a human span. As a weak human be-

---

[16]'foretold measurer of the Temple': 'metatura praedicta'. Cf. Lactantius,
Divine Institutes 4.11: Ezekiel 40.

ing he suffers in contradiction to his divine nature, so that immortality might be imparted to a humanity brought to nothing by the law of death. For this is the sovereign power of God, to enable something to be what it is not. **4.** This is our God, the co-eternal Son of the eternal God. This is both a human being and God because he stood as mediator[17] between the Father and humanity to prove flesh with its weakness and majesty with its power. This is our sun, the true sun, which with the abundance of its brightness lights the dazzling fires of the world and their sisters, the fires of the shining stars of the heavens. This is the one which set once for all and rose again, never to repeat its setting. This, I say, is the one crowned with a crown of twelve rays, that is the twelve apostles, the one who is drawn along its course around the world not by four dumb animals, but by the four Gospels with their proclamation of salvation. The prophet bears witness to the might of his apparel and chariot when he says, 'God will come like fire and his chariot like a storm to render his vengeance in wrath' (Isa 66:15).

II.13: SERMON ON THE PASCH

The preeminent day is here, dearly beloved brothers, the father of the ages, potent with the produce of every kind of fruit in his rich bosom and at every moment distributing the gifts of the four seasons. And so today for our *competentes* the winter of sin is finished; they will rejoice in the consecrated oil. Today smiling spring will make them into various kinds of flowers with their various gifts when they are immersed in the healing wave and rejoice in the harvest of cloudless summer and begin to eat the new bread. The autumn's new wine will not hinder them; they will be filled with it and happily drunk, and aglow with the warmth of the Holy Spirit. God the Father almighty will grant that no one among us will ever grow cold.

[17]Cf. Lactantius, *Divine Institutes* 4.25.5.

II.14: PASCHAL SERMON OR INVITATION TO THE FONT

Come on, brothers, parched by the longed-for craving of blessed thirst, hasten with desire and the speed of deer to the water of the life-giving font. Drink deeply, so that the water may satisfy you for ever, and know this above all, that this water must not be wasted nor be drunk a second time.

II.15: AGAIN AN INVITATION TO THE FONT[18]

Rejoice, O Christian, and bravely fear God if you wish to have no fear of the devil's fires. Behold the three children, protected by the mystery of their number but with one fortitude, are unharmed by the roaring flames and the red-hot oven. As they are burnt they sing a hymn. They dumbfound the barbarian king with their steadfastness. They are vindicated before their executioners. They see God. Death passes into life, fear into glory. Who would not wish thus to burn?

II.16: SERMON ON EXODUS

Time does not permit me to give the truth for the image. However why, O Jew, do you rejoice in what points out your crime? You serve for a long time in Egypt, not by compulsion but by justice. You were delivered from there; you did not escape by your own strength. The pillar of cloud led you by day, to show you are blind; the pillar of fire by night, to signify that you will burn. An angel went before your camp, lest you should anywhere find excuse for your crimes. You walk through the sea; to right and left the wave retreats upon itself and bears witness that 'your feet are swift to shed blood' (Ps 13:3). Finally you are received into the desert, where now

---

[18]This title in the manuscript is clearly wrong, perhaps from confusion with the opening words of some invitations, e.g., II.23.

you recognise that you have arrived; where indeed you drank water from the rock and tasted manna from heaven for this purpose, that you should know, you wretch, what you were to lose.

II.17: ON THE DAY OF THE PASCH

Not only can the Jews not celebrate a Pasch according to the Law, but also they retain nothing at all of godly religion. Understand this in a few words. The Temple of Solomon, in which they put their trust, has fallen. They themselves have turned over the altars of God. 'The Law and the prophets were until John' (Matt 11:13). Lamentation is imposed on their priests. Sacrifice is taken away. The oil of anointing has ceased. Circumcision is made void. The Sabbath is a thing of reproach. New moons and feast days are held in hatred. The Romans have power over their realm. Nothing, I reckon, remains to them which they can call their own, except that having ungratefully despised the saving Lamb, in bitterness these bitter people eat their vile lambs.

II.19: AGAIN ON THE DAY OF THE PASCH

1. Repeating his tracks in the solemn multiple circuit of the worn mile post, the charioteer of the eternal chariot, the day of salvation has come. The same as its predecessor and as its successor, ever new in its long old age, the parent of the year and the year's offspring, it precedes the seasons which it follows and gives birth to its own beginning from its end so as to sow the ages and bring them together. **2.** This is when, similarly, but once only, out of love for his humanity, its maker, our Lord and God, died and rose again *[occidit et exortus est rursum]*, never indeed to repeat his death *[occasus]*. This, I say, is when the darkness of the dead was plundered, when death was subdued, when hell was forced to pour out alive those people whom it had received dead. God the Father almighty will grant that we may celebrate it with our brothers always and everywhere, increased in faith, numbers, and love.

II.20: AGAIN ON THE DAY OF THE PASCH

1. How long, O Jew, will it be until you disperse the darkness of your stupid mind and recognise and acknowledge that the oracles of the Law are now fulfilled in Christ? But if you want to celebrate a Pasch according to the Law, as you understand it, you will require a lamb as is prescribed, one who joins the different natures 'of the sheep and goats' (Exod 12:5). Even your ancestors could not find it in their herds of animals. And if only you could find it! For you are worthy of such a sacrifice, since you think that your salvation lies in the entrails of an animal of a doubtful species. **2.** But it shows your gluttony that you kill so many animals at random; your futility, that you kill them in different places; your wretchedness, that you eat them with bitterness. I pass over the fact that the one who ordered the performance of the sacrifice rejected it as commemoration by the ungrateful, not a means of healing. I simply say this: At least fulfil the Law in its other respects, gird up your loins, put sandals on your feet, take your staff in your hands, and, if you wish to imitate your ancestors, set off into the desert.

II.21: SERMON ON ISAIAH

The text of sacred Scripture shows that the whole Jewish people have lost the security of their salvation. Here, gracious brothers, it is not strictness that condemns them before all, but love. For if a most patient and most gentle father has disowned someone, and if indeed the son stands convicted more by the approval accorded him than by accusations made against him, then he can expect no reward from anyone else. So God calls heaven and earth as witnesses of what he has suffered: earth in which everything is done, heaven under which it is done. He calls the Jews sons to emphasise their crime, he says he raised them up, to show their ingratitude. He sets above them the ox and ass so that, if they recover their senses, they might feel more pain from the comparison than they would from the punishment.

II.22: SERMON ON DANIEL

The three Hebrews, armed with the mystery of the revered number, were tender in age but firm in the strength of their faith. Glorying in the punishment that would support them, in their love for the worship of God they spurned adoration of the king's image even to the point that they spurned the king himself. Bursting with anger he ordered the oven to be heated to seven times its usual heat and, to leave nothing lacking in his raging madness, he is reported to have piled up the fire with pitch and flax. Heaven itself is lit up by the strange light and glows with balls of fire. The innocents are thrown in, and there meet the one for whom they are thrown in. And so they are received not by flames but by dew, by the honour of God, not punishment. O happy execution which in perfect safety is followed by immortality and the crown!

II.23: ON BAPTISM

Rejoice, brothers, your faith is giving birth to you. As you flee the world's snares, guilt, wounds, and death and implore the help of the divine majesty, hasten to the deep of the gracious font with all speed, not of feet but of the mind. Immerse yourselves straightway, you who will live safe and sound by the happy death of your old self.

II.24: AGAIN A SERMON ON BAPTISM

1. Let us rejoice, brothers in Christ, and with hymns, stringed instruments, tambourines, and songs let us give thanks to the eternal victor. He has carried out his promises and in his gracious judgement has, so to speak, presented us with truly golden keys: not indeed those which crimes receive as a dubious benefit, they spare the body but cannot free the soul, they dissemble and pass over sins, they do not take them away but keep them in, they release the guilty person in the same state as they found him, and for such a reason can be of no use to the one who stands surety. But our keys bring out everything, whatever they find, and they allow nothing to remain, but they open the innermost regions of the breast, carefully they drive out crimes of every kind and again carefully they shut the breast again to prevent the return of anything worthless that has been removed. **2.** What marvellous logic! What marvellous blessedness! The guilty person remains whole, but the guilt is punished in the guilty; in the person who is safe and sound, guilt dies the death that the person deserved. So it is that our confession has no need of torture. The guilty person confesses his crimes, not by the sweat of the torturer, but spontaneously so that he may become innocent. Brothers, what a precious mercy it is which provides pardon and healing. For in pardoning the poisoner, the murderer, the adulterer, the committer of incest and sacrilege, I cannot see what benefit is given unless their mind is healed. **3.** What deep loving wisdom of our deliverer! What unparalleled excellence! What sweet sentence! What necessary condemnation! The person is killed so that he may live. The executioner and the executioner's sword are not seen. The victim's wound does not open, no blood flows, his colour does not pale. He is the same and yet he is not the same. The old dwelling place remains, but there is a new inhabitant with a change in his way of life who shows to the unbelievers the dignity of his birth by virtues of every kind. Keep the integrity of your new life with its infancy remaining for ever throughout its course, and guard with all your might against ever recalling the memory of your former self.

II.25: SERMON ON THE PASCH

1. That the Jews cannot celebrate a Pasch according to the Law, realise, you who are learned in the Law, from the words of God himself. He calls their synagogue a 'robber's cave' (Jer 7:11), their priestly seat a 'pestilence' (Ps 1:1), their sacrifices a 'dog's slaughter' (Deut 23:18), their fasts a 'thing of hatred' (Isa 58:5), the people a 'brood of vipers' (Matt 3:7). After this what they put their hope in, I cannot guess, these people who place their salvation in the death of their herds. For, after they came out of Egypt where they conducted their imaginary Pasch, God says, 'I am full of the holocausts of rams and the fat of lambs, for who demanded these from your hands?' (Isa 1:11). **2.** Clearly, brothers, by condemning the thing by which their Pasch is performed, he has taken their Pasch away from them altogether. 'Yet they observe the image'. Not even that, for whoever does not love the truth falsely observes its image. Indeed this alone they perform well, that like 'ravening wolves' (Matt 7:15) they slaughter the innocent lambs.

II.26: SERMON FOR THE DAY OF THE PASCH
AS ABOVE

1. As the sacred reading bears witness, Israel the people of God was oppressed most bitterly in Egypt by Pharaoh and his people with the great yoke of captivity. God ordered them to set out, under the leadership, that is, of Moses and Aaron, and with a pillar of cloud showing the way by day and also one of fire by night. The sea is divided and to right hand and left the amazed water like a cliff is heaped up in solid piles. The people of God sails through on foot. What an amazing thing! For their enemies pursuing them, neither horseman nor ship can follow the path. Miriam with the women beats her tambourine, a hymn is sung, the people of God is freed when the waves are released and the road is wiped out along with the pursuer.

2. All this is to be understood spiritually; Egypt is this world, Pharaoh with his people the Devil and every spirit of iniquity. Israel is the Christian people which is ordered to set out and strive for the things to come. Moses and Aaron by the priesthood they embodied and by their number showed forth the mystery of the two covenants. The pillar which shows the way is Christ the Lord. The fact that he has a double appearance of cloud and fire symbolises the two judgements, one of water which has already happened, the other of fire, which is to come. **3.** We must understand the sea as the sacred font in which the servants of God are freed in the waters and, in the same waters which do not flee but carry them, their sins are destroyed.[19] Miriam who beats her tambourine with the women is the type of the Church who with all the churches she has borne sings a hymn and beats the true tambourine of her breast as she leads the Christian people not into the desert but to heaven.

II.27: SERMON ON DANIEL FOR THE PASCH

Keep watch, O Christian, throw off all heaviness of worldly sleep, open the ears of your heart and learn fortitude from the children. Do not reckon it was untrue, but see for what reason the fire withdrew from them. Understanding proclaims the truth. The one who baptizes with the Holy Spirit and with fire those who believe in him is now present in the number representing the Trinity. So see that it was performed as a mystery. They have been put in the oven and submerged in flames, at once the fires are cooled by a whisper of dew. Death retreats and changes its role; those who throw them into the fire are burned, the flame fawns before those thrown in and they sing a hymn. God is blessed by all creation. In the three exults one mind, one fortitude, one triumph. Life is improved by punishment. The king would not have envied the children, if he had not ordered them to be burnt.

[19]Reading with Dolbeau: 'iisdem quae non fugiunt'.

II.28: INVITATION TO THE FONT AS ABOVE

Come on, why do you stand there, brothers? Through your faith the life-giving water has conceived you, through the mysteries now it gives birth to you. Hurry as quickly as you can to what you desire. Behold, now the solemn hymn is sung; behold soon the sweet crying of infants is heard; behold from the single womb of their parent proceeds a dazzling throng. It is a new thing, that each one is born in a spiritual manner. Run freely to your mother who has no labour if she gives birth to more than she can number. Come in, then, come in, all of you happy ones, in a moment to be babes at the breast together.

II.29: PASCHAL SERMON

Welcome, my brothers in Christ, born today! Guard carefully, strictly and faithfully the royal favour of mercy which you have received. For every liability you owe has been cancelled. Rejoice freely! Now you owe nothing to the world. Behold, there is no weight or rattling of earthly chains on your necks. Your hands are not bound in any manacles, your feet are not burdened with any fetters. No terror distracts you; no squalor degrades you. You feared the one who knows your crimes: now you do not fear your conscience. For your old self has been happily condemned so that he may be forgiven, buried in the wave of the sacred waters so that he may be quickened in the nest of the tomb and taste the privileges of the resurrection.

2. Oh what goodness of our God! What pure love of our good mother! She has taken people different in race, sex, age, and rank; like an evil stepmother she kills them out of hatred of their crimes, like a loving mother she keeps them safe and does not bring back the dead to life before she has extinguished all the old poison, lest she give birth to anything less than pure. And lest she should seem to love anyone more or less than another, she grants to all one birth, one milk, one pay, one honour of the Holy Spirit.

3. How splendid it is, brothers, and how salutary, that you choose to admire the one who a short time ago you scorned, and to imitate the virtue of the one whose corruption you cursed. You were always horrified at his greed; now you are amazed at his pouring out his goods far and wide to the poor and needy. You knew him as a shrine of idolatry; now you rejoice that he is a temple of God. Indeed blessed is the one who always remembers that he is reborn; more blessed is the one who does not remember what he was before he was reborn; most blessed is the one who does not spoil his infancy with the advance of years.

II.30: ON GENESIS AS ABOVE

1. Nothing, dearly beloved brothers, is so necessary and useful above all else for a person who is born than that he should know himself. For it is madness itself to investigate an understanding of the secret of one's nature when one cannot give an account of one's life. For the elements were made and are seen by God more beautifully or truly than they can be described by human words.

2. And so, what especially applies to us, what is it that God says: 'Let us make humanity in our image and likeness' (and it says, 'God made humanity in the image and likeness of God') (Gen 1:26), and in another place it says, 'I am who I am and I do not change' (Mal 3:6)? Since this is so, how can a human being bear the image of God when his face is liable to every change and at every moment altered by labour, age, weakness, joy, sadness, sometimes deformed by thinness, sometimes enormous with fat, so that it is not at all certain that there are two people in the entire world with the same face. **3.** Since this is not the case with God, do we then not have the image of God? Far from it, brothers, of course we do, and indeed this is clear from the very fact that it is not seen by those who bear it. For the image of the incomprehensible God must be invisible, so it is not to be seen by mortal eyes. For when it enters the body and when it leaves the body, it cannot be spotted by anyone, and it has such power that, when it is enclosed within the walls of its dwelling place, it shows forth at every moment whatever it wills. So we must believe that the image of God is not this fleshly garment but the spiritual image of the heavenly person which of his abundance he lavishes on us from the sacred font. **4.** Paul clearly shows forth this matter when he says, 'Just as we have borne the image of the man of dust, so we shall bear the image of the man of heaven' (1 Cor 15:49). Those who bear it in holiness, as did the apostles and all the just, will bear not only the image, but even God himself, as it is written, 'You are the temple of God, and the Spirit of God dwells in you' (1 Cor 3:16).

Chapter Four
THE PASCHAL SERMONS

We have already learnt much about the sermons through examining the MS tradition, and we must now look at them in some detail. The greater part of this chapter will be devoted to examining the sermons of the paschal Vigil, taking each type of sermon in turn (i.e., all the proclamations together, all the sermons on Genesis, etc.). Each type of sermon is effectively a genre in its own right, not only with its contents guided by its position or the reading on which it is commenting, but also with its own level of formality or humour, its own sense of prejudice or triumph.

We will then look at a number of sermons that may well have been part of the catechetical course the candidates underwent both before and after baptism. There are only a few of these sermons, and we are much less confident in our conclusions than we can be with regard to those in the paschal Vigil.

As far as possible we will avoid commenting on the liturgical details or the theological views or imagery displayed here. They must wait until subsequent chapters, and if given free rein here would obscure our view of the sermons in themselves. The only exception is that we must look at the *disciplina arcani*, the rule of secrecy which surrounded the sacraments of the Church in the fourth century and which again and again influences the way in which Zeno discusses his subject.

1. THE *DISCIPLINA ARCANI*

The *disciplina arcani* was so general in the fourth century that we should have been surprised if Zeno's church in Verona did not practise it.[1] Keeping certain details of Christian worship and belief secret is totally foreign to us, but it must have been completely natural to the preachers and people of that time. For a candidate undergoing initiation, experiencing the unknown and learning its meaning were an integral part of becoming a member of the Church.

The *disciplina* was fairly precise in its terms of reference, though of course, since we are presented with an 'argument from silence', we are not always clear about the details of how it was practised. 'The secrecy extended to the Creed and the Lord's Prayer, the words, the sacred vessels and the species of the Eucharist, baptism and the rites of initiation'.[2]

Zeno explicitly mentions the custom of keeping certain aspects of Christian worship secret, and also many times his sermons show the influence of the *disciplina* in the allusiveness of his remarks.

The explicit mention of the *disciplina* comes in Zeno's sermon *De continentia* (II.7) when he is exhorting widows not to remarry, or at any rate not to marry a pagan husband. The problem, a natural one when secrecy cuts across a marriage, is treated also by Tertullian who is afraid that the pagan husband may find the Christian wife giving herself Holy Communion in the morning.[3] For Zeno in the fourth century the problem arises in much the same way:

> Let us suppose that, as often happens, feast days of the two religions coincide, and you have to go to church, he goes to the temples. How is each of you to arrange your offerings, how is it paid for, with what containers and which servants? There is no point, however careful you are. By leaving and

[1]For a survey of the *disciplina arcani* see *AIR,* 50-4.
[2]Ibid., 53.
[3]Tertullian, *Ad uxorem* 2.5.

returning to one and the same house they will be mixed up
by confusion or error. And his offering is public, yours is
secret. Anyone can know all about his, but yours cannot be
seen even by catechumens without sacrilege. It becomes a
dreadful state, that you cannot as a wife do what pleases your
husband. . . the whole house roars with your arguments,
God is blasphemed, and the man perhaps snatches your offering from you and beats you on the breast with it; and, with
the mess he has made of your face, in the end he does you
a favour when he forbids you to go to church.[4]

Evidently the wife was in no position to act without her
husband's consent and cooperation. He was not allowed to
see the *sacrificium* (presumably of bread and wine for the Eucharist) which she was to take to the church, and certainly
not allowed to glimpse the sacrament when she brought it
home for daily communion.[5] Zeno is categorical. It would
be sacrilege even for catechumens ('Christianis minime consecratis') to see the sacrament.[6] It is interesting that Zeno
seems to suggest that some confusion was possible between
the Christian and pagan sacrifices when they were brought
home—is this simply the habit of using the food sacrificed to

[4]'Proponamus itaque, ut saepe contingit, in unum sibimet convenire
diversae religionis diem, quo tibi ecclesia, illi adeunda sint templa. Quo
genere unusquisque suum sacrificium procurabitis, quo sumptu, quibus
vasis quibusve ministris? At si discrete fiunt ista, nihil prodest. Ex uno
enim proficiscendo et in unum remeando, si non confusione, vel errore
fiunt una. Quid, quod illius sacrificium publicum est, tuum secretum? Illius a quovis libere tractari potest, tuum etiam a Christianis ipsis minime
consecratis sine sacrilegio videri non potest? Postremo detestabilis est vivendi
condicio, ubi non licet facere uxori, quod marito placet. . . . tum tota
mugiet litibus domus, blasphemabitur deus arreptoque forsitan ipso sacrifi-
cio tuo tuum pectus obtundet, tuam faciem deformabit, praestans aliquando
et beneficium, cum te iubet ad ecclesiam non venire': II.7.14–15.

[5]For this custom at the time of Zeno, cf. Basil, *Ep*. 93; Jerome, *Ep*.
49 (48). 15.4–7.

[6]When in danger of shipwreck, Satyrus, a catechumen, asks Christians
on the boat if he may have a portion of the sacrament they are carrying
to help him in the danger. He does not propose to see it; it is tied up in
an *orarium* and fastened round his neck (Ambrose, *De Excessu Satyri* 1.43).

pagan gods such as we find in First Corinthians, chapters 8–10? Since the sacrament is snatched from the wife and used to beat her, the Ballerini suggest that it would have been contained in a box of some kind.[7]

In another place Zeno says of faith, 'Oh how public it is, when even the pagans speak about its secrets!'[8] The secrets of the faith were therefore obviously of interest, if only by exciting the curiosity of the outsider. On occasion, Zeno is quite prepared to tantalise the uninitiated. The classic example of this must be in II.6.8, where he is obviously being deliberately allusive and elusive: 'In addition I shall say what is the daily pay and what allowance is paid out: to everyone equally is given one loaf with wood, water with wine, salt, fire and oil, a new tunic and one denarius'.[9]

Löfstedt in his text makes a conjectural emendation of 'wood' to 'mark' (*ligno* to *signo*). However it is because Zeno is being deliberately difficult here that I am inclined to reject Löfstedt's emendation. This is not a place where the text needs to be rationalised; indeed, the more odd the better! It only remains for us to make sense of it, which is precisely what Zeno did not want his uninitiated hearers to do, but which we shall try to do when we consider it below among passages describing the whole rite.

What was the practical outcome of the *disciplina arcani* in the initiation ceremonies? Candidates needed to be told at some point what the meaning was of the rites they were undergoing. Chrysostom explained them shortly before the occasion of baptism. Ambrose only explained them afterwards. It would seem that Zeno, like the latter, would explain the rites only after the candidates were fully initiated. The custom

---

[7]The Ballerini (PL 11:310, 359) take 'panem cum ligno' in II.6.8 to refer to the box in which the sacrament is kept. But see my comments on the passage, below.

[8]'O quam publica, cuius fabulantur etiam profani secreta'!: II.3.10.

[9]'Dicam praeterea, quae cotidie merces, quae impendatur annona. Omnibus peraeque unus panis cum ligno datur, aqua cum vino, sal, ignis et oleum, tunica rudis et unus denarius.'

of having a sermon after the baptism would probably be based on the need for explanation. Delivered in the church after the baptism, no doubt with only the initiated present, the purpose must have been to explain something of what was about to happen in the paschal Eucharist or its meaning. Zeno does nothing of the kind, in any of these sermons. Indeed, in one of them he acknowledges the curiosity of the candidates: 'But I am well aware of your curiosity. With the taking away of your old life, which henceforth is forbidden you, perhaps you would like to know from us under which constellation and which sign your mother bore you together, so varied, so many and so different, in a single birth.'[10] But his explanation, in the form of an allegory of the horoscope, served no useful purpose in describing or explaining the ceremonies either of baptism or of the Eucharist.

We must therefore suppose that Zeno applied the *disciplina arcani* until after the completion of the whole rite of initiation, including the first Eucharist of the candidates. They would presumably, as in other churches, have been taught the Creed and Lord's Prayer during Lent, but the remainder could wait until afterwards. We do not possess any sermons of Zeno such as Ambrose's *De sacramentis,* where the meaning of baptism and the Eucharist is set out explicitly.

Therefore, when attributing sermons to particular points in the Lenten and Easter catechesis and in the Vigil service, attention must be paid to how they describe aspects of the rite. If they are elusive in their description, then they would probably have been delivered during Lent or at any rate in the presence of the uninitiated. Others which are more explicit in their quotations of the rite or in their explanation should be attributed to the post-baptismal catechesis of Easter Week. Of course we do not know how explicit a preacher was allowed to be and in what areas before he infringed the *dis-*

---

[10]'Sed curiositatem vestram bene novi. Veteris vitae usurpatione, quod quidem vobis ulterius non licebit, fortassis requiratis et a nobis qua genitura quove signo tam diversos, tam plures, tam dispares una uno partu vestra vos peperit mater': I.38.2.

ciplina. From II.6.8 we can see that Zeno was, if anything, inclined to tread on the boundary in an almost mischievous fashion. But his interpretation of Psalm 22, 'the cup signifies the Blood; the table, the Body; the oil, the gift of the Holy Spirit',[11] is so explicit that it must militate in favour of a post-baptismal setting. These cases will be discussed further below.

When we come to consider the details of the baptismal liturgy, the question of the *disciplina arcani* will arise very often, and influence our understanding of the performance of the liturgy.

2. THE SERMONS OF THE PASCHAL VIGIL

The sermons called paschal sermons in this study are those which, as described above, were delivered during the paschal Vigil. These comprise a sermon, called the proclamation (*Praefatio Paschalis*), to introduce the Vigil, sermons commenting on each of the readings during the Vigil (Genesis 1; Exodus 12; Exodus 14; Isaiah 1 or Isaiah 5; and Daniel 3), a sermon welcoming the candidates for baptism into the baptistery (invitation to the font: *Invitatio fontis*), and a final sermon after baptism when the candidates return to the church (post-baptismal sermon: *Post traditum baptisma*).

The sermons will be examined together according to subject matter in detail. But beforehand, previous attempts to compare the sermons will be summarised here. The similarities between sermons and their order in the manuscripts has dawned slowly on successive writers. The problems of individual sermons will be ignored here in order to keep clear the picture of the development.

It has been obvious to all readers of the sermons that a very large number of them are concerned with Easter and baptism, and that many are similar to one another in length, content, and style. The Ballerini recognised at least the similarity

[11]'Calix sanguinem, mensa corpus, oleum donum spiritus sancti significat'. I.13.10.

of content of many of the paschal sermons. When they departed from the manuscript order of the sermons and arranged them in subject order in their edition, they grouped some of the paschal sermons together with a small introduction, saying that, 'a number of short sermons, even though they are headed by different titles, all belong to the same season of Easter and contain references to baptism as going to be conferred or already conferred during this season. On this basis we believe that they should all be brought together'.[12]

The Ballerini put into this section the following:

> 8 sermons, *Invitatio ad fontem* II.xxx–xxxvii[13]
> 7 sermons, *Ad neophytos post baptisma* II.xxxviii–xliv[14]
> 9 sermons, *De Pascha* II.xlv–liii[15]
> 15 sermons, *De Exodo,* undifferentiated II.liv–lxviii[16]
> 8 sermons, *De Daniele* II.lxix–lxxvi[17]

The Ballerini of course saw that other sermons also referred to baptism, but felt either that their length precluded them from this section or that as editors they were not justified in removing the sermons from others of the same title.[18] Therefore the sermons *In Isaiam* are collected separately, in II.xxii–xxix.[19] In fact, all of these except xxii and xxix[20] fit into the

[12]'nonnulli breves tractatus,. . . etsi variis titulis praenotantur, omnes tamen ad idem paschale tempus pertinent, et baptismatis per hocce tempus conferendi vel collati mentionem fere continent, ex quo etiam simul omnes adferendos credidimus': PL 11:col 473f., esp. col 473A.

[13] = CCL I.12; 23; 32; 49; 55; II.14; 23; 28.

[14] = CCL I.24; 38; 41; 42; II.10; 24; 29.

[15] = CCL I.6; 16; 26; 33; 44; 57; 58; II.13; 19.

[16] = CCL I.8; 9; 18; 19; 28; 29; 46A; 46B; 51; 52; II.16; 17; 20; 25; 26.

[17] = CCL I.11; 22; 31; 48; 53; II.15; 22; 27. A ninth, II.lxxvii (= CCL II.18) is included in the Ballerini list here but is recognised by them to be on a different subject altogether.

[18]'Non tamen eos duximus transferendos, cum vel longiores sint multo, et de baptismate non nisi obiter meminerint, vel a proprio titulo ex.gr. In Isaiam sub quo alii tractatus non paschales habentur, haud disjungendos putarimus': PL 11:473B.

[19] = CCL I.10 (both together); 20; 30; 47; 60; 61; II.11; 21.

[20] = CCL I.60; 61.

series of paschal sermons. The Genesis sermons (II.i–v, ix, xix, xx) are likewise grouped with material not belonging to the paschal rites.

Bigelmair's findings are close to those of the Ballerini. He adds the readings on Isaiah to the same context of the Easter celebrations, and he differentiates between the Exodus sermons on Passover and those on the crossing of the Red Sea. However he does not add the sermons on Genesis.[21] He does identify the liturgical setting of the paschal sermons as having been the paschal Vigil, including their relation to the scriptural readings of the Vigil.[22]

With the advent of Löfstedt's edition, the sermons are found once again in the order in which they are found in the manuscripts, rather than in the subject order in which the Ballerini placed them. The interrelation of the paschal sermons (where we see the order: proclamation, on Genesis, on Exodus, etc.) is more clear. When Truzzi examines these sermons together he is struck by their distinctive brevity and the similarity of their treatment, extending even to some being copies of others. The phenomenon, he says, is unique among the Latin Fathers. He follows Löfstedt's thesis of the development of the sermons and the role of later liturgists in producing the order of sermons in the manuscripts. Truzzi includes the sermons on Genesis with the other sermons here, but believes that they were not composed originally for Easter but were adapted by liturgists to fit their needs for paschal ceremonies. He describes the Genesis sermons as *bozze*—incomplete drafts.[23] Because Truzzi follows Löfstedt in the idea of the reordering of the sermons, he need not attribute those on passages of Scripture to the Vigil service, but to other situations. The sermons on Exodus 12 and Daniel 3 are attributed to the Vigil, but those on Exodus 14 are attributed to the pe-

---

[21]Bigelmair, *Zeno von Verona,* 53.

[22]Ibid., 95. Given the prominence of the Genesis reading in Vigil lectionaries, it is curious that Bigelmair missed Zeno's sermons on that reading.

[23]Truzzi, 58–60.

riod after baptism, as are those on Isaiah 5. Truzzi does not suggest a setting for the sermons on Isaiah 1.[24]

The sermons as we find them in the manuscripts have therefore been recognised as set in the context of the paschal rites. Löfstedt's thesis of the development of the manuscript order has been rejected in this present study, and it has been suggested that the sermons as we receive them were originally composed for the paschal Vigil and come down to us substantially in the same form in which they were preached. We must now examine the sermons in detail.

(i) The Paschal Proclamation *(Praefatio Paschalis)*

I. TEXT

There are nine of these sermons: I.6; 16; 26; 33; 44; 57; 58; II.13; 19. All of these are between nine and fourteen lines long in Löfstedt's text, except for I.33 which is thirty-seven lines long. Despite this difference of length, I.33 from its context clearly belongs to this group of sermons.

I.44; 57; 58; II.19 can be compared with one another by synopsis. The beginnings of the first three are nearly identical, as a perusal of even the translations makes very clear. It has been suggested above that it is possible that I.58 was a draft which was never in fact preached. The reason is that this sermon, unusually, is to be found next to one which is based on it and is not, as is usually the case, in a different paschal group or at least elsewhere in the MS order. It would seem that Zeno wrote it out, and then rejected it but used part of it in I.57 in conjunction with a revised draft of I.44. The rejected draft was in some way preserved along with I.57, perhaps by being on the same piece of paper. Although I.58 was perhaps never preached, it was composed with delivery in mind, and can be examined here in the same way as the others.

---

[24]Ibid., 212–17, and the table of sermons in the Appendix.

The proclamations are notable for the grand style and the formality with which the bishop addresses the congregation; they well deserve the title of *praefatio* with its connotation of formal declamation. This grand manner is by no means sustained throughout the ceremonies; indeed the *praefatio* stands apart from the other sermons delivered, and, to the modern reader at any rate, might seem close to the *praefatio* of the Eucharistic Prayer or, on the paschal night, to the Exultet. (We have very little evidence of the style of the Eucharistic Prayer in Zeno's church, and we have no evidence as to whether an 'Exultet' was sung.) Truzzi aptly descibes the *praefatio* as a *salutatio* to the day of salvation: *dies salutaris*.[25] The term *praefatio* is itself of some interest. It would seem to have a double meaning, firstly of an introduction, and secondly of a public proclamation, which may be applied to prayers, and in Christian worship to other parts of the Eucharistic Prayer besides that today called the preface. Sometimes (as in the Gallican case) there is a sense of anteriority in the word, sometimes not.[26] In the present case, with the *Praefatio Paschalis* introducing the ceremonies we can hardly exclude the sense of anteriority, nor, given the formal style of the sermon, can we exclude the sense of proclamation. Liturgically its role seems to have been close to the Gallican use.

2. CONTENT

The sermons introduce the paschal liturgy, dwelling as they do on the day that is dawning and proclaiming the dawn as representing the new life of the baptised. This suggests that the paschal liturgy proper began at or near dawn. The sermon would have been preached to the whole congregation, referring to the *competentes* in the third person.[27]

[25]Ibid., 210.

[26]C. Mohrmann, 'Sur l'Histoire de *Praefari-Praefatio*', in *Etudes sur le Latin des Chrétiens,* vol. 2 (Rome, 1965) 291–305, (= *Vigiliae Christianae* 7 [1953] 1–15). The Gallican *praefatio* is described below when Zeno's rite is compared with other vigil liturgies.

[27]I.44.2; I.57; II.13.

In I.6 the benefits of Easter are promised to the whole Church: 'It grants pay to loyal priests, to subordinate ministers the advancement of promotion, the fruit of immortality for the baptised, healing for penitents, the way of light for catechumens, for the *competentes* the remission of all their sins'.[28]

Easter Day is presented as a New Year's Day, and with the new, young year emerging from the old, we recognise the image we might use today:

> The same as its predecessor and as its successor, ever new in its long old age, the parent of the year and the year's offspring, it precedes the seasons which it follows and sows the unending ages.[29]
> The great day has come, ever new in itself from its own sunset *[occasus]*. It follows what it has been before; it goes before what it will be. It is ever new and ever old. At every moment it changes not in nature but in number. It is the son of the hours and the father of all the ages.[30]

We are no distance at all from the modern motif of Father Time!

The setting and rising of the Day provide a link with the resurrection of Christ: 'Indeed it bears the image of the mystery of the Lord, for it announces the passion by its setting and the resurrection by its rising to new life, and thus it promises to us as well the gift of future blessedness.'[31] But

---

[28]'Namque piis mercedem sacerdotibus praestat, consequentibus ministris promotionis augmentum, immortalitatis fidelibus fructum, paenitentibus curam, catechuminis lucis viam, competentibus remissa omnium peccatorum'.

[29]'Idem sibi succesor idemque decessor, longaeva semper aetate novellus, anni parens annique progenies antecedit quae sequitur tempora et saecula infinita disseminat': I.44.1.

[30]Dies magnus advenit, suo semper novellus occasu. Quod praeterit sequitur, quod futurum est antecedit. In omnibus novus est et tamen in omnibus vetus est. Punctis omnibus commutatur, non natura, sed numero. Fit filius horarum, qui pater est omnium saeculorum': I.16.1.

[31]'Sacramenti dominici imaginem portat, nam occasu passionem resurrectionemque ortu redivivo concelebrat, per quem nobis munus futurae beatitudinis pollicetur': I.57.

elsewhere the 'once for all' nature of Christ's death and resurrection is clearly contrasted with the yearly return of the Easter
Day.[32] The risen Christ is described as 'the eternal day without any night'.[33] The newly baptised walk in the eternal light
of this day.[34] The return of the day bids us to celebrate the
event, and promises the benefits.[35]

Often the Easter Day is expressed rather as a cornucopia,
providing gifts to all types and conditions of people: 'potent
with the produce of every kind of fruit in his rich bosom'.[36]

As well as the theme of the day, there is also in I.33 and
II.13 that of the seasons. The former gives a very full account:
first the harshness of winter, the gentleness and new growth
of spring, the richness of summer, and autumn with new wine
and bread. Zeno then interprets them allegorically. Winter
refers to those who are enslaved by idolatry and the world.
Spring is the font giving the gifts of the Holy Spirit and new
birth. Summer is the people of God, and autumn refers to
martyrdom, where the grape juice being produced in the press
symbolises the blood of martyrs.

In II.13 the seasons are again symbolic. Here however the
treatment is much more brief and refers specifically (though
in veiled terms, because of the *disciplina arcani*) to the baptismal rites. The winter of sin is over. Spring is again the grace
of the baptismal font. Summer is the new bread they will eat
(i.e., in the paschal Eucharist) and autumn is the new wine.[37]

---

[32]I.16; II.19.

[33]'Eternus et sine nocte dies': I.33.4.

[34]I.33.4.

[35]I.26; I.57.

[36]'Omni genere fructuum fetibus pollens divite sinu': II.13 (cf. I.6 above).

[37]For another aspect of Zeno's interest in the seasons and the cycle of the year, see his treatment of the zodiac in the post-baptismal sermon I.38, discussed below.

(ii) The Sermons on Genesis *(De Genesi)*

I. TEXT

I.7; 17; 27; 45; 50; 56; II.12; 30.

This is the only group of sermons not recognised by either the Ballerini or Bigelmair as belonging to the paschal readings. However, the fact that there was a reading from Genesis 1 seems clear from the positions of the sermons I.7; 17; 27; 45 within the groups of paschal sermons, and I.50; II.12; 30 are also to be found within paschal groups. II.12 is in fact a dubious case and it will be discussed in some length below as to whether it is a sermon from the paschal Vigil. Truzzi acknowledges that some of the Genesis sermons have found their way into the series of paschal readings, but sees this as a transfer by a later editor of non-paschal material.[38]

The sermons are all between eleven and forty-one lines long in Löfstedt's text. I.27 is parallel with II.30, and I.17 with I.56.

All the sermons are entitled *De Genesi*, except I.56 *(Tractatus fidei)* and II.12 *(De nativitate domini et maiestate)*, and there are clear references to baptism in the parallel I.27.3, and II.30.3. It would seem to be clear that Genesis 1 was read at the Vigil as the first reading, and that the sermon would have followed it as a commentary. There are explicit references to Genesis 1:26,[39] and a passing reference to Genesis 2:7.[40] I.17 and I.56 begin with the word 'beginning': *principium,* no doubt a reference to Genesis 1:1. The reading therefore would seem to have covered at least Genesis 1:1-26 and may, less probably, have extended as far as 2:7.

2. CONTENT

The sermons on Genesis almost seem to fulfil a double role. They contain the exegesis that one might expect from a reading of Genesis 1, discussing the beginning of the world. Genesis

---

[38]Truzzi, 60–61 n. 69.
[39]I.27.2; I.45.1; II.30.2.
[40]I.56.3.

1:26 and the doctrinal disputes of the day also lead naturally to a defence of the Catholic doctrine of the Trinity and the incarnation. However, there is another, less explicit role of these sermons in that they refer to a series of historical events which are included in the patristic theology of Easter (namely creation, the incarnation, and the second coming), and bring them into the celebration. First we will consider the exegesis of Genesis 1.

I.27 and II.30 deal with the nature of humanity as the image of God. Zeno says that this cannot refer to a person's changing exterior appearance, but to the spiritual image of the heavenly person 'imaginem caelestis hominis spiritalem' which is given through baptism.

The sermons I.7; 17; 45; 50; 56 are all concerned with the divinity of the Son and the unity of God, maintaining the Catholic faith against Arian attacks. In I.45 this is argued from the text, 'Let us make humanity in our image and likeness' ('Faciamus hominem ad imaginem et similitudinem nostram'), to show that the likeness of the Father and the Son is the same, and their workings are indistinguishable: 'If, then, the equality of the Godhead cannot be distinguished in its external working, how can God possibly be inferior to himself in another person?'[41] Zeno goes on to say that there is no inferiority involved in the Son doing the Father's will.

This idea of the unity of the Trinity in action was evidently a commonplace in Catholic thought. Only a few years after Zeno, Ambrose says, 'You have been baptised in the name of the Trinity. In everything we have done the mystery of the Trinity has been preserved. The Father, the Son and the Holy Spirit are present everywhere; they exercise a joint causality, a single sanctifying action, although some aspects do seem to be peculiar to the individual Persons'.[42]

---

[41] 'Si igitur in opere extraneo paritas sacra distingui non potest, deus in alio se inferior esse quemadmodum potest?' I.45.2.

[42] 'Baptizatus es in nomine trinitatis. In omnibus quae egimus servatum est mysterium trinitatis. Ubique pater, filius et spiritus sanctus, una operatio, una sanctificatio, etsi quaedam veluti specialia esse videantur'. *De sac.* 6.5; trans. Yarnold, *AIR,* 150.

In I.7 God is shown to be superior to insensate chaos and therefore the sole beginning *(principium)*, while chaos, being shaped and growing old, cannot constitute the beginning. Zeno then goes on to discuss the procession of the Son from the Father, and of their relation as two seas joined by a strait which is the Holy Spirit, but sharing the same nature and substance.[43]

The themes of God as the *principium* and of the generation of the Son are found in I.17 and I.56. In both, Zeno begins by declaring explicitly that Christ is the *principium*, and, following Hilary (*De trin.* 3.8), 'From God, God is born, from the unbegotten the only begotten, alone from the alone, whole from the whole, true from the true, perfect from the perfect, having everything that is the Father's yet taking nothing from the Father'.[44]

I.56 goes on to describe the mystery of the creation of humanity, and questions how we can understand the secrets of God's nature when we cannot comprehend our own. This theme of the inexplicable mystery of God is very common in this group of sermons. In I.50, God is 'alone aware of his own secret nature', and Zeno condemns the foolish theories of the curious.[45]

II.12 does not fit into the pattern of the above sermons and indeed talks more about the incarnation and birth of Jesus than about anything directly concerned with the Genesis reading. Its title, *De nativitate Domini et maiestate,* is also unlike the others, which with one exception mention Genesis. It might be supposed that this sermon does not belong to the paschal Vigil at all but perhaps should be placed, in genre, with I.54; II.5; 8. Truzzi believes that it was originally preached in the context of a celebration of Christmas.[46] However there are

---

[43]I.7.3.

[44]'De deo nascitur deus, de ingenito unigenitus, de solo solus, de toto totus, de vero verus, de perfecto perfectus, totum patris habens, nihil derogans patri': I.17.2.

[45]Cf. I.17; I.45.1; I.27.1; II.30.1.

[46]Truzzi, 201–2.

signs that it was in fact preached as a commentary on the Genesis passage in the Vigil.

First, in the contents of the sermon, although the main emphasis is on the incarnation, there are some references that connect the sermon with the others in this genre. It shows a continuity of thought from I.17 where the temporal generation of the Son is discussed. We may be seeing here a progression of thought from one year to another. The bishop, reviewing a previous year's sermon, takes up a line of thought and enlarges it.

It is easy for us to be distracted by the birth and to think of Christmas. More central to the paschal Vigil, and equally important in the sermon, is the incarnation which in the fourth century was generally reckoned to coincide with the Pasch so that the date of Jesus' conception is also that of his death and the length of time of the incarnation could be calculated as a whole number of years. The date of Christmas is therefore held to depend on that of Easter, being nine months after the incarnation. T. Talley draws our attention to a Latin sermon, *De solstitiis,* which sets out explicitly the chronology as described above, but seems to have no awareness of the nativity being celebrated as a feast day.[47] It must be said that Zeno likewise never mentions or refers to Christmas, for all his interest in the incarnation. This is perhaps surprising since Christmas was celebrated in Rome by 336 and in Africa possibly from before the Donatist schism in 311.[48] Philaster of Brescia knew it in the decade after Zeno. But such are the facts of the case: we cannot go beyond the evidence but have to conclude that Zeno gives no evidence of a feast of the nativity; his interest in the incarnation is focused calendrically on the Pasch.

In addition to the appropriateness of the reference to the incarnation there are several typically paschal references in

[47]T. Talley, *Origins of the Liturgical Year,* 2d ed. (Collegeville, Minn., 1991) 91–99.
[48]Ibid., 85–87.

II.12. With regard to the reading, Zeno says that the earthly birth was out of 'love for his image',[49] which can only be a reference to Genesis 1:26. The description of Christ as the sun, 'which set once for all and rose again, never to repeat its setting',[50] is more clearly paschal in its reference. Both of these phrases find a parallel in a proclamation, II.19.2.[51]

Secondly, the position of the sermon in the MSS includes it in a group of Vigil sermons, II.10–II.16. Although this group is out of order it would, with the inclusion of II.12, be complete. In fact it would be remarkable, if II.12 were not of this series, that it happened to coincide with the the place of the missing Genesis sermon. The MS order does therefore support the inclusion of II.12 as the authentic Genesis sermon in this group.

So much for matters of the explicit commentary on Genesis and the question of the passage on the incarnation. Now we must consider the wider role of the sermons in the paschal celebration.

Having just been considering II.12 we may continue now with that sermon, noting how Zeno moves from the discussion of the incarnation into a graphic treatment of the birth, emphasising its difference from the normal rules of nature. This is very similar to the treatment we shall see in some of the invitations to the font, especially I.32. The Christian second birth is not like natural human birth, and in that respect we are prompted to see its origin in the human/divine birth of Christ.

Another prompt, as it were, is provided by I.7. At one level it is discussing various theories of the origin of the universe. But the first sentence of the sermon, 'No one can ever enjoy his goods in security unless he resists the enemy who attacks

[49]'amore imaginis suae': II.12.3.

[50]'qui semel occidit et ortus est rursum numquam repetiturus occasum': II.12.4.

[51]'Hic est, quo similiter, verum tamen semel, amore hominis sui eius artifex deus et dominus noster occidit et exortus est rursum, numquam repetiturus occasum'.

him', evokes the saying of Jesus, 'When a strong man, fully armed, guards his own palace, his goods are in peace', etc. (Luke 11:22). It suggests the second part of the verse, about the coming of the stronger one, and thus we have a whole complex of themes including the end of demonic influence now (in the exorcism of the candidates for baptism) and the end of the rule of Satan when the Lord comes like a thief in the night. The reading of Genesis is widened out from its temporal reference to cover past, present, and future and the whole of God's dealings with his creation. One might apply here the comment of P. Cramer, that Zeno 'causes the mind to leap back and forth from the brevity of the expression to the openness of the Biblical past. Reading him, we feel that instead of defining the Bible as Tertullian has done, he is releasing its possibilities.'[52]

In conclusion, Zeno's sermons on Genesis function as a necessary part of the paschal celebrations, since they include the important elements of creation and incarnation which are commemorated on this day and look even to the last day. To some extent the sermons are taken over, one might almost say distracted, by theological controversy, but that must not be allowed to blind us to their essential role as an organic part of the celebration.

(iii) The Sermons on Exodus 12 *(De Exodo)*

I. TEXT

I.8; 19; 28; 46A; 51; II.17; 20; 25
These eight passages are generally very short. Most are only fifteen lines long or less in Löfstedt's text, the shortest being nine lines (I.51) and the longest twenty (I.8).

Many of the sermons refer to Exodus in their titles. They are a commentary on a reading from Exodus 12, the institution of the Passover. There are many references to this read-

---

[52]P. Cramer, *Baptism and Change in the Early Middle Ages, c.200–c.1150* (Cambridge, 1993) 62.

ing scattered among the sermons, particularly to Exodus 12:5, the lamb being chosen 'from the sheep and goats', to its being 'without blemish' and 'male', and to the claim that it is the 'Pasch of the Lord': 'Pascha est domini' (Exod 12:11).[53] II.20 also mentions the Jews eating the Passover with their loins girded, shoes on their feet, and staff in hand, ready to leave (Exod 12:11).

2. CONTENT

However the key element in all the sermons is that of 'the Pasch according to the Law' ('legitimum pascha') (Exod 12:24) which occurs in all the sermons; indeed, in all except I.8 and II.20 these are the opening words. The theme is then applied to the whole of the Jewish sacrificial and religious system, and evidence, theological and otherwise, is adduced for its being no longer *legitimum*. Christ is the true Lamb, rejected by the Jews,[54] other animals are rejected by God,[55] festivals have similarly been rejected,[56] and circumcision likewise.[57] As evidence for all this, Zeno cites the domination of Jerusalem by the Romans, the ruin of the Temple, the end of the priesthood and of their altars.[58]

The same themes recur again and again. There is little direct copying here between sermons, rather this borrowing of themes. Nor is there much originality or depth of thought. This is primarily rhetorical anti-Semitism. II.20 concludes, 'If you wish to imitate your ancestors, set off into the desert'. This refers to no spiritual meaning of the desert, but is simply a cynical dismissal.

It is difficult to see any theological justification for this anti-Semitic gesturing which has rightly brought Zeno into disrepute with some modern-day writers. Liturgically it would seem

[53]E.g., I.8; 28; 46A; II.20.
[54]E.g., I.8; 28; 46A; II.20.
[55]E.g., I.19; I.46A; I.51; II.25; cf. Isa. 1.11, Jer 6.20.
[56]E.g., I.19; I.28; I.46A; II.17; cf. Isa 1.11, Amos 5.21.
[57]E.g., I.46A; II.17.
[58]E.g., I.19; 28; 51; II.17.

that a provision for the theme of the rejection of the Jewish nation is allowed for by the reading of Isaiah 1, though there is no reason to allow the theme to spread over into the two readings of Exodus as well. But Zeno allows the theme to run away with him, and defends the Christian 'legitimum Pascha' and the 'agnum legitimum'.[59]

(iv) The Sermons on Exodus 14 *(De sequentia Exodi)*

I. TEXT

I.9; 18; 29; 46B; 52; II.16; 26.
I.9 and II.16 are parallels.

The sermons, varying in length between nine (I.52) and twenty-six lines, all comment on the crossing of the Red Sea and the miraculous feedings in the wilderness (Exod 14–17). This is a very long scriptural passage, and it is likely that the Vigil reading would in fact have been much shorter. First, in two of these sermons, where Zeno refers explicitly to the contents of the readings, the narration of the events goes only up to the crossing of the Red Sea in I.29, and the song of Miriam in II.26. The last words of I.29, that the Jew 'still does not believe in God', seems to echo the last lines of Exodus 14: 'and the people feared the Lord, and they believed in the Lord and his servant Moses'. In the other sermons which do mention the divine feedings in the wilderness, the references are limited to the manna and the water from the rock, and not to the quail and the sweetening of the waters of Marah, which also come in this section.[60] Zeno also refers to milk and honey in this context,[61] although it is not mentioned with regard to the desert, and to the Jews reaching the Promised Land.[62]

[59]C.f. the Leonine Sacramentary 161, quoted by B. Botte, *Le canon de la messe Romaine* (Louvain, 1935) 43 § xi.
[60]I.9; 18; 46B; II.16.
[61]I.18; 46B.
[62]I.52.

It is therefore most probable that the actual Vigil reading covered only the crossing of the Red Sea itself. As we shall see, psalms were sung elsewhere between the readings, and it is quite possible that, as in other rites, the song of Miriam (Exod 15:1ff.) was sung as a canticle following the Exodus reading.

2. CONTENT

The theme of Zeno's sermons largely continues that of the sermons on Exodus 12: the rejection by God of the Jews. Also stressed is the distinction between the image *(imago)* of the Old Testament and the truth *(veritas)* of the Church.[63] Zeno therefore narrates the miraculous events with irony, if not sarcasm. The retreating of the waters of the Red Sea is portrayed not as making a way for the Jews but as retreating from their evil,[64] or so that they could suffer shipwreck on land—ruin in the desert.[65] In I.46B the manna and water are inferior to heavenly bread and baptism; in I.18 it is stressed that the Jews are not worthy of heavenly bread, and drink water from the rock in rejection of the true fountain (cf. Jer 2:13). In I.9/II.16 manna and water seem to have been given only to increase the pain of subsequent rejection.

Only II.26, and to a lesser extent I.46B, preserve a positive idea of the typology of the Red Sea and the desert. In the former we have a developed allegory of the rites of baptism: Egypt is the world and Pharaoh the devil from which Israel (i.e., Christians) escapes. Moses and Aaron represent the two Testaments. The column is Christ, and the fire and cloud refer to the judgements of water and fire. The sea is the font, and Miriam the Church which rejoices over the people to whom it has given birth in baptism. The people come not to the desert, but to heaven. R. Hillier's comments on I.46B bring out the originality of Zeno's exegesis as some-

---

[63]I.9/II.16; I.18; 46B. For *imago* and *veritas* see below.
[64]II.16.
[65]I.9.

thing distinctive among patristic writers, for he deals crea-
tively with the differences between baptism and the Red Sea
account by dwelling on these differences in order to demon-
strate the superiority of the Christian *veritas*.

> According to Zeno . . . the truth leaves allegory far behind.
> The Red Sea was no real baptism at all, for the Israelites did
> not pass through the water. . . Zeno then is willing to con-
> front head-on the difficulties and contradictions inherent in
> the use of the crossing of the Red Sea as a baptismal meta-
> phor. The saving event by which baptism is prefigured is not
> so much the crossing itself as the Exodus. The act of deliver-
> ance is figured in the escape rather than in the crossing of
> the waters. In this way Zeno avoids any accommodation of
> the biblical text: he does not make other characters the ob-
> ject of comparison leaving a convenient omission as regards
> the water, and categorically refuses to draw parallels implicit
> or explicit between the waters of the Red Sea and the waters
> of baptism. Instead the contrast is drawn between the dry feet
> of the Israelites and the water-loving Christians.[66]

(v) The Sermons on Isaiah *(De Esaia)*

The sermons here are unique among the groups of sermons
on the Vigil service in that the relevant reading of Isaiah was
changed during Zeno's episcopacy. Five readings are based
on Isaiah 1, and three on Isaiah 5. These two collections must
be examined separately.

(a) The Sermons on Isaiah 1.

I. TEXT

I.20; 30; 47; 61; II.21.

All these sermons are based on Isaiah 1, mainly on the first
two verses. In addition, II.21 refers to the ox and ass of Isaiah
1:3, and I.61.8 to Isaiah 1:8: 'the daughter of Sion will be
abandoned'.

---

[66]R. Hillier, *Arator on the Acts of the Apostles* (Oxford, 1993) 163.

All the sermons are very short, from eight to ten lines long, with the marked exception of I.61 which is seventy-five lines long and incomplete. It is possible that this sermon does not properly belong to the paschal Vigil. Although it is clearly on the reading used at the Vigil, its style as a straight commentary is somewhat out of character with the other sermons, though its content is perfectly appropriate. It is not part of any series of paschal sermons but seems to be completely detached. The length however need not disqualify it out of hand; II.11 on Isaiah 5 is seventy-one lines long. There can be no firm answer either way. If the sermon does not belong to the Vigil it could have been delivered in a catechetical session during Lent or the Easter Week. Nevertheless its content is sufficiently close to the other sermons on this reading for us to include it here, quite possibly as a proper part of the Vigil and certainly as relevant to it.

2. CONTENT

The theme of all these sermons, as in the reading, is that of God's condemnation and punishment of Israel for their faithlessness. There is very little of note in the sermons. Zeno dwells on the impiety of Israel, rejecting God their Father. This is put into the context of the history of the Jews as God's chosen people, and especially of the Exodus experience; the faithlessness is set against the marvels God has worked for them.[67] The earth and sky, invoked as witnesses in Isaiah 1:2, are said by Zeno to have fulfilled their witness in the darkness and earthquake at the crucifixion.[68] Elsewhere heaven is held to refer to the apostles, and the earth to the Gentiles, who hear God while the Jews do not.[69] Zeno tells his hearers that the condemnation of the Jews is to be taken as a warning for the Christian.[70]

[67] I.61.7–8.
[68] I.47; cf. Matthew 27:45, 51.
[69] I.61.3–4.
[70] I.30.

(b) The Sermons on Isaiah 5

I. TEXT

I.10A; 10B; II.11.

I.10B and II.11 are both based on Isaiah 5:1-7, the song of the vineyard, and Psalm 79. Only II.11 has a title referring to Isaiah. I.10B in the MSS was attached to I.10A, and only recognised as a separate sermon by Sparaver in 1695. Naturally it lacks a title. The reading and psalm can however be deduced from the contents of each of these sermons and can be seen to be the same.

I.10B begins by mentioning the 'discussion of the vineyard in the story' ('memoratae vineae disputatio'), and Zeno identifies it with the 'synagogue' which has spread far and wide but produced no fruit. There are echoes in his description of Psalm 79:12 where the shoots spread to the sea and the river, and also to Isaiah 5:2 where the vine produces no proper fruit. [71]

In II.11 Zeno again mentions the failure to produce proper fruit, and he describes the title of the psalm: 'To the end, for those who will be changed', similar to the Vulgate title of Psalm 79. [72]

It is clear from these references that both sermons are based on the reading of Isaiah 5 and the use of Psalm 79. What can be deduced about their place in the liturgy? Their position in the MSS is little or no help. I.10B is in the middle of a group, but there is another sermon *De Esaia* (I.10A) next to it. II.11 is also in the middle of a group, but one which is out of order. Any deductions should be made primarily from

[71]'Vinea dei quidem prior synagoga fuit, siluosis errantium palmitum crinibus vilis; quae cum per voluptuosa ac profana loca lasciva passim se fronde diffundit, generavit pro fructibus spinas, pro uva labruscam': II.11.2. Ps 79:12 (Vulg.): "Extendit palmites suos usque ad mare, Et usque ad flumen propagines eius'. Isaiah 5:2 (Vulg): 'Et exspectavit ut faceret uvas, et fecit labruscas'.

[72]'Inscriptio ipsa tituli psalmi lecti: In finem pro his qui immutabuntur'. Ps 79: 'In finem, pro iis qui commutabuntur'.

the contents of the sermons, while recognising that they share the same liturgical role.

I.10B is most explicit in this matter. Zeno says that a proper discussion of the vine is prevented by 'pressure of the mysteries to come'.[73] And later he says, 'So it is that today some of your number have been brought as new vines to the crossbar and to the joy of all have filled the Lord's wine cellar, aglow with the sweet stream of flowing new wine. God the Father almighty will grant that this comes to you also as your faith matures'.[74] It is clear from the context both of this sermon and of II.11 that Zeno is talking about the baptism of the *competentes*. Here he must be talking to the catechumens who are not being baptised in this particular year, for he looks forward to their baptism also. But though the verbs about the *competentes* are in the past tense, there is still the pressure of the coming mysteries, and the baptisms are happening *hodie* (today).

It seems best to understand the sermon as being delivered during the Vigil. It is not remarkable for Zeno to address specific groups during the services.[75] Catechumens would be present during the Vigil part of the service, but the *competentes* have already been set apart by fasting and preparatory rites, and no doubt they are sitting apart from the catechumens to whose number they no longer belong (cf. I.6 where the two groups are classed separately). Although they have not yet been baptised, Zeno has full justification for talking about them in this way to the catechumens.

It is most likely therefore that these two sermons were delivered during the paschal Vigil as commentaries on a reading of Isaiah 5 and the accompanying Psalm 79. Isaiah 5 is

---

[73]'urgentium sacramentorum pondus'.

[74]'Inde est, quod hodie vestro de numero novellae vites ad iugum perductae, scaturientis musti dulci fluento ferventes vinariam dominicam cellam communi gaudio repleverunt. Quod ut vobis quoque fide vestra adolescente contingat, praestabit deus': I.10B.3.

[75]Cf. below, the post-baptismal sermons, where he addresses the candidates on their return from baptism, except for I.41 where he talks to the congregation about the candidates.

to be found in other Vigil lectionaries, though usually as a canticle rather than a reading.[76] The place of these sermons in the Vigil is substantiated to some extent by the absence of a sermon on Isaiah 1 in the paschal group II.10–17, where II.11 would fill the gap. But in the group I.6–12 there is another sermon *De Esaia*, I.10A. Does this undermine the case for I.10B?

I.10A is a very short piece, more after the style of the sermons on Isaiah 1 than of those on the vineyard. It would at first sight appear to be a sermon on Isaiah 1 because of this similarity. In the MSS it is not separate from I.10B. They are held to constitute a single sermon, even in the Ballerini edition.[77] Löfstedt however divides them, following the example of Sparaver and others. The crucial clue is the use of *fratres*—'Memoratae vineae disputatio, fratres dilectissimi . . .'—which in Zeno is used to introduce sermons, not just new paragraphs. Certainly I.10B makes perfectly good sense without I.10A. Given Zeno's habit of joining one piece of a sermon on to another, we could have here a particularly clumsy join, but the use of *fratres* makes that unlikely.

What then of I.10A? These two sermons are found together in the middle of a paschal group. They fill the same liturgical slot. Did mere coincidence bring them together, one belonging here and one a stray? This would certainly be the case if one is based on Isaiah 1 and the other on Isaiah 5. Closer examination of I.10A, however, leads us to doubt its true subject matter. Unlike the (other) sermons on Isaiah 1, this one makes not a single reference, explicit or implicit, to the passage in question. It is like the sermons on Isaiah 1, but generalised. It recounts that the Jews have incurred the wrath of God, and Christians ought to take heed of doing the same. Thus it could fit either of the Isaiah passages.

This curious feature of the sermon, and its proximity to I.10B, leads us to conclude that it was drafted as a commentary on Isaiah 5. Evidently one or the other was found want-

---

[76]See below where Zeno's Vigil service is compared with other such rites.
[77]II.28; PL 11: col. 471–72.

ing and abandoned in favour of the other. Given Zeno's attraction to imagery, we may suppose that he found the latter sermon more satisfying. But the former would have been written on the same piece of paper and so was preserved when all the papers were collected together.

This hypothesis offers a further answer, this time to the inevitable question of which direction the change in the lectionary took. Was Isaiah 1 abandoned for Isaiah 5, or vice versa? Parallel lectionaries are not much use here. Both readings from Isaiah are attested, but our sources are all later, and we have no way of knowing what the local influences were on Verona ca. 370. However, the content of I.10A deals, as we have said, with Isaiah 5, but looks like a generalised version of the sermons on Isaiah 1. It must therefore be the case that the change was made from Isaiah 1 to Isaiah 5. Curiously, Zeno is content to compose a sermon on the new reading according to the pattern of those on the old lectionary, which does not suggest that he personally preferred to do away with Isaiah 1. What influences did make the change, we can only speculate.

2. CONTENT

These sermons, as mentioned above, are based on the song of the vineyard in Isaiah 5 and Psalm 79. In II.11 Zeno gives an extensive allegorical account not of the biblical material but of viticulture. The growth and cultivation of the vine is described, and interpreted as an allegory of baptism and the Christian life. This sermon will be discussed in detail below when we consider the baptismal liturgy. I.10B is altogether more brief. Zeno complains that there is not sufficient time to do justice to the theme. He restricts himself to the themes of Israel's rejection for not producing the proper fruits, and of the Church as God's vine, with the *competentes* as new branches. But in places this sermon has parallels with II.11: referring to the vine as 'hanging from the fertile wood',[78] which reflects the allegory of the vine's frames as the cross in II.11.2.

---

[78]'felici ligno suspensam'.

And in both the wine finds its way into the Lord's wine cellar. In II.11 the whole theme is properly developed and makes good sense. But in I.10B the references are more disjointed. We may speculate whether I.10B was based on II.11 and that, together with I.10A, it was composed after it.

(vi) The Sermons on Daniel *(Tractatus Danielis)*

Later we shall see how the martyrdom tradition affected Zeno's understanding of baptism. Here in the sermons on Daniel the theme is reciprocated, as it were, and the praise of the martyrs is sung in the language of baptism.

1. TEXT

The eight sermons (I.11; 22; 31; 48; 53; II.15; 22; 27) are all quite brief, between seven and thirteen lines long, and all clearly refer to the story of the three children in the furnace in Daniel 3. They all share the title *Tractatus Danielis,* except for II.15 which is entitled *Item invitatio fontis* in many of the MSS. This is clearly an error, perhaps because the opening words, 'Exulta, Christiane . . .' are similar to the invitations to the font, e.g., II.23: 'Exultate, fratres. . . .'[79]

2. CONTENT

The dominant theme in Zeno's sermons is a praise of martyrdom and of God's powers of deliverance: 'Whoever can believe in the martyrdom of the three children without terror can himself also obtain martyrdom'. 'Who would not wish thus to burn?'[80]

---

[79]II.18 has the title *Tractatus Danielis in Pascha,* but Zeno states that he is not talking about Daniel or Jonah or the three children, but about our Lord. This sermon is a mere fragment. It does not belong here, and it is difficult to make out the sense of its content or its proper context. The ascription of the title is clearly mistaken and may, like that of II.15, result from a careless reading of the sermon.

[80]I.22; II.15.

But every detail of the story is, for Zeno, full of baptismal imagery. He frequently describes the number of the children as a sign of the Trinity;[81] also the dew-like coolness in the furnace is a hint of baptismal water.[82]

In II.27 every aspect of the story is taken into a description of the events in the baptistery. The belief of the children in God is stressed, and their submersion (in the flames) is taken to refer to Matthew 3.11: 'he who baptises with the Holy Spirit and with fire'. The dew is mentioned. Death changes its role,[83] and the persecutors are burned (just as the Egyptians are drowned in the Red Sea) while the flames fawn before the children. They sing their hymn of triumph,[84] and their unity is stressed, 'one mind, one fortitude, one triumph'.[85]

(vii) The Invitation to the Font *(Invitatio fontis)*

I. TEXT

All these sermons (I.12; 23; 32; 49; 55; II.14; 23; 28) are extremely short, literally only a few lines long. They are not commentaries on a biblical reading but, as many of their titles state, are delivered in the baptistery inviting the *competentes* to the font. I.12 and I.23 refer in their titles to Psalm 41 which in the Roman Rite is sung on the way to the baptistery. In II.28 Zeno says, 'Behold, now the solemn hymn is sung' ('Solemnis hymnus ecce iam canitur'), though this may refer to other singing, perhaps during or even after the baptisms. In II.14 there is a clear reference to Psalm 41 when Zeno tells the *competentes* to come 'with the speed of deer' ('velocitate cervina'), and in II.28 they come to 'what they desire' ('ad

---

[81]I.22; I.48; I.53; II.15; II.22; II.27. Cf. Dan 3:50 Vulg: 'Angelus fecit medium fornacis quasi ventum roris flantem'.

[82]I.22.2; I.31; I.53.2; II.22.1; II.27.

[83]Cf. the treatment of the death penalty in the post-baptismal sermons (see below).

[84]Cf. the hymn after baptism.

[85]'una mens, una virtus, unus triumphus': cf. below, the theme of the unity of the baptised.

desiderata') (cf. Vulg: Ps 41.1: 'Quemadmodum desiderat cervus ad fontes aquarum'). So the sermon is delivered immediately on the arrival of the procession from the church.

2. CONTENT

'Now brothers, more quickly than I can say it, enter the heavenly gates'.[86] So Zeno begins one sermon, suggesting that he is addressing his hearers from inside the baptistery while they are still on the threshold. In I.23 he describes the baptistery, using the terminology of the baths. He invites them to have a good wash: 'Hurry for a good wash!' ('properate bene loturi').[87] The water is warmed—and alive with the Holy Spirit—and invites the candidates with its gentle murmur. The bath attendant *(balneator)* waits to baptise them, and also to provide the necessary anointing and washing: 'quod unctui, quod tersui opus est praebiturus', says Zeno, using the language of the baths in a quotation from Apuleius's *Metamorphoses* 1.7.2 but adding that the attendant will also provide a denarius signed with the union of the triple seal ('denarium aureum triplicis numismatis unione signatum'). So the attendant pays the customer! They will enter the font naked but when they emerge they will be dressed in white garments. In another sermon (II.28) the bishop describes the singing of hymns, the crying of infants, and the bright throng of the baptised.

The candidates hesitate when this scene greets their eyes.[88] Zeno tells them to hurry to the font.[89] There is one mention of the death of the old self in the font,[90] but for the most part the emphasis is on the theme of life. The water is alive with the Holy Spirit,[91] the font is identified with a mother—the

[86]'Iamiamque dicto citius aetherias portas, fratres, intrate'. I.49.

[87]Cf. J. Armitage Robinson, *The Passion of St. Perpetua* (Cambridge, 1891) 8. ' *"Salvum lotum"* is a phrase of the baths, to which καλως ἐλουσω properly corresponds.'

[88]I.55; II.28.

[89]I.23; I.49; II.14.

[90]II.23.

[91]I.23.

Church—who will give birth without grief on either side.[92] The diverse individuals become one new body.[93] Milk is mentioned in connection with the font.[94] The mother, having given birth to the neophytes, feeds them 'from the sweet-smelling rails of the holy altar'.[95] The cleanliness and joy of the new birth is contrasted with the filth, pain, and grief of earthly physical birth.[96]

The absoluteness of baptism is emphasised. The candidates are told to drink deeply and to fill themselves so that the water will satisfy them for ever, 'and know this before anything else, that this water must not be wasted nor be drunk a second time'.[97]

(viii) The Post-Baptismal Sermons *(Post traditum baptisma)*

1. TEXT

We have seven post-baptismal sermons: I.24; 38; 41; 42; II.10; 24; 29. They are all between twenty-five and thirty-four lines long in Löfstedt, except for I.38 which is fifty-three lines long. Sermons I.38; 41; 42 have all been removed from the paschal groups to which they had originally belonged and been placed in the non-paschal group C. The other sermons are all still to be found in their original groups. I.42; II.10; 24; 29 are all very similar and can be compared by synopsis. The other three sermons are different, indeed unusual if not eccentric, in their content and style.

2. CONTENT

In all of the sermons the tone is of joy and triumph as the bishop formally welcomes the newly baptised who have

[92] I.32; II.28; I.55.
[93] I.55.
[94] I.12; II.14.
[95] 'sacri altaris . . . a cancellis': I.32.
[96] I.32.
[97] 'fortiter bibite. . . vestra vasa replete, ut semper vobis aqua sufficiat. . . quia hanc nec effundere licet nec rursus haurire': I.12; cf. II.14.

returned from the baptistery and come before the congregation. 'Let us rejoice, brothers in Christ . . .';[98] 'Welcome, my brothers in Christ, born today . . .';[99] 'Rejoice, heavenly peoples, new children in Christ. . .'.[100]

The sermon is evidently delivered just before the paschal Eucharist. Gaudentius of Brescia has a sermon in this position in which he explains the meaning of the Eucharist,[101] and Chromatius's sermon 17A would fit well here. Perhaps the original purpose was, as in Gaudentius, that of explanation. However, it is evident that Zeno used the opportunity more for joyful and even light-hearted celebration.

I.42; II.10; 24; 29 are closely related to one another. I.42 in particular is clearly a combination of sections of the other three sermons.[102] All these sermons are concerned with baptism being seen in terms of guilt and punishment.

In II.29 Zeno assures the candidates that all their sins are forgiven. He pictures them as having been freed from imprisoning chains, from the terror and filth of prison and from their own conscience. The old self is condemned so that he may be forgiven; he is buried in the water so that he may rise from it in resurrection. In language reminiscent of the invitation to the font sermons, Zeno talks of the new unity of the baptised, all now born of the same mother and all receiving the same gifts: 'one birth, one milk, one pay, one honour of the Holy Spirit'.[103] This produces a change in the candi-

[98]I.41.1.

[99]II.29.1.

[100]I.38.1.

[101]'The second sermon (on Exodus) on the meaning of the mysteries, when the neophytes have returned from the font: not suitable for the catechumens' ('Tractatus Secundus < in Exodum > regressis a fonte neophytis de ratione sacramentorum, quae catechuminos audire non congruit'): CSEL 68:24.

[102]In Löfstedt, I.42, lines 2–5 = II.29, ll.2–5; lines 5–11 = II.10, ll.12–16; lines 11–26 = II.24, ll.14–20, 22–29. Löfstedt may be unjustified in emending the readings of I.42, lines 2–5 to agree with those of II.29.

[103]'Unam nativitatem, unum lac, unum stipendium, unam spiritus sancti . . . dignitatem'.

dates; from corrupt, greedy idolaters they have become virtuous, charitable worshippers of God. May they remember and preserve their new birth!

II.24 has very similar themes to II.29. But now the prison is a place which has little or no effect in discovering the sin or reforming the sinner. The 'golden keys', however, unlock the inner recesses of the heart, permit nothing to remain hidden but root out all sin and then shut the breast tight against the return of what has been cast out. Confession of sin is voluntary, and execution follows. The executioner's sword is not seen, and the body looks the same. But the old self is dead and the new self is born.

II.10 expands the theme of the fear of punishment; the guilty person smells the prison, senses the executioner and fears the judge, and suffers the utmost torture of the guilty conscience. But in God's court they have kept vigil and their pleas have been heard. A new kind of judgement is in force: confession leads to forgiveness, and denial to condemnation. The execution is described as in II.24 and it is said in addition that whereas water by nature drowns the living, the water of the font gives life to the dead, indeed it transforms them into true humans who will, if they preserve their new birth, become angels.

I.42 effectively copies the original greeting to the candidates from II.29, the new kind of judgement from II.10, and confession, execution, and the birth of the new self from II.24.

I.41 would seem to be addressed to the congregation, describing the newly baptised as they return from the baptistery.[104] They are likened to bread whose flour has been ground and purified. Salt is added, it is smoothed with oil and made into loaves of unleavened bread *(azymi)*. They are cooked in the font with a divine fire and raised without leaven. They are unblemished, milky in colour and flavour. Zeno emphasises that, contrary to appearances, they are all the same.

---

[104]'These whom you see. . .' ('Hi, quos videtis, . . .') §2.

They weigh the same, three pounds' weight, and are all sealed with the same weight-stamp *(numisma).*[105]

The other two post-baptismal sermons have both been discussed in considerable detail by other writers, and here it will suffice to give a summary of their descriptions.

I.38, by far the longest of the sermons here under discussion, is based on the symbolism of the twelve signs of the zodiac. Zeno takes one of the commonplaces of his sermons, that all the candidates for baptism, of diverse age, sex, and condition, now share the same mother and the same birth. He applies to all the candidates not one zodiacal birth sign but all twelve. The way in which he includes all the signs is effected with a remarkable sophistication examined in detail by Wolfgang Hübner.[106] Zeno's treatment of the signs depends both on current astrological tradition[107] and on biblical imagery.[108] The animal signs that are interpreted positively (Aries, Taurus, and Leo) are domesticated, as it were, by being represented in the sermon as young animals. The lust symbolised by Taurus is tamed: Zeno says the candidates take on Christ's yoke and make the ground of their flesh fruitful by subduing it.[109] Gemini, the sign of the twins who are represented hand-in-hand in concord, symbolises the two

[105]The whole passage may be compared with other sermons on the same theme: Gaudentius, *Tractatus II in Exodum* 32; Chromatius, *Sermon* 17A.2; Augustine's sermon on the same theme (which has a number of differences that will be discussed below under the theme of the unity of the newly baptised), Denis 6.1. *(Miscellanea Agostiniana* 1:30); *DBL* p. 106 (which wrongly attributes it to *Misc. Agost.* 2.6–19). We may be confident that we have here a commonplace of baptismal catechesis.

[106]Wolfgang Hübner, 'Das Horoskop der Christen', *Vigiliae Christianae* 29 (1975) 120–37.

[107]E.g., Taurus submits to the yoke and works hard. Virgo and Sagittarius are 'transition signs' and introduce ('foreshadowing': *praenuntians*; 'sends': *inmittit*) Libra and Capricorn. (The other two transition signs are Gemini and Pisces, and the four are meant to mark the transition between different times of the year.) Ibid., 129.

[108]E.g., Leo interpreted in the light of the reference in Genesis 49.9.

[109]'Terram vestrae carnis domando fecundantes'.

Testaments, and is set in contrast to Cancer. Leo stands for the resurrection, Virgo refers to Christ being born of a virgin, and Libra to his bringing justice. In contrast to these three good signs, Scorpio, Sagittarius, and Capricorn represent the harmful influence of the devil. Aquarius, symbolising baptism, conquers all and gathers into one the Jews and pagans, represented by Pisces (unlike Gemini a sign of discord, since the fish are opposite to one another). The sophistication of this sermon may conveniently be seen in Hübner's demonstration of the careful planning of the overall scheme, where positive and negative astrological signs are balanced with one another in their Christian interpretation:

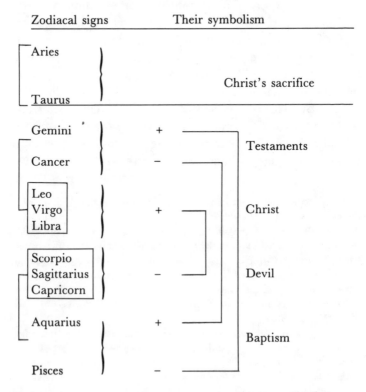

Zodiacal signs	Their symbolism
Aries – Taurus	Christ's sacrifice
Gemini + / Cancer –	Testaments
Leo Virgo Libra +	Christ
Scorpio Sagittarius Capricorn –	Devil
Aquarius +	Baptism
Pisces –	

Such a detailed working out of the symbolism shows that careful study and composition lie behind what may seem to be

light and trivial rhetoric. Once again we see evidence of the
care with which Zeno prepared the paschal sermons.

I.24, unlike some of the other post-baptismal sermons, is
still to be found in the paschal group of sermons to which it
originally belonged (I.16–24). This sermon has been studied
by Jean Doignon, who shows how its imagery is closely related to contemporary ideas of *refrigerium,* the condition of rest
for the dead in heaven.[110]

Zeno welcomes the newly baptised after they have passed
through fasting, the Vigil, and baptism. He declares, in a manner seen above in other sermons, that they are all full brothers
and sisters: 'germani fratres'. He invites them to the feast of
celebration, but the feast is not one of those in which over-
rich food is a burden on the stomach, and in which the new
wine is ruined by the aftertaste of the previous day's drinking; it is a heavenly feast, honourable, pure, wholesome, and
eternal. Zeno then lists various persons from the Old and New
Testaments who provide various foods for the feast. Melchisedek brings bread and wine, the three young men bring their
vegetarian diet, sprinkled with the salt of wisdom. Christ pours
on oil. Moses brings the year-old lamb, Abraham a calf, and
so on.

Zeno calls the present feast heavenly ('caelestis') and the
spoiling wine of the previous day worldly ('saecularis'), and
the two feasts are set as opposites symbolising the refreshment
of heaven and the inadequacy of earth. Doignon produces
parallels from other Christian writers to show that this symbolism is by no means novel,[111] and he also links the sweetness of the new wine ('musti vestri dulcedo') with the idea
of new wine providing *refrigerium,* 'refreshment', the word often
used in prayers and sentiments about the afterlife. Doignon
goes on to describe how some of the biblical characters listed

[110]Jean Doignon, 'Refrigerium et catéchèse à Vérone au IVe siècle', in
Hommages à M. Rénard, vol. 2 (Collection Latomus 102) (Brussels, 1969)
220–39.

[111]Tertullian, *De anima* 54.4; Augustine, *De Genesi c. Manich,* 2.10.14.

by Zeno as providing food for the feast themselves figure prominently in the symbolism of *refrigerium*.

It must be said that this sermon is less sophisticated in its construction and contents than is I.38 in its treatment of the zodiac. Also perhaps Doignon tries to prove too much. He is obviously correct in saying that Zeno is attacking the behaviour of worldly celebration, and is quite possibly right in saying that the bishop is pointing the finger at abuses of the contemporary *refrigerium* rites. It is not at all necessary to introduce a Donatist element into an Italian setting; Augustine is a good enough witness to the fact that the behaviour of Catholic Italy required tighter control from the bishops than did that of Donatist Africa.[112]

In his treatment of the biblical characters Doignon at times strains the connections with *refrigerium*.[113] In fact the list of characters is long and varied, and goes far beyond any theological or symbolic pattern. Perhaps Zeno is simply collecting together a list of characters connected, in whatever way, with food and feasting. We must remember that this sermon is very close to the spirit of the *Coena Cypriani*. We are not dealing with theology here so much as a humour which adds a new dimension to biblical hermeneutic, but which some may find trivialising or even impious. Was this the reason why this sermon was not included in the selected group of sermons (C)? Did the selector feel that here the great bishop's work was best forgotten? And what relation does the sermon have to the *Coena Cypriani*? Are these the only surviving examples of a lost genre of North Italian humour, or was the *Coena* writ-

---

[112]Augustine, *Confessions* 6.2: Monica newly arrived from Africa is evidently surprised that Ambrose has banned such commemorations.

[113]Doignon links Melchisedek with the *refrigerium* on the basis of the illustration in the mosaic of St. Mary Major in Rome, where Melchisedek is represented offering bread and wine. The wine is in a vase of a kind often represented in illustrations of the *refrigeria,* says Doignon. However the shape of vase is very common, being used even in representations of the Eucharist; cf. the mosaic of Melchisedek with Abel and Abraham in S. Apollinare in Classe, Ravenna (SL, plate 13).

ten in response to, or as a parody of this sermon? Whatever the answer, Zeno's statue still grins!

3. THE LENTEN AND POST-EASTER CATECHESIS

We must now turn from the sermons of the paschal Vigil to the rest of the sermons preserved, to see if we can identify any which might have been composed for the catechesis during Lent of the *competentes* or during the Easter Week of the neophytes.

There can be little doubt that, along with other Churches, Verona had an intensive course of instruction for the candidates for baptism based on the period of Lent. In I.37 Zeno interprets the parable of the good Samaritan:

> The inn-keeper is the teacher of the Law, who takes the two denarii, that is the saving precepts of the two Testaments, and receives the person who suffered the attack by the devil and his angels and this world into the inn, that is by the revered mysteries into the Church, where all God's animals resort, and heals him by the daily medicines of preaching.[114]

With Truzzi we identify the daily preaching described here as medicinal as being that of the Lenten catechesis.[115]

(i) Sermons from the Lenten Catechesis

Truzzi suggests that the course of teaching in the Lenten catechesis would have involved sermons on Old Testament

---

[114]'Stabularius doctor est legis, qui acceptis duobus denariis, id est duorum testamentorum salutaribus monitis, adgressuram hominem passum latrocinio diaboli angelorumque eius et huius mundi in stabulo, id est in ecclesia, quo pecora divina succedunt, venerabili sacramento susceptum cotidianis praedicationum medicaminibus curat': I.37.10.

[115]Truzzi, 204, n. 13. Compare Augustine's use of the same allegory where convalescence in the inn of the Church goes on for the rest of one's life: *Serm* 131.6. Cf. Peter Brown, *Augustine of Hippo* (London, 1967) 365.

figures, as was the custom of Ambrose.[116] He therefore attributes a number of Zeno's sermons to the Lenten catechesis: three *On Abraham* (I.43; I.59; I.62), one *On Jacob's Dream* (I.37), one *On Susanna* (I.40), *On Judah* (I.13), *On Job* (I.15). The *Sermon on the Prophet Jonah* (I.34.5–9) he attributes either to the end of the Lenten season or to the Vigil itself.[117] He also quotes De Paoli as attributing to the Lenten series I.3 *On Circumcision*; I.27 *On Genesis*; I.35 *Sermon on Psalm 100*; and II.30 *On Genesis*. Truzzi however seems to see no reason for these attributions.[118]

Of all these sermons some cannot be for the Lenten catechesis. I.27 and II.30 are, as we have already seen, sermons for the Easter Vigil. I.13 and I.37, and possibly also I.43, we shall identify as part of the post-Easter catechesis. This leaves us with sermons I.15; 34; 35; 40; 59; 62 as possible candidates. We must now examine these in turn.

I.34, *Sermon on the Prophet Jonah,* does make good sense as a sermon in the Lenten catechesis. After a preamble (§ §1–4, which Truzzi thinks is wrongly attached to this sermon but which I believe to be correctly, but badly, attached),[119] Zeno recounts the story of Jonah, and presents the allegorical interpretation. Jonah is Christ, thrown out of the synagogue which has already cast the prophets overboard. Jonah spends three days and three nights in the monster, and Christ goes down to hell. Jonah proceeds to preach to Nineveh, which represents the Church. The people of Nineveh put away their

---

[116]Ambrose, *De mysteriis* 1.1.

[117]Truzzi, 205–7.

[118]Ibid., 208 n. 18.

[119]Ibid., 57. §§1–4 do indeed seem to be a sermon on Psalm 129, and bear resemblances to Hilary's commentary on that psalm, e.g., the quotation of Romans 11:33, cf. Hilary *Tr. in Ps.* 129.1. But Truzzi is wrong to say that there is no connection with the sermon on Jonah. The appeal 'De profundis clamavi ad te, domine' makes excellent sense as a preamble to the story of Jonah. The digressions on Peter and Paul are curious; perhaps Zeno is here borrowing from a previous sermon, perhaps he is simply digressing. But the link with Jonah is real and there is insufficient evidence to doubt the integrity of the sermon.

idolatrous practices and do proper penance, as do we, says Zeno, in order to avoid the temptations of our present time and the punishments of the judgement to come.

Very similar in length and treatment of the subject matter are I.15, *On Job*; I.35, *Sermon on Psalm 100*; and I.59, *On Abraham*. In I.15, the history of Job is recounted, and Job is said to be a type of Christ. The allegory is developed in various ways. I.35, quoting the verse from Psalm 100, 'I will sing of your mercy and judgement, O Lord', sets out three forms of judgement: approval of the just, mercy and correction to the sinners, and eternal punishment for the impious who do not belong to the Church. The threefold distinction is in fact based on Psalm 1:5: 'The wicked will not stand in the judgement, nor sinners in the counsel of the righteous'. Psalm 100 is mentioned because it was the psalm used on the occasion of the sermon.[120] I.59, *On Abraham*, develops the story of the sacrifice of Isaac with special reference to the miraculous birth of Isaac, drawing a parallel with that of Christ.

In fact there is nothing in any of these sermons that can be taken as firm evidence that they are part of a Lenten or post-Easter catechesis. It is certainly possible, but they could quite easily be ordinary Sunday sermons. The fact that Ambrose included Old Testament types in his catechesis must not be taken to imply that all discussions of Old Testament figures took place only in the Lenten catechesis, in Milan or in Verona.

The sermons I.62, *On Abraham*; and I.40, *On Susanna*, are relatively short, at thirty-nine and twenty-nine lines respectively in Löfstedt's text. They have much the same treatment as the sermons above, describing the persons and events in a graphic style, but it is hard to see how such short pieces could constitute a catechetical course. These are probably better understood as short sermons for other occasions.

The much longer sermons, those on doctrinal matters (I.2, *On the resurrection*; I.3, *On circumcision*; I.36, *On faith, hope and*

---

[120]See § 1.

love; II.3, *Sermon on faith*;[121] II.4, *On the spirit and the body*) and
those on virtues and vices (I.1, *On chastity*; I.4, *On patience*;
I.5, *On greed*; II.1, *On justice*; II.7, *On continence*) look very much
like a planned-out course of teaching. They could well have
been part of a catechetical course, but there is no firm evidence either way.

In conclusion, it is very difficult to decide whether a sermon belongs to the Lenten catechesis or to some other situation. I.34, on Jonah; I.15, on Job; I.35 and I.59, on Abraham
make good sense within the terms of Ambrose's custom of
discussing Old Testament figures. The long sermons on doctrine and morals could well belong to the Lenten catechesis.
But in the end we are only guessing.

(ii) Sermons from the Post-Easter Catechesis

While identifying the Lenten catechesis is so much a matter
of guesswork, we do have a particular advantage when looking for post-Easter catechesis, namely that it was freed from
the *disciplina arcani*. Indeed the very point of the teaching during this period was that only after baptism were the candidates considered worthy or able to learn particular details of
the faith.

A number of sermons by other contemporary bishops can
be attributed to the Easter Week when catechesis would continue for the neophytes.[122] In Milan the *disciplina arcani* meant
that the content and meaning of the rites could be discussed
only after they had happened and, from Zeno's comment to
the neophytes about their curiosity,[123] it is clear that a similar pattern existed in Verona. But whereas Ambrose gives a
clear, detailed description of the rites, those sermons which
have come down to us from Zeno are more in the pattern of

---

[121]Truzzi, 56, believes II.3 to have been a letter rather than a sermon.

[122]Cf. Ambrose, *De sacramentis*; Gaudentius, *Tractatus Paschales*; Cyril of
Jerusalem, *Mystagogic Catecheses*: SL, 61–64.

[123]'sed curiositatem vestram bene novi': I.38.2.

Gaudentius, who teaches his neophytes through interpretation of Old Testament passages.

We shall identify only three sermons as clearly belonging to the post-Easter catechesis, and so we do not have enough to reconstruct the shape of the Easter Week either in terms of its liturgy or as to how Zeno completed his instructions of the neophytes.

I.25 is clearly a sermon from the period immediately following the baptisms. Zeno addresses his listeners as 'new Christian' ('novelle Christiane'), and as 'my sweetest flowers' ('dulcissimi flores mei'), terms used in the paschal sermons for the newly baptised.[124] He also refers to the 'white soul' ('candidus animus'), which may be corrupted: 'Aegyptiacos de candidis.'[125]

The theme of the sermon is the proper form of sacrifice to God. Starting with Psalm 49: 7, 12-15 (which seems to have been read as a lesson beforehand)[126] Zeno exhorts the neophytes to offer a 'sacrifice of praise'. He condemns the sacrifices of pagans as detestable to God, and those of Jews as having been rejected by God. Using Malachi 1:10f. he claims divine approval of the Christian sacrifice of praise. This he identifies not with bloody animal sacrifices but with the spiritual offering of oneself with pure minds and deeds. For the sacrifice to be acceptable, Zeno warns his hearers against tolerating pagan shrines on their property, and also against the abuses of offerings to the dead,[127] taking auspices, and every kind of immorality.

The end of this sermon connects the sacrifice of hearts and minds to that of the Eucharist. Quoting Leviticus 7:19ff., which is used by Cyprian to warn against unworthy reception of the Eucharist,[128] Zeno likewise declares that receiv-

[124]I.25.3.

[125]I.25.9.

[126]'praesenti lectioni': § 1.

[127]For the abuses of offerings to the dead, see Doignon, *'Refrigerium'*, 220ff.

[128]Cyprian, *Testimonia* 3.94.

ing the sacrifice unworthily is as serious as offering an unworthy sacrifice. Truzzi suggests that this sermon, with its discussion of the proper sacrifice, is connected with the custom which we know occurred in Milan that the newly baptised did not share in the offertory until the Sunday after Easter.[129]

Sermon I.13, *On Judah,* has references to the newly baptised, and also mentions details of the rites of initiation which might normally have been subject to the *disciplina arcani.* For both these reasons, this sermon would be best understood as part of the post-baptismal catechesis.

The theme of the sermon is an allegory of Judah, his sons Er, Onan, and Shelah and their relations with Tamar. Judah represents the patriarchs and prophets. Er as the first-born son represents the earliest race on earth, the demigods and kings who corrupted the earth and were wiped out by God. Onan represents the Jews. Just as he wasted his semen on the ground, so the Jews neglected the word of God and deserve his judgement. Shelah is the new people of God from the Gentile races. Tamar is the Church. The allegory becomes very complicated, but moves on to the pledges given to Tamar by Judah when he has intercourse with her. The necklace represents the law which decorates the heart, not the neck. The staff, being of wood, represents the cross. Zeno then refers to Psalm 22 with its mention of the table prepared, the anointing with oil, and the cup, and says, 'And so, brothers, the cup signifies the Blood; the table, the Body; the oil, the gift of the Holy Spirit.'[130] This mention not just of bread and wine but of Body and Blood, along with the identification of the oil with the Holy Spirit, is extraordinarily explicit. It is hard

---

[129]Truzzi, 218 n. 72: Ambrose, *Exp Ps. cxviii,* prol. 2.

[130]'Virga tua et baculus tuus ipsa me consolata sunt. Parasti in conspectu meo mensam adversus eos qui tribulent me. Inpinguasti oleo caput meum et poculum tuum inebrians quam praeclarum. Utique, fratres, calix sanguinem, mensa corpus, oleum donum spiritus sancti significat, virga cum baculo crucem, in qua deus pro homine pendere dignatus est': I.13.10.

to see how such an interpretation would not have been subject to the *disciplina arcani*.

The ring is a sign of faith ('signaculum fidei'): like a coin,
we are marked and sealed with the likeness of Christ, and
through the Holy Spirit bear his image. Tamar's innocence
points to the effect of baptism, 'since whoever is born again
of water and the Holy Spirit ceases to be what he had been
and begins to be what he used not to be'.[131] The number of
the objects by which Tamar frees herself from punishment
points to the threefold baptism: 'The Church herself in truth,
in the name of the Father and of the Son and of the Holy
Spirit, not only extinguishes the present fires of the devil but
also will overcome the fires of the Day which is coming.'[132]
This again, mentioning the words of baptism, must come
within the bounds of the *disciplina*. Zeno finishes by addressing his hearers, telling them that the Church has been glori-
fied by their joining it—'glorificata vestri numeri incrementis
ac fidei'—another reference that shows that this must be post-
baptismal.

Thus with great ingenuity Zeno deduces the natural and
supernatural history of all humanity from Genesis 38.

I.37 is another allegory, ostensibly *On Jacob's Dream*, but
in fact interpreting a large number of different verses. It would
seem to have been delivered after the baptism because it
describes the ceremonies of renunciation and warns the hearers
not to go back on their promises.

The sermon would seem to have followed a reading of
Jacob's dream of the ladder in Genesis 28, since Zeno refers
to the dream right at the beginning of the sermon but does
not describe nor interpret it until the end. His first concern
is to explain how pairs of things can represent a unity. Jacob's
ladder signifies the two Testaments (he does not say why).

---

[131]'quia renatus per aquam et spiritum sanctum desinit esse quod fuerat,
et incipit esse quod non erat': I.13.12.

[132]'Ecclesia ipsa veritate, in nomine patris et filii et spiritus sancti, non
tantum diaboli praesentes ignes exstinguit, sed etiam futuri diei iudicii incendia superabit'. I.13.13.

The sword in Revelation 1:16 has two edges but one hilt: the sword is the Holy Spirit and its oneness is that of the Father and the Son; the two edges of the sword are the two Testaments. The same is signified by the tongs in Isaiah 6.6f.: the lips which need to be purified are the two races of Jews and Gentiles which are joined into one Christian people by the touch of the coal—the word of God. A quill pen has a twin nib: even so the Testaments go together.

Zeno now introduces the miracle of Peter catching the fish to pay the temple tax (Matt 17:26). Yet again the Testaments are signified, by the two denarii. An allegorical interpretation of the miracle goes to some length discussing the mission to the world and the commission to baptise, and then we return to the two Testaments with Psalm 22:4; the rod and staff also foretell the crucifixion of Christ. Then we return to the denarii. They appear (why?) in the parable of the wise scribe being like the householder who brings out things new and old (representing the Testaments). The two denarii appear in the story of the good Samaritan:

> The person who suffered the attack is recognised as Adam, the robbers were the devil and concupiscence, the Samaritan is the Lord. . . . The inn-keeper is the teacher of the Law, who takes the two denarii, that is the saving precepts of the two Testaments, and receives the person who suffered the attack by the devil and his angels and this world into the inn, that is by the revered mysteries into the Church, where all God's animals resort, and heals him by the daily medicines of preaching.[133]

---

[133]'Homo enim adgressuram passus Adam esse cognoscitur, latrones diabolus et concupiscentia, Samaritanus dominus . . . Stabularius doctor est legis, qui acceptis duobus denariis, id est duorum testamentorum salutaribus monitis, adgressuram hominem passum latrocinio diaboli angelorumque eius et huius mundi in stabulo, id est in ecclesia, quo pecora divina succedunt, venerabili sacramento susceptum cotidianis praedicationum medicaminibus curat': I.37.10.

And at last we arrive at the explanation of Jacob's ladder. The angels who ascend and descend are good and bad respectively, but they are not angels but human beings.

> We recognise those who ascend and descend to be there as examples. The ones who descend are those who renounced the world but turn back to the world. But the ones who ascend are the righteous who by their good conduct are taken up the rungs of their spiritual journey of daily observing the divine precepts until they reach heaven.[134]

Zeno ends the sermon by summarising the unity of all the pairs mentioned, and listing the names of the rungs of the ladder as various virtues. The uprights are the two Testaments, the ladder itself is the cross by which Christ opened a way to heaven for all who follow him.

We see two major themes. The unity of the two Testaments is obviously a burning issue and occupies much space. The interpretation of the reading concentrates on the rejection of the world and the journey to heaven, with the implied exhortation to the neophytes not to abandon their resolve: Remember Lot's wife![135]

I.43, *On Abraham*, is a fourth sermon that possibly belongs here. It simply tells the story of the sacrifice of Isaac, but it is incomplete. The final extant paragraph begins to set out the secrets of the Law and their understanding ('legis arcana et intellectum'), which suggests that Zeno might be using this story to explain some detail that might fall under the *disciplina arcani*. If so, this sermon would belong to the post-Easter catechesis. It may well originally have been much longer than it is now, for Zeno has only just begun his explanation, so that it could have been similar in length to the other sermons

---

[134]'Sed ascendentes et descendentes qui sint, in exemplis agnoscimus. Descendentes sunt, qui saeculo renuntiantes rursus revertuntur ad saeculum. . . Ascendentes vero sunt iusti, qui probis moribus per gradus divinorum observantiae praeceptorum cotidie spiritalis itineris gloria feruntur in caelum': I.37.12.

[135]I.37.12.

belonging to the post-Easter catechesis. The line of thought developing is the identity of the lamb caught in the thicket with Christ the true sacrifice on the cross.

Truzzi suggests that the two sermons I.13 and I.37, which I have described above as belonging to the Easter Week, should be understood as part of the Lenten catechesis. Also he suggests that sermon II.11 may have belonged to the Easter Week series.[136] This is one that I have placed in the Vigil series, and have discussed there.

In conclusion, some sermons are identified as being from the post-Easter catechesis on the basis of their contents. I.25; I.13; and I.37 all have references to the audience as though they were recently baptised, and also, except in the first sermon, references to the sacraments which we might expect to be within the bounds of the *disciplina arcani*.   The contents of the sermons are not greatly different from those we have considered as possible Lenten catechesis. They all concern the fulfilment in the New Testament Church of Old Testament typology.

4. THE OVERALL VISION OF THE SERMONS

We have seen in this chapter both the variety and the consistency of the bishop over some eight years of preaching. In our own day we may be surprised at the amount that Zeno was prepared to copy of his earlier material and, presumably, the satisfaction of his congregation in hearing only minor developments in his themes.

During the Vigil itself there is considerable change of mood. The solemn formality of the proclamation moves to the theological seriousness of the Genesis sermons. The sermons on the Exodus and Isaiah readings can be chilling to the modern reader for the passion of their anti-Semitism, but we may equally wonder at the informality of the allegory of viticulture, and doubt whether Zeno is really serious in his sermons

[136]Truzzi, 205, 216.

on Daniel. The invitation to the font is of a different genre again, and all of Zeno's triumphalism, humour, and eccentric imagination are to be found in the widely varying post-baptismal sermons.

The sermons in their various ways deepen the congregation's vision, understanding, and appreciation of the paschal mystery. The Genesis sermons introduce a wide variety of themes all of which dwell on motifs important for the feast. By attacking the Jewish faith Zeno establishes the superiority of the Christian revelation, and by fêting the martyr he celebrates the Christian's victory over the world. In all these there is a tension between the sinful world, which caused the Jew to fall and is poised even now to tempt and pull down the unwary Christian, and the power of God which always breaks in unexpectedly and which is continually, steadily, and triumphantly building a new creation. By God's grace we recognise that new creation as it unfolds and gives meaning to all that has foreshadowed it.

But the most frequent theme throughout is that of baptism. Whatever the sermon, Zeno can find a way of hinting at it, describing it (in veiled terms because of the *disciplina arcani*, and to tease the uninitiated), or discovering it even in the most unlikely places through typology and allegory. Baptism at Easter is what the faithful (unless they underwent clinical baptism) would remember and on later Easters celebrate; it is what the *competentes* would now be about to achieve after months or years of preparation; it is what the catechumens and outsiders had to realise they lacked.

Other sermons of catechetical instruction, whether before or after Easter, are more difficult to identify and themselves tell us little about the faith or practice of the Church in Verona. Typology is always a major theme: the purpose and unity of all the Scriptures lie in their being fulfilled in Christ, in the New Testament and the Church. Christian doctrine and morals are set out systematically in a number of long, developed sermons, but whether these were part of the catechetical scheme we have no way of knowing.

This chapter has been devoted primarily to describing the sermons in themselves. We must now turn to analyse what they tell us about the liturgy that was their context and then about the preacher's themes and the images he used in portraying the communication of redemption on Easter Day.

Chapter Five
THE PASCHAL AND BAPTISMAL LITURGY

1. A SUMMARY OF THE RITE

Obviously with so many sermons delivered during the Easter cermonies there are very many references, explicit and implicit, to the details of the paschal service and the rites of initiation. We do not have from Zeno anything like the descriptions given by Ambrose, discussing the ceremonies afterwards and explaining their meaning. For the most part we have only chance references given at the time. The result is that Zeno's descriptions can be extremely vivid. We are not listening to explanations after the event, but are following the candidates through their initiation, hearing the very words that they hear as they wait during the Vigil, as they first step into the baptistery, as they return joyfully to the church for the paschal Eucharist. But, as we shall see below, there are other moments when the bishop has given no sermon, and at that point his silence leaves us ignorant. It is very rare indeed for us to find any evidence of the content of prayers or of liturgical formulae.

Because of the complexity of the material which we must consider, it is best to summarise the rite as reconstructed first, and then look at the evidence afterwards. Although this reverses the actual process of research and discovery, hopefully it will enable the reader to follow the details of the argument more closely and it will prevent 'the wood being lost for the trees'.

Zeno often refers to the catechumenate. He gives us no clues about admission to the catechumenate, or rules or pastoral practice concerning it. We do hear of the 'salt of wisdom' which in the Western Church is administered to the catechumens. Catechumens who were not being baptised in a particular year are mentioned as being present during the (first part of the) paschal Vigil. Zeno looks forward to the time when they too will be baptised, but does not say whether it is their tardiness or the length of a period of catechumenate which prevents their being baptised that year.

The *competentes,* the candidates for baptism, underwent certain examinations before their initiation. There would be forms of scrutinies and exorcism such as we read of in other contemporary churches, and in the course of this the candidates were possibly anointed more than once. There is no description in Zeno of a *traditio* or *redditio* of the Creed and Lord's Prayer. The *competentes* prepared for the paschal service with fasting and sharing in the Vigil leading up to the service.

It was probably on the Saturday that there was a final service of preparation with anointing and a form of renunciation. The anointing was (at least) of the breast. The renunciations are several times mentioned, and I speculate that the candidates were bidden to renounce the devil, his pomps, the world ('diabolo . . . pompis eius . . . saeculo').

On the night of the Saturday through to the dawn of Easter Day the Church met together to share in the celebration of the resurrection. The Vigil service preceded the rites of baptism. There is no evidence of any ceremonies connected with lights or a paschal candle, nor would we expect there to be since they would have been performed by a deacon and not by the bishop. Zeno does mention the brightness of the Vigil, so the presence of lights was important at least in setting the scene.

Towards dawn the service of readings began with the paschal proclamation, proclaimed by the bishop in honour of the day being celebrated. There were five readings from the Old Testament, and we know about them from the short sermons delivered by the bishop after each one of them: Genesis 1, Exodus

12, Exodus 14, Isaiah 1 (in later years Isaiah 5), and Daniel 3. The reading of Exodus 14 was possibly followed by the canticle, the song of Miriam. Psalm 79 certainly followed the reading of Isaiah 5. There is no mention of any other canticles, or of prayers that may have accompanied the readings. We can make no arguments from this silence.

After the last reading, that of Daniel, and Zeno's accompanying sermon and any prayers, preparations would be made for the baptism. Zeno is silent here, and we have to reconstruct the order from parallel rites, and from hints in his own sermons. The catechumens are dismissed since they could not remain to witness the later rites. The candidates go through to the baptistery, and the faithful remain in the church, probably singing the song of the three children while they wait for the return of the baptism party and the start of the paschal Eucharist.

We meet the candidates again as they enter the baptistery singing Psalm 41 and they see the font. The water is blessed, possibly using a cross that is dipped into the water, but the blessing does not interrupt the proceedings at all. Quite possibly the bishop had gone on ahead to perform the blessing. The water of the font has also been warmed.

After a greeting from the bishop the candidates immediately strip. They enter the font and are immersed (by a deacon?), using the interrogatory form of the baptismal formula. Once they have been immersed and probably before leaving the font they are anointed (presumably by the bishop) and the sign of the cross is made on them. They leave the font and put on white garments. Singing a hymn and possibly carrying lights, they return to the church in procession.

While the baptisms have been taking place, the congregation in the church are probably singing the canticle of the three children, divided into three parts with intervening silences. It is during the last part that the bishop and candidates return, and so the hymn they are singing may well be that canticle. Zeno delivers a final address before proceeding with the Eucharist in which the newly baptised share for the first time.

In the baptistery there is no evidence of any ceremony of the washing of feet, nor is there any mention of an imposition of hands after the baptism. The whole rite is described as a unified whole, perhaps all taking place in the font itself. There is no mention of or room for separate ceremonies. There is no *Effeta* rite such as we find in Ambrose. There is no mention of the inclusion of milk and honey in the paschal Eucharist.

2. SERMONS DESCRIBING THE WHOLE PROCESS OF INITIATION

Some of Zeno's sermons describe the initiation rites all together, in more or less detail, and these help us to gain a general overview of the shape of his liturgy. All of these however must be read with some caution. Some allegorise non-liturgical features, namely the four seasons, viticulture, and the making of bread, and the shape of the description may follow the thing allegorised rather than the liturgy. In addition, because of the *disciplina arcani,* the sermons seem to be made deliberately confusing for the uninitiated.

(i) An Allegory of the Seasons

II.13, a paschal proclamation, allegorises the seasons:

> And so today for our *competentes* the winter of sin is finished; they will rejoice in the consecrated oil. Today smiling spring will make them into various kinds of flowers with their various gifts when they are immersed in the healing wave and rejoice in the harvest of cloudless summer and begin to eat the new bread. The autumn's new wine will not hinder them; they will be filled with it and happily drunk, and aglow with the warmth of the Holy Spirit.[1]

[1]Competentibus nostris finitur hiems hodie peccatorum. Oleo confecto laetabuntur. Hodie eos etiam ver arridens diversos in flores diverso charismate redditurum, cum salubri unda perfusi, limpidae aestatis messe

The seasons are made to fit four aspects of the initiatory rite; an anointing, the baptism, the bread (presumably of the Eucharist), and wine. But from this sermon we cannot discover much about the details or emphasis of the liturgy. There is no real reason from this sermon to suppose that the Communion of the bread and wine were divided liturgically or theologically, and so we may be sceptical also about the precise liturgical point of the anointing.

(ii) An Allegory of Viticulture

II.11 is an allegory of viticulture: the shoot of the vine is measured and cut to size for planting; the candidate undergoes similar 'sizing up' ('legitimo examinis numero examinatus'). The trench signifies the font receiving the shoots and giving them life with water from heaven. The upright post which supports the vine is the sign of the cross, without which the Christian cannot live or acquire immortality, and the training of the vine along the horizontal bars shows the height of the way and life of heaven. The vine is tied on, representing the renunciation of worldly deeds and being spiritually tied by the ritual questions. Sins are pruned off by baptism and the Holy Spirit. The sap of the vine weeps when it is pruned; the divine streams of heavenly teaching drip from the person who has been washed. The buds of the vine burst open ('oculis ruptis') pointing to the spiritual opening of the eyes. The leaves feed and defend the vine, even as the divine commands defend the Christian who follows them. The horizontal bar is called a yoke ('iugum') and signifies the carrying of one's cross in the path of Christ in one's daily life. The sun and the rain represent temptation, and then the Christian is brought to his crown. The vintage is the day of persecution; the wine press is the place of execution and the workmen the persecu-

---

gaudentes panem novum coeperint manducare. Quos autumnale quoque non morabitur mustum, quo repleti inebriatique feliciter spiritus sancti calore fervebunt.

tors. The new wine is kept in the owner's cellar to mature, and the martyr proceeds to heaven and becomes an angel.

This sermon is most striking in the way in which it includes the moral aspects of the Christian life and the eschatological fulfilment in death. But the earlier part of the sermon mentions also many parts of the initiatory rite: the examination of the candidates, the font and life-giving water, the sign of the cross ('signum crucis dominicae'), a renunciation of the world ('renuntians saeculo sponsione facta') and being spiritually tied by ritual questions, the purging of sin by baptism and the strength of the Holy Spirit, the 'divine currents of heavenly doctrine', the spiritual opening of eyes.

Most of this is clear enough. But do the ritual questions which bind the candidate refer to an interrogatory form of the baptismal words such as we find in Ambrose, or to a separate form of adhesion? Is the spiritual opening of the eyes an actual ceremony, like Ambrose's *Effeta* rite, or simply the end result of the initiation, enabling the new Christians to understand what they have undergone? These questions cannot be answered adequately by consideration of this sermon alone.

(iii) An Allegory of Wheat

In I.41 those undergoing initiation are, when they arrive back in church after their baptism, likened to wheat that is being made into flour. Weeds and chaff are removed, the wheat is ground and sifted and made into white flour ('mirifico splendore'), without any adulterating yeast. Salt is added, it is raised with oil ('oleo gremiali': we have been unable to find what is signified by 'gremiali'), duly prepared and made into loaves of unleavened bread ('panes azymos'). They are cooked—in the font ('non furno sed fonte')—by divine fire. Their colour and flavour are milky. They all weigh the same. 'All that are used at the table are three pounds' weight, and signed with the one measure of the sacred stamp' ('Tripondes sunt omnes, numismatis sacri una libra signati qui mensae deserviunt').

Again much is clear. A removal of weeds and chaff points to the preparation of the catechumens with renunciations, exorcisms, etc. The cooking in the font with the divine fire would point to the gift of the Holy Spirit there. Attending at the table must refer to the ensuing Eucharist. Salt and oil seem to be used in the rites, but their precise role is unclear. The milky colour of the candidates at the end of the initiation can be taken to refer to the white garments. Does the milky flavour ('sapor') refer to the aroma of the oil of anointing? And the significance of the 'three pounds' weight, signed with the one measure of the sacred stamp' will need to be examined in greater detail.

(iv) The Christian's 'Daily Pay'

Sermon II.6 is not an Easter sermon at all, but one marking the dedication of a church. Here the Christian's 'daily pay' is enumerated:

> In addition I shall say what is the daily pay and what allowance is paid out: to everyone equally is given one loaf with wood, water with wine, salt, fire and oil, a new tunic and one denarius; whoever receives it freely and does not scorn what he has received, but persists in his work right to the end, will dwell in the tower when it is completed and possess inestimable riches.[2]

[2]'Dicam praeterea, quae cotidie merces, quae impendatur annona. Omnibus peraeque unus panis cum ligno datur, aqua cum vino, sal, ignis et oleum, tunica rudis et unus denarius; quem qui libens acceperit acceptumque non spreverit, sed in labore usque ad ultimum perduraverit, turri completa inaestimabiles divitias in ea commanens possidebit': II.6.8.

'Ligno' is the reading in the MSS. Löfstedt's text has the conjectural emendation 'signo' for 'ligno'. The emendation is, I feel, out of place here. Zeno is clearly being deliberately difficult, and so a *lectio difficilior* is quite in place. Löfstedt's conjectural emendation would presumably point to the use of a mark of some kind, applied to the bread perhaps. In his critical apparatus he cites the sign of the stamp on the coinage in I.41, but does not attempt to give an interpretation of enigmatic references. The discus-

The description of the daily pay is reminiscent of the provision for the Temple in Ezra 6:9. But other themes enter here. The willing acceptance of the denarius and working faithfully to the end point to the parable of the husbandmen in Matthew 20:1-16.[3] The completion of the tower is a reference to a vision in Hermas 3.8. The list of objects paid to the workmen can easily be read as representing objects used in the rites of initiation. Bread and wine refer to the Eucharist, water to baptism. Salt and oil occur again, as does the enigmatic coinage. The new tunic is most probably the white garment. The fire and wood could have been used to heat the baptismal water, but this would be very prosaic. Fire could signify the Holy Spirit, but then it would be symbolic of the Divine Person rather than, with the rest here, of a physical object. More probably it can be taken as evidence for the use of lights in the initiation, no doubt carried by the candidates from the baptistery into the church. The wood can refer to the cross, as it does in II.11.

In conclusion, all these descriptions of the rite in its totality do assure us that in the Easter ceremonies Zeno followed the pattern, well known to us from other sources, of baptism followed directly by the paschal Eucharist. Preparatory rites are also mentioned: the candidates are 'sized up' and purified (the removal of chaff). The rite includes renunciations and binding interrogations, and also anointings at some point or points,[4] the use of salt, the cross or sign of the cross, and

---

sion of the denarius below will show that the reference to I.41 cannot be used to support Löfstedt's emendation. The Ballerini have an alternative emendation—'lino'—referring to the cloth which was used to wrap up the Eucharistic bread when it was taken home by the congregation (col. 358-59). Both these emendations are possible. However neither are directly supported by the MSS or by parallel references elsewhere in Zeno. Given a reasonable explanation both for the meaning of the wood and for its place in this enigmatic list, it would seem best to reject both 'lino' and 'signo' in favour of the MSS reading 'ligno'.

[3]Cf. Augustine, *Ep*. 55. 17. 31.

[4]There would seem to have been some variety in the number of anointings in different areas of the Western Church, and we have no evidence

other features which must be discussed in detail. But before considering individual features of the rite, the shape of the liturgy in the baptistery must be made clear.

3. THE RITE IN THE BAPTISTERY SEEN AS A WHOLE

It is our purpose here simply to discuss problems about the overall shape of the liturgy in the baptistery rather than the details. This will involve a survey of the practices in other churches and of the development of aspects of the rite in the West.

In the privacy of the baptistery Zeno describes fairly explicitly what is about to happen. Although he does not go into every detail, and presumably the *disciplina arcani* still applied in some respects to the candidates until the completion of the rites of initiation, the bishop need not be as reserved as he had been in front of the full congregation previously. What he describes, therefore, and also what he fails to say, is especially notable.

The candidates arrive before the font singing Psalm 41.[5] They are bidden to enter the font at once. There seems to be time only for undressing: 'Now, brothers, more quickly than I can say it, enter the heavenly gates and plunge into the life-giving vessel of the everlasting waters'. 'Hasten with the desire and the speed of deer'. 'Hurry, hurry for a good wash'.[6]

There hardly seems room even for a blessing of the water. Indeed, I.23 suggests that the water is already blessed and

---

of what custom Zeno followed. Cf. Canon 8, *Canones ad Gallos,* ed. H. T. Bruns, *Canones Apostolorum et conciliorum,* vol. 3 (Berlin, 1839) 278–79; *DBL* 229.

[5]Cf. e.g., the title of I.23: *De psalmo xli;* II.14: *Velocitate cervina convolate.*

[6]'Iamiamque dicto citius aetherias portas, fratres, intrate aeternique gurgitis alveo genitali condentes.' I.49; 'cupiditate ac velocitate cervina . . . convolate': II.14; 'Properate properate bene loturi': I.23.

endowed with the working of the Holy Spirit when the candidates enter the baptistery.[7]

Likewise, when the candidates come up from the font, there seems to be no room for subsequent rites: 'You will indeed go down naked into the font, but soon you will rise from there robed in white, dressed in heavenly vesture'. 'Soon you will come forth all new, all robed in white, all rich with the gift of the Holy Spirit'. 'Behold, now the solemn hymn is sung; behold, soon the sweet crying of infants is heard; behold, from the single womb of their parent proceeds a dazzling throng'.[8]

All this suggests that the rite was effectively concluded when the candidates came out of the font. All that remained to be done was the dressing in white garments. So 'font-centred' is this liturgy that G. W. H. Lampe understands Zeno as believing with Cyril of Jerusalem that the gift of the Spirit is received through the sign of water. Lampe quotes, 'omnes Spiritus sancti munere mox divites processuri', and adds, 'i.e., from the actual font, not from their initiation as a whole'.[9]

Two problems arise from this presentation. First, are there any other rites besides that of the baptismal dipping? Secondly, if there are other rites, where can they have taken place, given that there seems to be little room for them according to the descriptions given by Zeno?

It will be seen below that there were indeed other rites, namely a post-baptismal anointing and sealing. Their position in the rite, however, in order not to conflict with the 'font-centred' liturgy, can be best understood as being linked very closely to the immersions. In practice short accompanying rites need not detract from the central rite. We have nothing here of the scale of the washing of the feet such as we see in Am-

---

[7]'Aqua viva spiritu sancto . . . iam vos invitat'.

[8]'Nudi demergetis, sed aetheria veste vestiti mox candidati inde surgetis': I.23; 'Novelli omnes, omnes candidati, omnes spiritus sancti munere mox divites processuri: I.49; 'Solemnis hymnus ecce iam canitur, ecce mox infantum dulcis vagitus auditur, ecce parientis uno de ventre clarissima turba procedit': II.28.

[9]G. W. H. Lampe, *The Seal of the Spirit,* 2d ed. (London, 1967) 203.

brose. Furthermore it would seem very likely that the post-baptismal anointing and sealing could reasonably have oc-cured in the font itself.

We might bear in mind the commentary on Tertullian's description of baptism by Ernest Evans, where he picks up the problem of what we read into the description. 'What was the precise significance of these post-baptismal ceremonies is not clearly stated: perhaps, as Fr. Refoulé remarks of one of them, they were ceremonies still in quest of their own mean-ing'.[10] Tertullian was inclined to try to give meaning to each ceremony, but Evans comments,

> It may not be necessary to follow him in his attempt, not very convinced or convincing, to assign each several effect, each several grace of God, to its own particular ceremony: the one all-inclusive act of washing in water with the spoken word of the trinitarian formula may be supposed to effect not only the removal of sins and regeneration to newness of life, but also to carry with it those further graces of which the subsidiary ceremonies may have been (in their origin) illustrative tokens rather than effective signs.[11]

Zeno does not share Tertullian's need to explain each ceremony separately. Nor would it be entirely accurate to imagine the subsidiary ceremonies as being illustrative.[12] But the centrality of immersion makes it quite natural that he should seem to ignore or even, as Lampe wrongly supposes, be ignorant of these subsidiary rites.

In order to establish what rites may lie behind Zeno's chance descriptions, it is necessary here to survey the evidence in other rites for possible parallels to Zeno's liturgy. It will be seen below that Zeno gives no evidence for more than a single post-baptismal anointing, nor does he mention a laying on of hands.

[10]Ernest Evans, *Tertullian's Homily on Baptism* (London, 1964) xxviii.
[11]Ibid., xxix.
[12]We shall later describe these ceremonies as being effective rites but 'by extension' as it were from the immersion rather than detracting from it.

Any parallel would need to be for a single anointing and sealing. Parallels will be found both for a single post-baptismal
anointing and for an anointing that happens in the font itself. Thus it will be seen that Lampe's description of the candidates as endowed with the Spirit as they leave the font is
correct, but that he is wrong in concluding that there was no
anointing.

At first the evidence for a single anointing does not seem
to be very encouraging. In Milan only a few years later we
have the well-known example of Ambrose who after the post-
baptismal anointing has a further ceremony of sealing by the
bishop which probably involved a further anointing.[13] This
echoes what we know from Hippolytus in earlier days,[14] and
the Gelasian Rite later on,[15] while Roman canons make it
clear that presbyters may anoint on the head but may not in
the absence of the bishop sign the brow, this being done later.
A twofold rite after baptism is therefore again attested.[16]

Meanwhile in Africa, Tertullian, Cyprian, Optatus, and
Augustine all witness in various ways to a laying on of hands
as well as a post-baptismal anointing,[17] and this seems to be
the case in France also, being mentioned by the first Council
of Arles and by Hilary of Poitiers.[18] Nearer to Zeno, Chromatius of Aquileia mentions a laying on of hands as well as
a post-baptismal anointing.[19]

However, other sources point only to a single post-baptismal
anointing with no other rite. The later Gallican rites, Gregory
of Tours and pseudo-Germanus of Paris, know only the
anointing.[20] In Northern Italy the Ambrosian Rites have a
single post-baptismal anointing and sealing, as does the

---

[13]*De sac.* 3.8–10; cf. *AIR* 33.
[14]Hippolytus, *Ap. Trad.* 22.1–3; *AIR* 38–39.
[15]I.44; *DBL* 188.
[16]L. L. Mitchell, *Baptismal Anointing* (London, 1966) 92–102.
[17]Ibid., 80–85.
[18]Ibid., 123.
[19]Chromatius, *Sermon* 14.4; 15.6.
[20]*BA*, 121.

eleventh- or twelfth-century MS published by the Henry Bradshaw Society as *North Italian Services.*[21] Pseudo-Maximus of Turin has a single anointing.[22]

How is this evidence to be read? The early evidence generally has more than just a single anointing. The later sources seem to favour the simpler single rite. Usually a ceremony might be expected to become more rather than less elaborate through the years.[23] But not all churches necessarily followed the same rite, and some churches could even have varied their practice. It is possible that the later rites do provide some evidence for early practice. For example the Ambrosian Rites have a single post-baptismal anointing. Do they reflect the custom of that church except under Ambrose himself who boasted of following the Roman liturgy, which in this case is more elaborate?

The decline of the paschal episcopal baptisms and the rise of the presbyteral baptisms and the more common baptism of infants is a clear cause at least in some cases for the development of a simpler rite. The Roman bishops restricted the presbyters' functions and therefore the usual baptismal liturgy. Quite conceivably the whole rite was simplified over the years. This, at least broadly, is Mitchell's view. Discussing the equating of the single post-baptismal anointing with Roman episcopal consignation, or 'confirmation', he says, 'When we consider Gallican, Ambrosian and Mozarabic practice together, we see a substantial agreement. . . . The *spiritale signaculum* described by St Ambrose, like the laying on of hands known to St Hilary of Poitiers, has disappeared'.[24]

There is however a piece of early evidence that may complicate this picture of early liturgical elaboration and later simplification. Fragment 7 of the Mai fragments of an Arian

[21]*North Italian Services of the Eleventh Century,* ed. C. Lambot (London, 1931) 34. *BA,* 151–52.

[22]Pseudo-Maximus, *Sermon* 7.1. Cf. *BA,* 152–53.

[23]Cf. A. Baumstark, *Comparative Liturgy,* trans F. L. Cross (London, 1958) 20.

[24]*BA,* 150.

sermon (probably from the Danube area in the late fourth or early fifth centuries) quotes among various orthodox prayers the following: 'The God and Father of our Lord Jesus Christ who granted you regeneration by water himself anoints you with the Holy Spirit etc'. ('Deus et pater domini nostri Iesu Christi, qui te regeneravit ex aqua, ipse te linet spiritu sancto et cetera').[25]

This prayer is easily recognisable as related to that used by Ambrose and also by the Gelasian rites and the Ambrosian and Gallican rites for the post-baptismal anointing. However this prayer alone explicitly links this anointing with the gift of the Holy Spirit, and has been considerably reshaped in order to do so.[26] The wording given by the writer concludes with 'et cetera'. Mitchell conjectures that it may have gone on to list the sevenfold gifts of the Holy Spirit.[27] If so, this would again be a considerable reshaping of the prayer.

Mitchell believes that the formula is in fact a late one, showing the effects of the simplification of the rites after the time of Ambrose when the post-baptismal elements are conflated. However, can a late date be supported? For among the other prayers quoted by the Arian are two Eucharistic Prayer fragments of an early form, omitting the Sanctus which we know was certainly included in some Western Eucharistic Prayers about 400.[28] Mitchell's reason for a late date does seem to

---

[25]*Scriptorum Veterum Nova Collectio* iii/2 (Rome, 1828) 222–3, quoted in *BA*, 122. For a full translation of the liturgical section of the Mai fragment, see G. P. Jeanes, *The Origins of the Roman Rite* (Alcuin/GROW Liturgical Study 20, Bramcote, 1991) 41–42.

[26]The prayer of the Mai fragment has clearly been reshaped not only in making more explicit the gift of the Holy Spirit in the anointing but also, in order to do this, in suppressing mention of the Holy Spirit in the paired 'ex aqua et Spiritu Sancto' which is based on John 3:5 and found in other instances of this prayer. Ambrose contrariwise has an extremely short ending to his version of the prayer, evidence perhaps of a similar rationalising of the rite, avoiding description of the oil of anointing as chrism? Cf. *BA*, 122.

[27]*BA*, 90.

[28]For the development of the place of the Sanctus in the Italian Eucharis-

be in order to fit the Mai fragment into his pattern for the development of the liturgy. It is at least equally probable that here is genuine early evidence for a simple rite, representing either an ancient usage or a development separate from that which we see, for example, in Ambrose and Chromatius.

I believe that the Mai fragment is early, and that in all likelihood there was considerable diversity of practice in fourth-century Northern Italy and its environs. It is at least as likely that the later Ambrosian and Gallican liturgies reflect early usage as that they were simplifications of earlier practice.

I also believe that the baptismal rite practised by Zeno was of a simple form, that it involved a single anointing after baptism for the gift of the Holy Spirit at or in the font. The evidence for this will be seen below. Here we have a context in which such a (necesarily hypothetical) reconstruction makes good sense. In all probability the Mai fragment represents a variant form of the older 'granted you regeneration by water and the Holy Spirit', altered to fit an explicit pneumatological understanding of the chrism. We shall see below what form of formula Zeno himself may have known.

If there was in Zeno's liturgy a single anointing with a pneumatological significance, is there any reason for saying that it happened in the font itself rather than just in the baptistery room or in some other part of the buildings? The Mai fragment gives an important parallel for such an anointing, but there is no evidence for where it happened except that the prayer as reshaped is parallel to that of the first anointing in Ambrose, which in both *De sac.* and in *De myst.* occurred while the candidate was still in the font. In both the pattern is: immersion; coming to the bishop; anointing; coming up out of the font.[29]

---

tic Prayers see B. D. Spinks, *The Sanctus in the Eucharistic Prayer* (Cambridge, 1991) 93–98.

[29]*De sac.* 2.24: 'Ergo mersisti, venisti ad sacerdotem . . .' (the formula of anointing), 'unctus es; . . .; 3: Discussion of anointing, and of the immersion; 3:4: 'Ascendisti de fonte, quid secutum est? Audisti lectionem' (for the washing of the feet).

The situation of the anointing would then be very similar
to that portrayed in the Arian baptistery in Ravenna, where
John the Baptist lays a hand on Jesus standing in the water
and the dove of the Holy Spirit descends on him.[30] It makes
sense of Zeno's descriptions of what happens in the baptistery
to suppose that the post-baptismal anointing occurs in the font
immediately after immersion, indeed that in the thought of
the bishop it was one with immersion.

This discussion of the context of the ceremonies associated
with immersion emphasises the problems we are facing in
reconstructing Zeno's liturgy. The various actions were by
no means of equal importance, and those of lesser importance
were strictly dependent on and subordinate to other more important ceremonies. In the baptistery the rite of immersion
was all important, and the sealing with chrism was subordinate
to it. The stripping and the dressing in a white garment framed
the entire action and, it will be seen, were taken to represent
the difference between one's condition before and after
baptism.

The attention of the bishop in his sermons is so exclusively
on these few ceremonies in their respective order of importance that it is hard to imagine anything else happening in
the baptistery room. The renunciations and pre-baptismal
anointings must have occurred elsewhere, before the candidates entered the baptistery. There is no evidence at all of

---

De myst. 28: 'Descendisti' (the immersions); 29: 'Ascendisti ad sacerdotem' (the anointing); 30. 'Ascendisti de fonte. Memento evangelicae lec-
tionis' (of the washing of the feet). The use of 'ascendisti' precludes the
possibility that here 'fons' can mean the baptistery rather than the font
proper.

[30]David Talbot Rice, *Byzantine Art,* 4th ed. (Harmondsworth, England,
1968) 155. The representation of the baptism of Christ in the Neonian baptistery is unfortunately of little help here. John the Baptist is represented
as pouring a liquid (water or chrism?) over the head of Christ as the latter
stands in the Jordan. However the mosaic has been largely restored, and
it is likely that originally the Baptist was not in the act of pouring, but
rested his hand on Christ's head as he does in the Arian baptistery. Cf.
G. Bovini, *Ravenna Mosaics* (Oxford and New York, 1978) 19.

more than one post-baptismal anointing or of a washing of feet.[31]

4. PREPARATORY RITES

Zeno mentions the preparation for the paschal service: 'After the chaste fast of holy expiation has been most devoutly accomplished, after the sweet vigils of a night dazzling with its own sun . . .'.[32] The 'vigil' refers of course to the Vigil service and no doubt to the practice of watching through the whole of that night. The abundance of artificial light is attested by the description.

The fast is not described in detail. Its being 'chaste' suggests that the candidates had to refrain from sexual relations.[33] For the term 'expiation' ('expiationis'), we may compare Pope Siricius (ca. 385) who says that candidates for baptism were 'expiated' by exorcisms and daily prayers and fasts.[34]

The daily catechesis during Lent has already been discussed above, with the problem of identifying any such surviving sermons.

Penitence is a common theme in the Lenten preparation. I.34, attributed by Truzzi to this context, ends with the people of Nineveh doing proper penance, and Zeno's congregation are exhorted to do the same in order to escape present temptation and future judgement.[35] And in another sermon, at-

[31]P. F. Beatrice (*La lavanda dei piedi* [Rome, 1983] 99–100) purports to find evidence for the washing of the feet from the fact that the bath attendant in I.23 is 'girded up' ('praecinctus') as was Jesus at the Last Supper. He admits the evidence is hardly sufficient; I entirely agree.

[32]'Post devotissime completa expiationis sacrae casta ieiunia, post clarissimae noctis suo sole dulces vigilias. . .': I.24.1.

[33]Pesci, 'De Christianarum', 37; but see Truzzi, 207–09 n. 25. Cf. I.1.21: 'Per [pudicitiam] legitima ieiunia celebratur'.

[34]Siricius, *Ep. ad Himerium Tarraconensem* 2.3, trans. Jeanes, *The Origins of the Roman Rite,* 8. Cf. H. A. Kelly, *The Devil at Baptism* (Ithaca and London, 1985) 115.

[35]I.34.9.

tributed by Truzzi to Lenten catechesis but by me to the Easter
Week, the allegory of Tamar touches on the role of penitence
in the context of initiation, in enabling the candidate to efface
present sins and to repel those of the future.[36] The baptismal
rites themselves are seen as a judgement on the sinner's previous life, in which the sinner has to accept condemnation in
order to receive forgiveness. As we shall see, the theme of penitence carries through the rites to the renunciations and anointings, and the gift of forgiveness is celebrated in the sermons
after the baptism.

There is no evidence of the ceremonies by which the candidates progressed in status to be catechumens and then *competentes*. Zeno is, to our knowledge, the earliest of the Latin
Fathers to use the term *competentes* for the candidates preparing for baptism at Easter.[37] Ambrose refers to *competentes* only
a few years later,[38] and the term is commonly found in the
West except in Rome where they are called *electi*.[39] It is curious that Chromatius seems to address his candidates as *filii
catechumeni* on the very eve of baptism.[40]

5. PRE-BAPTISMAL ANOINTING AND RENUNCIATION

A pre-baptismal anointing accompanies the renunciations in
other Western rites, and I believe that Zeno follows this common tradition.[41]

The rite of renunciation and anointing is not described explicitly at any point by Zeno. We have seen above when the
overall shape of the rite in baptistery was discussed that there

[36]I.13.12.
[37]E.g., I.6.
[38]Ambrose, *Ep.* 76 (20).4.
[39]J. D. C. Fisher, *Christian Initiation* (London, 1965) 30.
[40]Chromatius, *Sermon* 15.6.
[41]Cf. Ambrose, *De sac.* 1.4–5 (but *De myst.* 5 does not mention the anointing at all); John the Deacon 6, *DBL* 156; Gelasian Sacramentary 1.42.

was no room for the renunciations there, and evidently it took place earlier at some point when the bishop did not deliver an explanatory sermon.

One position for such ceremonies that we find in parallel rites is that of Saturday during the day, and in all likelihood this was the position Zeno knew. It is then that in the Gelasian Sacramentary the renunciations occur, with both the *Effeta* rite and the anointing of the breast and back.[42] In Ambrose also we have the *Effeta* rite on the Saturday, but the renunciations with their accompanying anointing of the whole body occur later *ad fontem,* it would seem in an ante-room to the baptistery immediately before the baptism during the night.[43] Tertullian speaks as though the rites could be repeated, once in public at a point before the baptistery, and then immediately before baptism.[44] But there is no evidence in the writers of Zeno's day for such repetition.

(i) The Pre-Baptismal Anointing

> And so today for our *competentes* the winter of sin is finished; they will rejoice in the consecrated oil. Today smiling spring will make them into various kinds of flowers with their various gifts when they are immersed in the healing wave and rejoice in the harvest of cloudless summer and begin to eat the new bread. The autumn's new wine will not hinder them.[45]

The oil comes first in a list of four stages of initiation the candidates undergo. Zeno is linking the oil with the end of the winter of sin. Properly that might be linked with baptism

[42]Gelasian Sacramentary 1.42.

[43]*De sac.* 1.2–5.

[44]Tertullian, *De corona* 3.

[45]'Competentibus nostris finitur hiems hodie peccatorum. Oleo confecto laetabuntur. Hodie eos etiam ver arridens diversos in flores diverso charismate redditurum, cum salubri unda perfusi, limpidae aestatis messe gaudentes panem novum coeperint manducare. Quos autumnale quoque non morabitur mustum. . .': II.13.

itself, but the font in this sermon stands as spring. Apart from the mere notion of gladness, it is hard to see how Zeno should link a post-baptismal anointing with the end of the winter of sin, enough for it to be moved from its liturgical order in Zeno's sermon and still be understood by the congregation. The end of the winter of sin might therefore be seen more appropriately in the pre-baptismal anointings.

A remarkable parallel for this may be found in the blessing *(confectio)* of the exorcised oil in the Gelasian Sacramentary. The oil is for the putting to flight of the devil, and 'for the adoption of flesh and spirit for those who are to be anointed by it for the forgiveness of their sins. May there be made in them a pure heart, sanctified for every spiritual grace'.[46] Most clearly paralleled here is the forgiveness of sins. But the parallel by no means ends there. It will be seen when we consider the exorcisms that in rites that mention the devil the explanation of the rites tends to talk about sin or the world. The dispelling of the winter of sin in Zeno's sermon therefore may well refer to the expelling of the devil in the rite, such as we find in this pre-baptismal anointing.

While this remains the most likely solution, it cannot be without the following reservations. Applying the reference to the pre-baptismal anointing requires an unusual, though not impossible, understanding of the sermon. The natural reading would place the use of the oil in the future along with baptism and Eucharist. Against this understanding Zeno says not that the *competentes* will receive the oil in the future, but that they will rejoice in it. It is possible therefore that he means that they will understand in the future what they have already received on the Saturday—the pre-baptismal anointing. This understanding is made more possible by the subsequent repeating of 'today'. Zeno is understood as saying, 'Today the winter of sin is finished: the candidates will rejoice in the

---

[46]'In adoptionen carnis et spiritus eis qui ex eo ungueri habent in remissionem omnium peccatorum; efficiatur in eis cor purum ad omnem gratiam spiritalem sanctificatum': I.41.

oil [they have received already]; today spring will make them bloom as flowers through the font. . .'.

The interpretation of this sermon is made very difficult by the fact that it is shaped by the seasons rather than by the liturgical structure. The forgiveness of sins in the spring is a most natural counterpart to winter gloom suggesting the old life of sin—but why connect this forgiveness with the oil of gladness, for this is what is suggested by, 'they will rejoice in the consecrated oil' ('oleo confecto laetabuntur': Ps 44:8; Heb 1:9). Augustine seems to refer the oil of gladness to the post-baptismal anointing.[47] And Chromatius of Aquileia says of the post-baptismal anointing, 'We always have the oil on our heads, if we guard the saving chrism which we received. and so we will not be put to shame in the day of judgement, but rather be counted worthy to rejoice with the saints'.[48]

These do not seem necessarily to be witnesses of liturgical forms, but they still show something of their understanding of the post-baptismal anointing as the 'oil of gladness', and so weaken the case that Zeno must be referring to a pre-baptismal anointing. For a parallel for the oil of gladness as the description of the pre-baptismal anointing, we have to turn to Pseudo-Germanus, a southern French writer of ca. 700, who describes the oil for pre-baptismal anointing as the 'oil of gladness' in terms of Psalm 44, and says that it is for healing the wound of sin.[49]

A second passage in Zeno gives strong evidence of a pre-baptismal anointing, especially when we read it in the context of other descriptions of anointings.

The anointing of the ears, nostrils, and then breast is said

[47]Augustine, *Enarratio in Ps. 108.26:* 'sive per aquam. . . sive per oleum propter exsultationem et inflammationem caritatis, significetur Spiritus sanctus.' Cf. Heb 1:9 Vulg. For 'oleum laetitiae' rather than 'exsultationis', cf. Vulg. Ps 44:8; Cyprian, *Test.* 2.60.

[48]'Habemus semper et oleum in capite, si chrisma salutare quod accepimus custodiamus, et sic in die iudicii non confundemur, sed potius collaetari cum sanctis. . . merebimur': *Sermon* 14.4.

[49]*DBL,* 164; *BA,* 116–18.

by John the Deacon to fortify the candidates against this world
and to teach them to be faithful in following Christ.[50] This
is very close to the Gelasian Rite, where the ears and nostrils
are touched with spittle and the breast and back are anointed.
The spoken formula for the ears and nostrils includes both
Effeta and a putting to flight of Satan, and the anointing accompanies the renunciation of Satan.[51] This is similar also
to the *Effeta* anointing in Ambrose of the ears and nostrils,
followed, at least in *De sacramentis,* by a subsequent anointing
'as an athlete' ('quasi athleta').[52]

It is a pre-baptismal anointing of the breast that best explains Zeno's description of the golden keys: 'But our keys
bring out everything, whatever they find, and they allow nothing to remain, but they open the innermost regions of the
breast, carefully they drive out crimes of every kind and again
carefully they shut the breast again to prevent the return of
anything worthless that has been removed'.[53]

We have here the expelling of the sinful (no doubt with an
exorcistic formula) and the sealing up of the breast by the same
anointing. Such a description fits extremely well the anointing of the candidates at the time of their renunciation of Satan
and the world. In Zeno, as in John and the sacramentary,
the sinful is renounced by the candidate and at the same time
expelled and its return prevented by the rite of anointing.[54]

We have no mention in Zeno of the idea of *Effeta* connected
with this anointing, any more than we do in John. It would
go beyond the evidence to suppose that so close a parallel can

[50]John the Deacon, *Letter to Senarius* 5; trans. Jeanes, *Origins of the Roman Rite,* 16; *DBL,* 156.

[51]I.42, trans. Jeanes, *Origins of the Roman Rite,* 16; *DBL,* 183.

[52]*De sac.* I.4.

[53]'At vero nostrae [claves aureae] acervatim absolvunt quicquid invenerint nec aliquid subsicivi esse patiuntur, sed pectorum aperiunt cuncta
penetralia, diligenter universa crimina expellunt ac rursus diligenter accludunt, ne quid illo vel frivolum, inde quod excluditur, revertatur': II.24.1.

[54]Cf. Optatus, *De schismate Donatistorum* 4.6. See below, the theological
discussion of the exorcisms and renunciations.

be drawn with Ambrose and the Gelasian Rite, and we must content ourselves with an anointing for exorcism, however interpreted, for the remission of sins, and for protection against future sin. As to what parts of the body were anointed, we have clear evidence of an anointing of the breast in Zeno, as we have in John, but no evidence concerning the back. The anointing of the senses (ears and nostrils) figures in John, Ambrose, and the Gelasian Rite, but is not mentioned by Zeno. His almost total silence concerning preliminary rites leaves the possibility that an anointing of the ears and nostrils did occur earlier, but we have no way of knowing.

(ii) The Renunciations

[The vine] is tied on with bands, while the one who renounces the world by his bond is spiritually bound by the sacred questions.[55]

The inn-keeper . . . receives the person who suffered the attack by the devil and his angels and this world into the inn, that is by the revered mysteries into the Church.[56]

[Of Jacob's ladder] Those who descend are those who renounced the world and again return to the world.[57]

The rite of renunciation is widely known both in the East and in the West. In the East it was followed by a rite of adhesion to Christ, separate from the formulae of the baptismal immersion. In the West the renunciations are attested, again for example in Tertullian and in Ambrose. There is no direct evidence for a separate rite of adhesion, for that seems to be understood as part of the meaning of the baptismal immersion with its interrogatory formulae. Thus we find Am-

[55]'Ligaturis adstringitur, cum renuntians saeculo sponsione facta spiritaliter sacris interrogationibus obligatur': II.11.5.

[56]'. . . adgressuram hominem passum latrocinio diaboli angelorumque eius et huius mundi': I.37.10.

[57]'Descendentes sunt, qui saeculo renuntiantes rursus revertuntur ad saeculum': I.37.12

brose proceeding from the renunciation directly to his description of the baptism: 'You turned to the east, for the person who renounces the devil turns to Christ and sees him face to face. What did you see? Water'.[58]

The lack of an explicit description of any actual rite of adhesion, in *De Sacramentis* or anywhere else in the West, leads one to suppose that entry into the baptistery and the interrogatory words of baptism are the liturgical expression of the adhesion to Christ.[59] The 'sacred questions' referred to by Zeno are most probably therefore those of the baptismal formula.[60] The rite of renunciation would have preceded this.

As for the words of renunciation used by the Church in Verona, the allegory of the good Samaritan in I.37 describes the assault as having been made by the devil, his angels, and the world ('diabolus, angeli, mundus'). This looks very much like a formula of renunciation and so may be taken to represent at least approximately that used in Verona. I say approximately because we already have in the other quotations cited above the use of 'saeculum' rather than 'mundum'.[61] Also 'angeli' could be a paraphrase for the very frequent 'pompae' attested to by, among others, Cyprian[62] and Chromatius,[63]

---

[58]'Ad orientem converteris: qui enim renuntiat diabolo ad Christum convertitur, illum directo cernit obtutu. Quid vidisti? Aquas': *De myst.* 7–8. We find in Tertullian the same progress from the renunciations to the interrogations of baptism: 'When we approach the water, there, as also shortly beforehand in the church under the bishop's hand, we affirm that we renounce the devil and his pomp and angels. Then we are immersed three times, giving a fuller answer than the Lord prescribed in the gospel' ('aquam adituri ibidem, sed et aliquanto prius in ecclesia sub antistitis manu, contestamur nos renuntiare diabolo et pompae et angelis eius. Dehinc ter mergitamur amplius aliquid respondentes quam dominus in evangelio determinavit'): *De corona* 3.2–3.

[59]But Yarnold (*AIR*, 18 n. 6) sees indirect evidence of a separate rite of adhesion, e.g. in the quote from Ambrose, *De myst.* 7.8.

[60]Cf. Cyprian, *Ep.* 69.7, where the interrogations would seem to refer to the credal formula. Also *Ep.* 75.10.

[61]Cf. I.60 for the 'saeculum' as the place where the devil is at home.

[62]Cyprian, *De dom. orat.* 19.

[63]'saeculo et pompis atque operibus eius': Chromatius, *Sermon* 14.79.

though not Ambrose.[64] For a parallel for renouncing the devil's angels, we have to go back to Tertullian.[65]

The formula at Verona might therefore quite possibly have been,

'Abrenuntias diabolo?'	'Abrenuntio'.
'Abrenuntias pompis eius?'	'Abrenuntio'.
'Abrenuntias saeculo?	'Abrenuntio'.

But whatever the precise wording, the mixture of renouncing the devil and the world without distinction is unusual among the writers we have seen. For Tertullian has a renunciation only of the diabolic sphere, and Chromatius only of the world. Ambrose retains both aspects but in an untraditional twofold scheme.

(iii) *Effeta/Apertio*?

From the one who is washed drip the divine currents of heavenly teaching, the buds being opened, that is the eyes spiritually opened ('ruptis oculis, id est spiritaliter patefactis').[66]

Does Zeno, in describing the opening of the buds on the vine, here point to a rite of opening the eyes or senses of the candidates parallel to the *Effeta* ceremony in Ambrose? This is a very ambiguous description. There is no other suggestion of such a rite anywhere in Zeno. It is most probable therefore that he is not describing such a rite but means just what he says. The eyes of the candidates are opened spiritually.

---

[64]*De sac.* I.3.5. Ambrose has a twofold formula, renouncing 'diabolo et operibus eius' and 'saeculo et voluptatibus eius'.

[65]Tertullian, *De corona* 2.2, quoted above, and *De spectaculis* 4.1: 'When we enter the water we profess the Christian faith in the words of its rule; we affirm that we have renounced with our own lips the devil, his pomp and angels' ('Cum aquam ingressi, Christianam fidem in legis suae verbis profitemur, renuntiasse nos diabolo et pompae et angelis eius ore nostro contestamur').

[66]II.11.5.

The rites of initiation provide, as part of their function, spiritual illumination, but there is no specific rite to that effect.[67]

6. FROM THE CHURCH TO THE BAPTISTERY

The candidates arrive in the baptistery singing Psalm 41, and after being greeted by the bishop they promptly strip and are baptised.[68]

The last thing we know of in the church is the reading from Daniel and Zeno's accompanying sermon. It would have been forbidden to outsiders and catechumens (those who were not being baptised) to witness anything to do with the rites of initiation. Certainly they would have been dismissed at some point before the candidates returned from the baptistery, and would presumably have left at about the same time as the candidates departed with the clergy to the baptistery. In the church only the faithful would remain until the paschal Eucharist.

The period of waiting in the church may have been covered by the singing of the canticle of the three children. This reading is notable in the liturgical order of various rites. It is found in the Gelasian Sacramentary and in some Spanish Rites, but not in the Gregorian Sacramentary or in the Ambrosian Rite of Beroldus.[69] What is remarkable about the Daniel reading is that it is always the very last of the readings of the Vigil. Genesis 1 is fixed as the first reading; Daniel 3 wherever it

---

[67]This interpretation finds a parallel in Ambrose elsewhere than in the *Effeta* ceremony. 'You went there, you washed, you came to the altar, you began to see what you had not seen before: that is to say, through the font of the Lord and the preaching of the Lord's passion your eyes were opened' ('Isti, lavisti, venisti ad altare, videre coepisti quae ante non videras, hoc est: per fontem domini et praedicationem dominicae passionis tunc aperti sunt oculi tui; qui ante corde videbaris esse caecatus, coepisti lumen sacramentorum videre': *De sac.* 3.15 (trans. Yarnold, *AIR* 127).

[68]Pesci, 'De Christianarum', 37, by a curious misreading of II.11.4 has the candidates carry a wooden cross in their procession to the baptistery.

[69]Cf. the survey in J. W. Tyrer, *Historical Survey of Holy Week* (Oxford, 1932) 156–57, and my survey (based on his) below.

occurs is fixed as the last. No other reading has the same position in all the various liturgies of the paschal Vigil.

There are parallels for this use of the canticle. The Armenian lectionary in Jerusalem uses the song of the three children, broken into three parts, after the Vigil readings.[70] 'And while the hymn is said, at midnight, the throng of the newly-baptised enters with the bishop.'[71] It would seem, therefore, that the song of the three children was used in some way to cover the period of time taken by the baptisms.

In the West, litanies are recorded as being used in the same way. In the Gelasian Rite, after the last of the 'paschal prayers' the rubric states that the clergy and candidates proceed to the font while a litany is sung. After the baptisms are completed, the clergy wait in the vestry until the beginning of 'the third litany' which is timed by the appearance of a star in the sky. It is during the singing of this litany that the bishop ascends his throne in order to sing 'Gloria in excelsis Deo'.[72] Psalm 41 is included in the Gelasian lectionary for the Vigil, but now, like the readings, has a prayer attached, and so must have been recited like those readings, and would not have covered any action or movement.[73]

The *Ordines Romani* 23 and 24 give a more detailed description. The bishop and candidates proceed to the font, where a threefold litany is sung by the choir. During the baptisms, the choir returns to the church and sings a sevenfold litany, a fivefold litany, and a threefold litany. Periods of silence are kept between the litanies, and during the last litany the bishop enters and, when it is finished, begins the Mass.[74] In the light of the *Ordines*, we may suppose that there was the same ar-

[70]J. Wilkinson, *Egeria's Travels to the Holy Land,* 2d ed. (Warminster, England, 1981) 276.

[71]Ibid., 270.

[72]I.43-44; *DBL,* 186, 188.

[73]I.43, *DBL,* 185-86.

[74]*Ordo Romanus* 23 (a description of the papal rite), 28, 32 (M. Andrieu, *Les 'Ordines Romani' du Haut Moyen Age* [Louvain, 1961] 273); *Ordo Romanus* 24 (a Roman suburbicarian church?), 44, 51, 54 (ibid., 295-97).

rangement of litanies in the Gelasian Rite, and the litany that accompanied the movement to the baptistery was not one of the three litanies.

Even with the attraction of the number three, the similarity of the Roman arrangement to that of the Vigil in Jerusalem is striking.[75] Daniel 3 was not a feature of the Vigil in the Gregorian Sacramentary or in the *Ordines,* and so the song of the three children would not have had a natural place following the readings. In the Gallican rites, Daniel 3 with its canticle is found in the lectionaries.[76] We may guess therefore that there too, at least in the early days, the song of the three children was used, divided into three parts as exemplified in Jerusalem, and paralleled by the litany in Rome. It is notable that the 'Gallican' Egeria confirms the close relationship of the Jerusalem rites with her own. For after the baptism, and the prayer in the Anastasis, the bishop returns with the candidates 'where all the people are keeping the vigil in the usual way'.[77]

This use of the song of the three children to cover the period of the baptisms could well have been the arrangement known by Zeno. He also has Psalm 41 covering a movement into the baptistery, but this would be rather like the use of the litany not included in the three in the *Ordines Romani.* The most natural explanation might be that after the reading of Daniel and the bishop's sermon, the catechumens were dismissed, the candidates were then led through to the baptistery singing Psalm 41, and the congregation remaining in the church kept vigil singing the song of the three children.

[75]A. J. MacGregor suggests other links between the Roman and Jerusalem paschal Vigils, *Fire and Light in the Western Triduum* (Collegeville, Minn., 1992) 431ff.

[76]The *Lectionary of Luxeuil* has the song included within the reading, but, as we shall see in the comparison of Vigil rites, there is strong evidence that it was originally a separate canticle.

[77]Egeria 38.2; Wilkinson, *Egeria's Travels,* 139.

7. THE BLESSING OF THE FONT

The water of the font was blessed. In I.23 the water is 'living with the Holy Spirit' ('viva spiritu sancto') and in I.61 Zeno says, 'What of the bitter water made sweet by the rod: the water which we would drink when our Gentile bitterness has been purged by the wood of the cross?'[78] This passage is very similar to Ambrose in his description of the blessing of the font: 'It is bitter water. But once it has received the cross of Christ, the heavenly sacrament, it begins to be sweet and agreeable to the taste'.[79]

The cross is mentioned both in Zeno and in Ambrose. In II.6.8, according to the MSS, the requirements for baptism include 'bread with wood' ('panem cum ligno'), and the latter would point to the use of an actual physical cross.[80] This has been suggested as possible in the case of Ambrose.[81] The picture of the baptism of Christ in the Baptistery of the Orthodox in Ravenna has a rustic John the Baptist, clad in his camel skin, wielding a most inappropriate heavily jewelled cross.[82] John clearly represents the bishop. The cross must have been prominent in the rites to have been included thus in the picture.

When did the blessing of the font occur? Zeno's exhortation to the candidates to come to the font with haste would have been somewhat lame if they then had to wait for a lengthy blessing to be said. Also when they first enter the baptistery Zeno describes the water as already 'living with the Holy Spirit'. Perhaps the bishop went on ahead to bless the font before the arrival of the candidates. In *De sacramentis* 1.18 the

[78]'Quid per lignum amara aqua dulcis effecta, quam per lignum crucis amaritudine gentilitatis exclusa bibituri essemus?': I.61.8.

[79]'Amara ergo aqua, sed ubi crucem Christi, ubi acceperit caeleste sacramentum, incipit esse dulcis et suavis': *De sac.* 2.13; trans. Yarnold, *AIR*, 113–14.

[80]See the discussion of this passage above (p. 164, n. 30).

[81]*AIR*, 24.

[82]*SL*, plate 5.

exorcism and blessing of the font occurs 'when the bishop enters' as though that happened separately.[83] In the later Ambrosian Rite the bishop certainly goes to the baptistery before the clergy and candidates in order to bless the water.[84]

The water of the font was evidently warmed, no doubt after the manner of the Roman baths.[85]

8. STRIPPING

You will indeed go down naked into the font, but soon you will rise from there robed in white, dressed in heavenly vesture.[86] Steadfastly and faithfully throw off that old self of yours with his filthy garments.[87]

Zeno speaks as if the candidates have not yet stripped, and he assures them that they will have clothes to wear after baptism. As far as we can tell, the stripping was performed quickly and without ceremony.

9. IMMERSION

The candidates are bidden to immerse themselves in the water of the font.[88] The physical difficulties of immersion in ancient fonts is well known to modern writers, but Zeno along

[83]*AIR*, 106.

[84]*Beroldus*, ed. M. Magistretti (Milan, 1894) 111–12 (*DBL* 151–52). *Manuale Ambrosianum*, ed. M. Magistretti (Milan, 1905) part 2, pp. 205–7; *DBL* 137–40.

[85]Cf. I.23; I.32. Pesci says, 'Zeno nos docet de opportunitate vel necessitate calefaciendi aquam fontis in quem baptizandi nudi demergebantur, ad morbos vitandos': 'De Christianarum', 37.

[86]'In fontem quidem nudi demergetis, sed aetheria veste vestiti mox candidati inde surgetis': I.23.

[87]'Constanter igitur ac fideliter hominem istum vestrum veterem foeterosis suis cum pannis abicite': I.49.

[88]II.23: 'vos constanter immergite'; II.13: 'salubri unda perfusi'; I.44: 'sacri oceani lacteo profundo dimersi'. Cf. I.57; I.12: 'fortiter bibite'.

with other ancient writers gives no hint of it.[89] From his various allusions, it would seem that the candidates were immersed in a flowing stream of water, presumably from a fountain of some sort. The water is evidently moving when the candidates enter the baptistery.[90] When they are immersed, a stream of water is said to flow over them: 'Immerse yourselves with all haste in the wave, let its stream run over you'.[91]

The precise words used at the administration of baptism are not known to us. Naturally they were based on Matthew 28:19 but, as has already been discussed, they were of the interrogatory form common in the West.[92]

Who was the minister of baptism? In I.23 Zeno mentions the bath attendant, girded up and waiting for the candidates,[93] which suggests that he is referring to a priest or deacon in the water with his clothes tied up. But in the sermon he implies that it is the same person who then administers the anointing and sealing, which suggests that he is also referring to himself, the presiding bishop. We can only conclude that his description is based on the association with the baths and not necessarily on a particular individual in front of the candidates.

10. THE POST-BAPTISMAL ANOINTING

Immediately after the candidate has been immersed, and before he has left the font, he stands before the bishop for anointing. Zeno's description of this part of the rite is overshadowed by the importance of the immersion itself, but there are still clear references to the anointing.

[89]*AIR*, 25; J. G. Davies, *The Architectural Setting of Baptism* (London, 1962) 23ff.

[90]'Aqua . . . blando murmure iam vos invitat': I.23.

[91]'Superfluentis amnis undae subiecti': I.12. Pesci: 'Vos constanter immergite, salvo salutis statu' (Serm. XXXIV) [II.23] quae verba innuunt alium ritum pro aegrotis': 'De Christianarum,' 37. I suspect however that Zeno is referring to their spiritual rather than their physical state.

[92]I.13.13: 'Ecclesia ipsa veritate, in nomine patris et filii et spiritus sancti'; II.11.5: 'sacris interrogationibus obligatur'. Cf. *SL*, 137.

[93]I.23: 'balneator praecinctus'.

Zeno mentions quite clearly an anointing for the gift of the Holy Spirit. In an allegory on Psalm 22:5, identified above as part of the post-baptismal catechesis, he says, 'Oil signifies the gift of the Holy Spirit'.[94] Oil is not the only thing said by Zeno to signify the Holy Spirit, but this passage witnesses to the use of oil among the rites. It is most natural to identify this with the anointing referred to as happening immediately after baptism. It is to be noted that Zeno's interpretation of this anointing is pneumatological, like that of the Mai fragment but unlike that of the first post-baptismal anointing in Ambrose[95] and in John the Deacon[96] where it has a royal and priestly significance. In Ambrose the pneumatological interpretation is given to the second anointing. Mitchell suspects that there is an episcopal consignation known to John the Deacon which by his time is already a separate event.[97]

Another reference to anointing is less clear: 'Now the bath attendant is girded up and waiting for you, ready to provide the necessary anointing and washing, and also a golden denarius signed with the union of the triple seal'.[98]

When Zeno mentions 'unctus' he is probably actually referring to the post-baptismal anointing. Here he is quoting Apuleius's *Metamorphoses* 1.7.2, and so the strange phrase, 'quod unctui, quod tersui', depends on his literary source. The description and order of anointing and cleansing would seem to reflect Apuleius rather than the liturgy, and to fit with the overall picture used by Zeno of the baptistery as a bathing place.

Can the anointing and sealing be described separately in the same passage? Certainly they must have been separate actions. Ambrose describes the oil running down to the

[94]'Oleum donum spiritus sancti significat': I.13.10.

[95]*De myst.* 29–30.

[96]John the Deacon, *Ad Senarium* 6.

[97]*BA*, 99.

[98]'Iam balneator praecinctus exspectat, "quod unctui, quod tersui" opus est praebiturus, sed et denarium aureum triplicis numismatis unione signatum': I.23.

beard,[99] so there must have been oil poured on the head, and not just applied by the hand while making the sign of the cross. Such a pouring would have a precedent as far back as the *Apostolic Tradition*.[100]

Anointing and sealing were not only physically distinct actions; they could be thought of separately. It is admittedly half a century later that, in his letter to Decentius, Pope Innocent I declares that a presbyter may baptise in the absence of a bishop and anoint with chrism which has been consecrated by a bishop, but only a bishop may sign the brow.[101] But we have very similar issues in Jerome's *Dialogue with the Luciferians*, written in the 370s or 380s, and so very close in date to Zeno. In this work it is acknowledged as a general rule that the gift of the Holy Spirit is reserved to the bishop.[102]

A not altogether appropriate quotation of Apuleius therefore leads Zeno here to describe the baptism, post-baptismal anointing, and the sealing in a somewhat clumsy and misleading fashion. But while the order is misleading and the distinction between anointing and sealing quite unusual, it is perfectly understandable in the light of the customs of the day.

But we must remember that for Zeno the anointing does not stand on its own, but is held within the flow of the baptismal rite: 'So steadfastly and faithfully throw off that old self of yours with his filthy garments; soon you will come forth all new, all robed in white, all rich with the gift of the Holy Spirit'.[103] When he brings the candidates into the baptistery he makes no distinction between the different parts of the rite. The baptism and its attendant ceremonies, including the post-

[99]*De myst.* 29–30.

[100]Hippolytus, *Ap. Trad.* 22.2. This anointing might be referred to by Zeno himself in I.24.2: 'oleum Christus infundit'.

[101]Ed. R. Cabié, *La lettre du Pape Innocent 1er à Décentius de Gubbio* (Louvain, 1973) 22–24.

[102]See Mitchell (*BA*, 93ff.), who also gives evidence that the rule dated from the beginning of the fourth century.

[103]'Constanter igitur ac fideliter hominem istum vestrum veterem foeterosis suis cum pannis abicite, novelli omnes, omnes candidati, omnes spiritus sancti munere mox divites processuri': I.49.

baptismal anointing for the Holy Spirit, are regarded as one continuous whole.

We must now look at two aspects of the post-baptismal anointing, the use of the sign of the cross and the symbolism of the denarius. These are very important in Zeno's understanding of the rites of initiation.

11. THE SIGN OF THE CROSS

There are various references in Zeno to signing the candidates with the sign of the cross: 'Brothers, we are circumcised by this sacrament, both men and women. We are numbered among God's people not by the scar but the sign of the Holy Spirit'.[104] The sign of the cross is connected explicitly with the Holy Spirit, pointing to its connection with the anointing at baptism which as we have already seen carries the same significance. Zeno does not divide the sense of the sealing from that of the anointing, and the two would have been performed together. '[Among the astrological symbols] Of necessity the two Pisces follow in one sign, that is, the two peoples from Jews and Gentiles who live by the water of baptism, having been sealed by one sign into the people of Christ'.[105] This quotation gives less of the use of the sign of the cross, more its role as conveying something of the identity of the baptised, and showing that it had an integral part in the baptismal rites.

However, most references to the sign of the cross are connected with the symbolism of the denarius.

12. THE DENARIUS

Now the bath attendant is girded up and waiting for you, ready to provide the necessary anointing and washing, and

[104]'Hoc nos, fratres, sacramento tam viri, quam feminae circumcidimur. Hoc spiritus sancti non signaculo, sed signo censemur': I.3.21.

[105]'Uno sequuntur duo Pisces in signo, id est duo ex Iudaeis et gentibus populi baptismatis aqua viventes, in unum populum Christi uno signo signati': I.38.7.

also a golden denarius signed with the union of the triple seal.[106]

To everyone equally is given . . . one denarius; whoever receives it freely and does not scorn what he has received, but persists in his work right to the end, will dwell in the tower when it is completed and possess inestimable riches.[107]

And lest she should seem to love anyone more or less than another, she grants to all one birth, one milk, one pay, one honour of the Holy Spirit.[108]

[Of the neophytes, likened to loaves of bread] All that are used at the table are three pounds' weight, and signed with the one measure of the sacred stamp.[109]

All these references to coinage and payment obviously belong together in Zeno's symbolism. Various possible interpretations have been put forward.[110]

The Ballerini (in their commentary on II.6.8) suggest that an actual denarius was handed to the neophytes, and quote parallels. They admit that these are somewhat late in date but think that this does not disprove the same practice in Zeno. Indeed, everything else in the list is present physically. Why not the denarius?[111] However, when commenting on the golden denarius of I.23, the considerable expense of a literal interpretation leads the Ballerini to suspect allegory, as does also the description, 'signed with the union of the triple seal'

---

[106]'Iam balneator praecinctus exspectat, "quod unctui, quod tersui" opus est praebiturus, sed et denarium aureum triplicis numismatis unione signatum': I.23.

[107]'Omnibus peraeque . . . unus denarius; quem qui libens acceperit acceptumque non spreverit, sed in labore usque ad ultimum perduraverit, turri completa inaestimabiles divitias in ea commanens possidebit': II.6.8.

[108]'Ac ne quem plus amare videatur aut minus, unam nativitatem, unum lac, unum stipendium, unam spiritus sancti praestat omnibus dignitatem': II.29.2.

[109]Tripondes sunt omnes, numismatis sacri una libra signati, qui mensae deserviunt': I.41.3.

[110]Discussed by Truzzi, 215-16.

[111]PL 11:360-61.

('triplicis numismatis unione signatum'). Parallels are quoted for the coin representing the Eucharist or the triple grace of baptism, confirmation, and Eucharist. Perhaps, they conclude, it is merely a mystical representation of the physical coin.[112] But it is difficult to see evidence for the denarius representing the Eucharist, still less the triple but anachronistic baptism-confirmation-Eucharist.

M. Righetti suggests that a medal of some kind was handed over, described as a denarius by Zeno but with religious symbols stamped on it.[113]

Pesci disagrees. 'Saint Zeno is speaking only of baptism, which he describes using the imagery of the baths. And so, even as we have said that the bath attendant is the bishop, so we must understand the denarius to represent baptism, and indeed it is golden, to extol the royal magnificence of this bath. And since baptism is conferred in the name of the most holy Trinity, so the person baptised is said to be signed with the "union of the triple seal" '.[114]

In the absence of some contemporary evidence for such a practice, it is highly unlikely that any actual denarius or medallion was handed over. The reference to the triple seal gives the clue, and in the allegory of the loaves in I.41 we see that the mark of the stamp, 'numisma', is applied to the candidates. It refers to the spiritual seal.

Pesci is vague at this point. Correctly he says that the denarius applies to baptism and he mentions 'sealing'. However baptism proper is administered by dipping or pouring. The seal can hardly refer to this, but to the well-known post-baptismal rite of making the sign of the cross on the forehead of the candidate. That the denarius is 'signed with the union of the triple seal' and the candidates are 'three pounds' weight' points to the use of a Trinitarian formula or a Trinitarian understanding of the signing.[115]

---

[112]Ibid., 481–82.
[113]M. Righetti, *Manuale di storia liturgica*, vol. 4 (Milan, 1959) 132–33.
[114]Pesci, 'De Christianarum', 38.
[115]Cf. e.g., Hippolytus, *Ap. trad.* 22.2; the Mai fragment; and even *De*

Zeno is not alone in describing the spiritual seal as a denarius. Augustine talks of us being sealed like the denarius with the image of God when we are born again, and he applies to this the saying, 'Render to Caesar what is Caesar's, and to God what is God's'.[116]

The signing in itself would seem to require no physical object like the water for baptism. It might therefore be supposed that the denarius for Zeno represents the action of signing and nothing else. However the point made by the Ballerini in their commentary on II.6.8 remains. The list is of actual physical objects. We may possibly except 'ligno/signo',[117] depending on our reading of the text and our interpretation, and also 'ignis' could perhaps refer only to the Holy Spirit. But both of these quite probably and the others certainly refer to objects and not to actions or interpretations. Dipping and raising, wombs and tombs are not included in the list. Therefore does the denarius refer, as well as and through the action of signing, to a physical object?

Given its place in this context, it is quite possible that, at least here, Zeno means it to refer also to the oil or chrism used at this point, and its different role (it is always blessed separately in the ancient rites) and perhaps its different phys-

---

myst. 42: 'Signavit te deus pater, confirmavit te Christus dominus et dedit pignus spiritum in cordibus tuis'.

[116]Augustine, *En. in Ps.* 4, 8; discussed by B. Busch, 'De initatione Christiana secundum Sanctum Augustinum', *Ephemerides Liturgicae* 52 (1938) 464–65.

[117]Löfstedt in his critical apparatus for II.6.8 quotes the 'numisma' of I.41 to justify his conjectural emendation of 'panem cum ligno' to 'panem cum signo', presumably taking it as evidence for some marking or signing of the Eucharistic bread. This is not at all necessary. The 'numisma' need not refer specifically to the Eucharist any more than the other stages which the wheat has undergone on its progress to the altar. Indeed according to the allegory the 'numisma' is merely the final stage of the bread-making progress. The marking is of a weight stamp applied to ordinary bread, not of a religious symbol. When allegorised it is seen to apply to the sealing in baptism, not to the details of the Eucharist. Therefore Löfstedt is probably wrong in his understanding of this passage.

ical nature (chrism, not olive oil, cf. Ambrose) would distinguish it from the 'oleum' already mentioned in the list.

The description of the denarius in II.6.8 looks beyond the rites: 'Whoever receives it freely and does not scorn what he has received, but persists in his work right to the end', would seem to be a reference to the parable of the labourers in the vineyard in Matthew 20:1-16; Christians are not to grumble about their 'pay' but to continue faithfully in their labour. And the eschatological element is there: the golden denarius looks forward to the inestimable riches of heaven.

13. A POSSIBLE FORMULA OF CHRISMATION

> The luxuriant shoots are cut off with a pruning hook: that is, all the sins are removed altogether by baptism and the strength of the Holy Spirit.[118]

Zeno's allusive style teases us into seeing all kinds of connections: let us simply note this one as a possibility. The pairing of baptism and the Holy Spirit evokes the language of Titus 3:5 and John 3:5, the two scriptural verses that underlie the chrismation formulae in the ancient Latin Rites. In the *Apostolic Tradition* (in the Verona text) we find the bishop's post-baptismal prayer begins thus: 'Lord God, who made them worthy to receive remission of sins through the washing of regeneration of the Holy Spirit. . . '.[119] And Ambrose in *De sacramentis* has the following formula for the bishop's anointing at the font: 'God the Father almighty who has granted you regeneration of water and the Holy Spirit and has forgiven you all your sins, himself anoints you to everlasting life'.[120] It is this version of the formula which became

---

[118]'omnia omnino peccata baptismate spiritusque sancti vigore amputantur'. II.11.5.

[119]'Domine Deus qui dignos fecisti eos remissionem mereri peccatorum per lavacrum regenerationis Spiritus Sancti': *Ap. trad.* 21.

[120]'Deus pater omnipotens qui te regeneravit ex aqua et spiritu sancto concessitque tibi peccata tua, ipse te unguet in vitam eternam': *De sac.* 2.24.

general in later rites; therefore it is usually taken to be the normal one and that attested by the *Apostolic Tradition* to be the exception.

Obviously in such an obscure reference discrimination is difficult, but Zeno's description of the role of baptism and the Spirit as primarily effecting the forgiveness of sins naturally evokes the liturgical form found in the *Apostolic Tradition*. The words in the sermon can then be understood as a paraphrase (subject to the *disciplina arcani*) of 'remissionem mereri peccatorum per lavacrum regenerationis Spiritus Sancti'.

Whatever the interrelation of the two liturgical forms and their long-term development, it is quite possible that they were both in use in north Italy in the time of Zeno. For quite apart from the survival of the manuscript of the *Apostolic Tradition* in a library somewhere, the Bobbio Missal preserves a most curious conflation of the two formulae: 'May God the Father of our Lord Jesus Christ, who has regenerated you by water and the Holy Spirit, and who has given you remission of sins through the washing of regeneration and of blood, himself anoint you with his holy chrism to eternal life'.[121] The reference to 'blood' is obviously to avoid a repetition of 'Holy Spirit'; the very nature of the duplicated phrase implies that whoever compiled this formula was liturgically familiar with both variants (this is not a literary work!), and wished to incorporate them. Therefore there is nothing remarkable in the possibility that Zeno should refer to one that is comparatively very rare in surviving manuscripts. And although the difference between the formulae is small in the extreme, this possible variety helps us towards an understanding of the pluriformity of early Italian liturgy.

---

[121]'Deus pater domini Iesu Christi qui te regeneravit per aqua et spiritu sancto quicquid tibi dedit remissione peccatorum per lavacrum regeneracionis et sanguene ipse te liniat crisma suo sancto in vitam eternam': *Bobbio Missal* 248, ed. E. A. Lowe (London, 1920) 75 (HBS 58).

14. THE WHITE GARMENTS

You will indeed go down naked into the font, but soon you will rise from there robed in white, dressed in heavenly vesture.[122]

First it was not Aries but the Lamb who received you; he rejects no one who believes in him. He has clothed your nakedness with the shining white of his wool.[123]

The use of white garments by the newly baptised is mentioned by Zeno, as is to be expected since they are so well known in the early Church. In the list of objects in II.6.8 is the 'tunica rudis', the new garment, referring to the white robe of the baptised.[124]

15. PROCESSION FROM THE FONT

Soon you will all come forth all new, all robed in white, all rich with the gift of the Holy Spirit.[125]

---

[122]'In fontem quidem nudi dermergitis, sed aetheria veste vestiti mox candidati inde surgetis': I.23.

[123]'Primos vos, qui in se credentem reprobat nullum, non Aries sed agnus excepit, qui vestram nuditatem velleris sui niveo candore vestivit'. I.38.3.

[124]Alternatively, if 'rudis' is meant in the sense of a rough or coarse garment, it may refer to an aspect of the rite of renunciation of the Devil and the exorcisms, when in some churches the candidate stood barefoot on a rough rag or a 'tunica' made of animal skin (F. Van der Meer, *Augustine the Bishop* 359; *AIR*, 9–10, re Theodore of Mopsuestia, Chrysostom, Augustine.) However there is no other evidence for this in Zeno. It is probably best to understand 'rudis' in the first sense, of the new (white) garment. This interpretation is clear enough in itself, requires no extra hypotheses about the rites (for a rough garment is not mentioned elsewhere by Zeno) and keeps the list of II.6.8 complete. It would have been strange if Zeno in mentioning the goat skin, of no importance elsewhere, omitted the white garment from his list.

[125]'Novelli omnes, omnes candidati, omnes spiritus sancti munere mox divites processuri': I.49.

Behold, now the solemn hymn is sung; behold soon the sweet crying of infants is heard; behold from the single womb of their parent proceeds a dazzling throng.[126]

[Of the Jews at the Red Sea] Finally after the sea they came to the desert, but we after baptism come to Paradise.[127]

Miriam who beats her tambourine with the women is the type of the Church who with all the churches she has borne sings a hymn and beats the true tambourine of her breast as she leads the Christian people not into the desert but to heaven.[128]

The happy sunset invites [the *competentes*] so that, immersed in the milky depth of the sacred ocean, and rising from there, new with the new day, and, radiant with their own light, they may come with us in a safe course on the heavenly path of immortality to the time of promise where one rises for ever.[129]

The candidates, once they are dressed, go in triumphal procession from the baptistery back to the church. Zeno describes this as an entry into paradise or into heaven. We may guess that as the candidates join the main congregation this procession provides a climax within the rites of initiation.

In II.26 Zeno refers to the singing of a hymn in this procession. In II.28 he talks as though a hymn is being sung during the baptism itself, but he does preempt the procession here, so the singing may not actually begin until after the baptism.

Some of the above descriptions of the procession as 'the dazzling throng' and 'radiant with their own light' may sug-

[126]'Solemnis hymnus ecce iam canitur, ecce mox infantum dulcis vagitus auditur, ecce parientis uno de ventre clarissima turba procedit': II.28.

[127]'Denique illi post mare ad eremum pervenerunt, nos post baptismum ad paradisum pervenimus': I.46B.3.

[128]'Maria, quae cum mulieribus tympanum quatit, typus ecclesiae fuit, quae cum omnibus ecclesiis, quas peperit, hymnum canens et pectoris verum tympanum quatiens populum Christianum ducit, non in eremum, sed ad caelum': II.26.3.

[129]'[Competentes] felix invitat occasus, ut sacri oceani lacteo profundo demersi, surgentes inde novello novelli cum die, sua luce radiantes nobiscum possint inmortalitatis per aerium tramitem cursu servato ad repromissionis tempus, ubi in perpetuum quis oritur, pervenire': I.44.2.

gest more than just the white garments, namely that lights
are being carried by the candidates. While there is no firm
evidence for this, the mention of 'ignis' among the objects
of initiation in II.6.8 does make this more likely. It could refer
to the Holy Spirit or to fire warming the font, but both these
interpretations seem wrong. If the former, then it would be
out of place in this list by not referring to a physical object
of initiation. If the latter, it would be oddly prosaic. It could
also refer to the lights of the Vigil service, but these are hardly
pertinent to initiation as such. The most likely reference is
therefore to the other known use of fire, namely in the lights
carried by the candidates after baptism. The pseudo-
Ambrosian *De lapsu virginis,* ascribed now to Nicetas of Remesiana, mentions the candidates' candles and there are other
references from the period.[130]

16. THE PASCHAL EUCHARIST

The procession leads back to the church where the final post-
baptismal sermon *(post traditum baptisma ad neophytos)* is delivered by the bishop. Then the Eucharist follows, justifying
Zeno's claim that the candidates have now marched to paradise ('ad paradisum').[131] In I.24 the heavenly feast is described
in a highly fanciful fashion, beginning with the provision of
bread and wine by the 'pater familias', that is, Melchisedek.
In I.32 the Church is described as a mother who gives birth
to the baptised and feeds them from the 'cancelli' of the altar.

There is no evidence of a cup of milk and honey in the
paschal Eucharist. Milk and honey are not prominent in the
list of foods in I.24, as they might have been expected to be.
In I.46B.3, where the font and the Eucharist are paralleled
to the Jewish experience in the wilderness, the milk and honey

---

[130]Pseudo-Ambrose, *De lapsu virginis* 5.19. See *SL,* 141; MacGregor, *Fire
and Light,* 478.
[131]I.46B.3.

of the Jews is allegorised as the blessedness of eternal life, without any hint of a liturgical usage.[132]

We have already mentioned the custom in Verona, as elsewhere, of laity bringing bread and wine to the Eucharist. Ambrose declares that the baptismal candidates did not share in this custom until the Sunday after Easter.[133] We do not know what the practice was in Verona, but we do know that the *disciplina arcani* covered the Eucharistic elements, and so if the delay in Milan was because of concern for the *disciplina*, we may suppose that it applied in Verona as well.[134]

17. THE EUCHARISTIC PRAYER IN VERONA[135]

Zeno nowhere quotes a Eucharistic Prayer explicitly, but in a number of places in his sermons he does seem to refer to portions of a Eucharistic Prayer parallel to the sections 'Unde et memores' and 'Supra quae' of the Roman Canon and, less closely in some respects, to the Eucharistic Prayer quoted by Ambrose.

(i) A Reference to Melchizedek Parallel to That in 'Supra Quae'

In his sermon I.3.5, on circumcision, Zeno gives a list of figures in the Old Testament who were uncircumcised yet were counted acceptable by God:

---

[132]This stands in contrast with the so-called Verona Sacramentary, 205 (ed. Mohlberg, 26) (actually recording Roman usage) where the Roman custom of administering milk and honey to the neophytes is testified.

[133]Ambrose, *Exp. Ps. 118,* prologue 2; cf. *SL,* 141.

[134]Zeno says that the offering was secret even to 'Christianis minime consecratis', (II.7.14), which could, but need not, include the *competentes* on the eve of baptism.

[135]This discussion of the Eucharistic Prayer used by Zeno is based on my article, 'Early Latin Parallels to the Roman Canon? Possible References to a Eucharistic Prayer in Zeno of Verona', *Journal of Theological Studies* n.s. 37 (1986) 427–31.

What of the fact that Abel was found to be righteous without this wound? What of the fact that Enoch is read to have been taken up whole by God? What of the fact that uncircumcised Noah was appointed by God in the raging flood to be the heir and father of the human race? What of the fact that Melchisedek, the high priest himself most acceptable to God ['summus ipse sacerdos deo acceptissimus'], was ignorant of this scar?

The phrase 'summus sacerdos' referring to Melchizedek is paralleled in the section 'Supra quae' of the Roman Canon, 'summus sacerdos tuus Melchisedech', and likewise 'summus sacerdos Melchisedech' is found in the version of the Eucharistic Prayer quoted by Ambrose in *De sacramentis* 4.27. Other instances are known in the Mozarabic liturgy.[136] Could Zeno be referring to the Eucharistic Prayer used in his time in Verona?

This is made more probable by the fact that Zeno describes Melchizedek as 'deo acceptissimus'. Although Ambrose quotes a different form here, this description by Zeno has its parallel in the Roman Canon where the theme of the section 'Supra quae' is that of the acceptance by God of the offerings: 'digneris . . . accepta habere sicuti accepta habere dignatus es munera . . . Abel, et sacrificium Abrahae et quod tibi obtulit summus sacerdos tuus Melchisedech'. The same theme of acceptance is found in the Mozarabic prayers.

Both these features, Melchizedek being described as 'summus sacerdos', and his being 'deo acceptissimus', while they can be paralleled in the liturgy, are not to be found in the literary sources which Zeno seems to have used for this sermon.

The list of righteous people goes back to that in Hebrews 11:4ff., where Abel is called 'iustus' and is said to have offered acceptable sacrifices, and is accompanied by Enoch, who was

---

[136]Ed. M. Férotin, *Le liber Mozarabicus sacramentorum* (Paris, 1912) 262 n. 627; quoted by B. Botte, *Le canon de la messe Romaine* (Louvain, 1935) 43; and a similar one translated by R. C. D. Jasper and G. J. Cuming, *Prayers of the Eucharist, Early and Reformed*, 3d ed. (New York, 1987) 158.

pleasing to God, Noah the heir of righteousness, then Abraham and Sarah, Isaac and Jacob, and other heroes of Jewish history. Melchizedek is not found in this list, but of course he has a prominent place elsewhere in the epistle.

In Hebrews and in Genesis 14 Melchizedek is not directly called a high priest, as Ambrosiaster points out in his famous comment: 'Likewise the Holy Spirit is sent as a priest, and is called the priest of the most high God (not the high priest as our people claim in the oblation)'.[137]

Apart from the Bible we know of three possible literary sources or parallels for Zeno that would be relevant to this part of his sermon. It can be seen that none of them is a source for Zeno's description of Melchizedek. In his *Adversus Iudaeos*, Tertullian writes, 'And Melchisedek, the priest of God most high, was appointed to the priesthood of God while uncircumcised and not observing the sabbath'.[138] Cyprian writes of 'Melchisedek the priest, according to whose order Christ was promised'.[139] And Gregory of Elvira writes that 'The circumcised Abraham himself offers tithes to the uncircumcised Melchisedek, and presents an offering of gifts to the uncircumcised priest of the most high God'.[140]

Zeno's description of Melchizedek as 'summus sacerdos deo acceptissimus' has approximate parallels (Tertullian and Gregory: 'summi dei sacerdos'; Tertullian: 'Deo posse placere') but it is still remarkable that for a precise parallel both to the title and to the idea of acceptance we must turn to the liturgy of the Roman Canon and the Mozarabic Rites.

[137]'Similiter et spiritus sanctus missus quasi antestes sacerdos appellatus est excelsi dei non summus sicut nostri in oblatione praesumunt': Ambrosiaster, *Quaestiones V. ac NT* 109, 21.

[138]'Melchizedek quoque, summi Dei sacerdos, incircumcisus et non sabbatizans ad sacerdotium Dei allectus est': Tertullian, *Adversus Iudaeos* 2.11–14.

[139]'Melchizedek sacerdos, secundum cuius ordinem Christus repromissus est': Cyprian, *Test.* 1.8.

[140]'Ipse Abraham circumcismus Melchizedek incircumciso decimas offert et summi dei sacerdotem incircumcisum munerum oblatione prosequitur': Gregory of Elvira, *Tract. Orig.* 4.11.

As a small but additional factor, Zeno uses 'ipse' in describing Melchizedek: 'summus ipse sacerdos'. This suggests that his congregation was familiar with this figure and his role.[141]

In conclusion, Zeno in I.3 refers to Melchizedek with a title and a role corresponding not to his biblical and literary sources for this sermon, but to what we know of the Eucharistic Prayers of his day. His references to Melchizedek also seem to presuppose that his congregation were familiar with the figure and his role, and therefore that Melchizedek for them was more than a merely literary figure. All this makes it very probable that Zeno is in this sermon quoting, at least approximately, the Eucharistic Prayer of his Church in Verona.

(ii) A Reference to Abraham Parallel to That in 'Supra Quae', and a Reference to 'Immaculata Hostia' Parallel to That in 'Unde et Memores'

Two other possible parallels with the Eucharistic Prayer are to be found in sermons on the sacrifice of Isaac. This theme is found in four places in Zeno, in sermons I.4.13–5; I.43; I.59; and I.62. Although the treatment is roughly similar, the sacrificial language varies considerably. In the section of I.4, in some twenty-five lines, 'victima' occurs twice, and 'sacerdos', 'ara', 'immolatio', 'displicere', and 'sacramentum' once each. In the forty lines of I.62 'victima', 'ara,' and 'sacrificium' occur once each. However in I.43 we find a par-

---

[141]This familiarity has been seen elsewhere in Zeno. In I.24.2 'the *pater familias* lavishes upon you precious bread and wine from his store.' The *pater familias* can here refer to none other than to Melchizedek, with a reminiscence of Genesis 14:18. (This is the interpretation of most commentators, e.g., the Ballerini brothers, PL 11:484 n. 9; J. Doignon, 'Refrigerium et catéchèse à Vérone', 231. F. Sparaver [PL 11:577] suggests that the *pater familias* should be identified with Christ, but Doignon would make this only a secondary identification.) Such a direct and yet familiar reference—Zeno feels no need to name the *pater familias*—brings us close to the prominence of Melchizedek with Abel and Abraham in the Ravenna mosaics of a century and a half later, themselves in all probability reflecting a popular piety.

allel to the Eucharistic Prayer: 'Abraham patriarcha noster' (cf. 'Supra quae', *De sacramentis* 4.27; 'sacrificium patriarchae nostri Abrahae'). And in this sermon of seventy-four lines, 'sacrificium' occurs four times, 'placere' twice, 'probatus' once, 'victima' ten times, 'hostia' once, 'immolare' four times, 'immolatio' once, 'offerre' three times, and 'sacramentum' and 'mysterium' once each.

To describe Abraham as 'patriarcha noster' without comment or explanation is perhaps curious. It is, therefore, quite likely that in the context of stressing the sacrificial aspect of the offering of Isaac, Zeno is recalling a reference to the Eucharistic Prayer of his Church—the sacrifice of our patriarch Abraham.

In sermon I.59.2 we read of Isaac, 'the innocent martyr is offered, a spotless victim, a victim not unready', and, including the words in this phrase, the sermon has in its eighty-two lines 'hostia' four times, 'victima' three times, 'ara' twice, 'immolare' five times, 'immolatio' once, 'offerre' twice, '(ne) displicere' once, and 'sacerdos' twice.

The words 'immaculata hostia' are to be found in 'Supra quae', but they are said by the *Liber Pontificalis* to have been added by Pope Leo.[142] They do occur earlier in 'Unde et memores' (as 'hostiam immaculatam') and in a similar position in *De sacramentis* 4.27 (as 'immaculatam hostiam'). This is still in the context of Abraham's offering of Isaac; the 'immaculata hostia' of the Eucharist is offered and the prayer made for its acceptance just as God accepted the Old Testament offerings.

Therefore, in addition to a reference to Melchizedek in the Eucharistic Prayer and the theme of the acceptance of the offerings, it is probable that we have here a similar reference to the words of the Eucharistic Prayer: 'sacrificium patriarchae nostri Abrahae' and 'immaculata hostia'.

Could all these references be to a prayer outside the Eucharistic Prayer itself? A similar prayer is found in the Lit-

[142]I.239. Quoted by Botte, *Le canon de la messe Romaine*, 43.

urgy of Basil as an offertory prayer,[143] and this could conceivably be the case in Verona. However in the Latin West we know only of the instances of this prayer of offering being included in the Eucharistic Prayer, and it would be more reasonable to suppose that Zeno's prayer has approximately the same position as it has in Ambrose and at Rome, as also in Ambrosiaster—'in the oblation'.

We depend in this kind of study on finding parallels to known formulae. With such indirect allusions we have little hope of identifying any quotations of a Eucharistic Prayer which differ from those already known. However, even within this limitation, if this discussion points us in the right direction, we notice two interesting conclusions.

First, we have here a source for a Latin Eucharistic Prayer of the style of the Roman Canon which is at least approximately contemporary with those quoted by Ambrose and Ambrosiaster and quite possibly earlier than both. Certainly Zeno's dates, discussed above, provide us with the earliest dated reference to the Eucharistic Prayer.

Secondly, in being identified as a parallel to the Roman Canon in respect of the theme of the acceptance of the offerings, Zeno's Eucharistic Prayer differs from that of Ambrose. In the latter the theme is slightly but significantly different, being that not of the acceptance of the offerings but of their being taken to the heavenly altar. The relation of the prayer quoted by Ambrose to the Roman Canon is a difficult question. Evidence of a version earlier than Ambrose that agrees not with his prayer but with the Roman Canon is neither startling nor unforeseen, but at the same time it is of some historical importance. Perhaps the place, Verona, is as important as the date, testifying to the geographical extent of this type of prayer at so early a date.

[143]Ed. F. E. Brightman, *Liturgies Eastern and Western,* vol. 1 (Oxford, 1896) 319–20.

18. OTHER CEREMONIES AT EASTER

In the vast majority of his sermons, the only group that Zeno refers to in the congregation is that of the candidates undergoing baptism that year. There is one important exception, where he describes the benefits of Easter Day as applying to all the various parts of the Church: 'The day of salvation has come, lavish with every kind of gifts for all who attend on the Lord's mystery. For it grants pay to loyal priests, to subordinate ministers the advancement of promotion, the fruit of immortality for the baptised, healing for penitents, the way of light for catechumens, for the *competentes* the remission of all their sins'.[144]

There is a mixture here of general grace given, as it were, in reward to the priests, in the fruit of immortality to the baptised faithful, 'fideles', and in the way of light to the catechumens; also there is a reference to rites based around Easter in the ordination of clergy and the reconciliation of penitents just as the baptism of the *competentes* is set fully within the liturgical practice and theological understanding of the Easter Day. We know of the tradition of later times of the ordination of clergy being held on Easter Day, and Zeno is our earliest authority for the custom.[145]

The reconciliation of penitents being linked to Easter Day might seem to be at variance with later custom where the liturgical rite occurred on Maundy Thursday.[146] However, as the

---

[144]'Dies salutaris advenit, officiis sacramenti dominici omnibus omni genere munerum largus. Namque piis mercedem sacerdotibus praestat, consequentibus ministris promotionis augmentum, inmortalitatis fidelibus fructum, paenitentibus curam, catechumenis lucis viam, competentibus remissa omnium peccatorum': I.6.

[145]Cf. Ballerini, PL 11:505–6, n. 4; P. Jounel, 'Les Ordinations', in A. G. Martimort, *The Church at Prayer,* vol. 3 (ET London, 1988) 152; Truzzi, 210.

[146]Cf. Gelasian Sacramentary I.38; Ambrose, *Ep. 20 ad Marcellinam* 26: 'Erat autem dies quo sese Dominus pro nobis tradidit, quo in ecclesia poenitentia relaxatur'. The Ballerini PL 11:506–7 n. 5, misunderstand 'tradidit' and make the reconciliation on the Friday.

Ballerini suggest, it is quite likely that the fruit of reconciliation, receiving Communion, happened only at the paschal
Vigil.

Although we have only this one sermon mentioning additional rites (and certainly we need not expect ordinations to
occur every year though penitents may have been regularly
reconciled) we do have here ample evidence of the variety of
ceremonies that were included in the paschal season and that
found their climax in the rites of Easter Day.

19. THE VIGIL IN THE CONTEXT OF OTHER RITES

(i) The Use of Sermons Accompanying the Readings

The readings in the Vigil service at Verona are known to
us from Zeno's sermons. The latter are as a liturgical form
unique. We have many sermons from paschal Vigils and Eu-
charists, among which, very close to Zeno in geography and
chronology, are those of Gaudentius of Brescia and Chromatius of Aquileia. They both have sermons introducing the
Vigil which perform the same liturgical function as do Zeno's
Praefationes,[147] and sermons after the baptism and introducing the Eucharist which occupy the place of Zeno's post-
baptismal sermons, but which are less eccentric and more
didactic than those of Zeno.[148]

If Gaudentius, Chromatius, or any other bishop preached
sermons after each of the readings of the Vigil we have no
record of it. Other liturgical sources mention only the use of
canticles, psalms, and prayers, with or without set introductions, but nothing after the form of Zeno's sermons. The
closest that we get to such material is the use of *praefationes*
in the *Missale Gothicum* (we shall note also the similar usage
in the *Missale Gallicanum vetus*). These *praefationes* are set in-

[147]Gaudentius, *Tr. Pasch.* 1; Chromatius, *Sermons* 16, 17.
[148]Gaudentius, *Tr. Pasch.* 2; Chromatius, *Sermon* 17A.

troductions to collects. They do not comment on readings or liturgical actions as do Zeno's sermons, but their positioning is significant. There are a pair at the very beginning of the Vigil before the blessing of the paschal candle. These are entitled *Praefatio in vespera Paschae* and *Praefatio ad inicio noctis sanctae paschae*. Then follow twelve *praefationes* and collects to accompany the readings. After a section for signing the candidates with the sign of the cross we find the blessing of the water which is preceded by another *praefatio* and collect. Finally the Mass begins, as usual, with a *praefatio* and collect.[149] Thus the *praefationes* occupy the same positions as Zeno's sermons in his liturgy, and of course occur at the beginning of the Vigil and of the Mass where we know sermons were preached more widely than just in Verona. There may well be a link here, but whether it was common to preach rather than use set *praefationes* or whether Zeno's habit of preaching after each reading was his own personal adaptation of the *praefationes* we cannot say.

Zeno's sermons show no evidence of collects accompanying the readings, but neither do they preclude them. Given that they are found so widely in other liturgical sources, and that the *Missale Gothicum* also joins its *praefationes* to the collects, it is perfectly possible that Zeno knew a similar pattern where the collect followed after his sermon.

There is a difference between Zeno and the later Gallican liturgy in that the *praefatio* in the baptistery for the former would have been after the blessing of the font, while in the latter it comes beforehand.

With regard to the position of Zeno's *Praefatio Paschalis* my conjecture is that it came not at the beginning of the Vigil where the Gallican liturgies have the blessing of the candle (whether or not Zeno knew of such a blessing) but at the beginning of the Vigil readings. There are three reasons for this. First Zeno's *praefatio* is celebrating the Easter Day rather than the evening or beginning of the night as do those in the later

---

[149]*Missale Gothicum*, 30–33.

liturgy which are connected with the blessing of the candle. Secondly the *Missale Gallicanum vetus* has thirteen *praefationes* and collects where we should expect twelve for the Vigil readings.[150] Thirdly the first *praefatio* in this series, and its equivalent in the *Missale Gothicum's* twelve, are similar in tenor to Zeno's *praefatio*. The *Missale Gothicum's praefatio* reads thus:

> ORATION FOR GIVING THANKS. PREFACE. As we have reached the Easter day which we have looked forward to and desired, dearly beloved brothers, let us give thanks to God the Father almighty, that he has called us to this same day through his Son our Lord Jesus Christ whom he gave as a sacrifice for us to eternal salvation. For this let us with faithful thanksgiving praise, bless and give honour to the most blessed name of God the Father in the Son and of the Son in the Father and the Holy Spirit for ever and ever.[151]

It is therefore likely that, even if it may have changed its role, its origin was that of introducing the Vigil readings at the dawn of the Easter Day, and that Zeno gives us an early example of this practice.

(ii) The Selection of Readings in Various Lectionaries

The selection and order of readings in the Vigil service as witnessed to by Zeno find no perfect equivalent in other rites, but there are a number of rites with which we can make interesting comparisons. First, we may note the list of readings that are found in the various Vigil services.[152]

1. Gen 1:	Creation
2. Gen 2-3:	The Fall

---

[150]*Missale Gallicanum vetus*, 26.

[151]*Missale Gothicum* 33.226.

[152]Readings 1–17 are taken from the list made by Tyrer, *Historical Survey of Holy Week*, 156–57; 18–22 are added to cover the Armenian lectionary (see Wilkinson, *Egeria's Travels*, 276). Tyrer says that readings 7, 8, 12, and 17 are always accompanied by a canticle, and readings 15 and 16 are sometimes. In the synopsis I have only noted the variations with regard to 15.

3. Gen 6–8:	The Flood
4. Gen 22:	Temptation of Abraham
5. Gen 27:	Jacob and Esau
6. Exod 12:	The Passover
7. Exod 13–15:	The Red Sea
8. Deut 31–32:	The (second) song of Moses
9. Josh 3–4:	The passage of Jordan
10. 2 Chr 34–35:	Josiah's Passover
11. Isa 1:	Exhortation to repentance
12. Isa 4:	Judgement and salvation, with chapter 5 (the song of the vineyard) as canticle
12a. Isa 5:	The song of the vineyard (as reading)
13. Isa 55:	Come ye to the waters
14. Ezek 37:	The valley of dry bones
15. Dan 3:	Nebuchadnezzar and the three children
15 + C	as above, followed by a canticle (song of the three children)
15C	as above, with the song included in the reading
16. Jonah	(various parts)
17. Hab	(parts)
18. Isa 60:1-13:	Arise, shine; for your light has come
19. Job 38:1-28	God answers Job
20. 2 Kgs 2:1-22:	Ascent of Elijah
21. Jer 31:31-34:	A new covenant
22. Josh 1:1-9:	God's commands to Joshua

The readings may be tabulated in the various lectionaries as follows:[153]

[153]The *Missale Gothicum* and *Missale Gallicanum vetus,* which have been seen to be similar to Zeno in the matter of the *praefationes,* do not describe the readings and so are not included in this tabulation.

Zeno	1		6 7		11/12a				15 + C?	
Luxeuil[154]	[][] 3 4 5 6 7		14 11 +12a 9 16						15C	
Ambrosian[155]	1	4	6 7 13	11					Ps 42	
Gregorian[156]	1		7		12 13					Ps 42
Gelasian[157]	1 3 4		7 13 14		12 6	8	15			Ps 42
Mozarabic[158]	1 3 4		6 7		12 14 17 16	15 + C				Ps 42
Spanish[159]	1 2 13 3		7 4	8	5	6	10 14	15 + C		
Armenian[160]	1	4	6 16 7 18	19	20	21	22	14	15 + C	

The tabulation immediately shows how Zeno shares in the universal custom of having the readings of Genesis 1 (1) and Exodus 14 (7). Other readings are more or less common, but it would be best to compare the readings in Zeno's lectionary one by one.

The reading of Genesis 1 is to be found in all the rites compared, no doubt including *Luxeuil* which suffers a lacuna here. The Red Sea (7) is also found in all the rites. It would have included the canticle 'Cantemus Domino' (Exod 15:1ff.) in Zeno as in all the other rites.

The Passover reading (6) however is not to be found in the Gregorian or Gelasian Rites. Of course this had been the reading underlying the sermon of Melito, *On the Pasch*,[161] and the reading is preserved in the Gallican and Mozarabic Rite and in Beroldus, as well as in the Armenian Rite. Its disappearance is as remarkable as its retention, and may perhaps point to the growing influence of Maundy Thursday and the link of the Last Supper to the Passover meal. The end of the unitive celebration of Easter meant, in Rome at least, the trans-

[154]Ed. P. Salmon, *Collectanea Biblica Latina*, vols. 7, 9 (Rome, 1944–53) 7:97ff.

[155]*Beroldus:* ed. Magistretti, 110–11.

[156]Ed. Deshusses (Friburg, 1971) 183–85.

[157]Ed. Mohlberg, 70–72.

[158]*Missale mixtum*, PL 85: col. 446ff.

[159]*Liber comicus*, ed. G. Morin (Maredsous, 1893) 171ff.

[160]Wilkinson, *Egeria's Travels*, 276.

[161]Melito of Sardis, *On Pascha*, ed. S. G. Hall (Oxford, 1979) 2.

ference of the Passover away from Easter Day itself to the preceding Thursday.[162]

The readings of Isaiah 1; 4; 5 (numbers 11, 12, 12a in the list) require considerably more comment, both because of the complexity of the details of how these readings feature in the various lectionaries and because Zeno himself bears witness to a change of the reading during his episcopate. As concluded above, the original reading of Isaiah in Zeno's lectionary was Isaiah 1. This was replaced by a reading of Isaiah 5 with Psalm 79 used as the canticle.

Luxeuil has the readings set out in full, unlike the other documents which have only the 'incipits'. Its reading of Isaiah 1 (beginning at verse 1) includes the song of the vineyard in Isaiah 5 as well.[163] *Luxeuil* does not record the canticles. Similar to *Luxeuil* and to Zeno is Beroldus, who has a reading of Isaiah 1 beginning with 'Levamini mundi' ('Wash and be clean': v. 16), but we do not know whether the reading included the song of the vineyard as well. For a canticle, Psalm 41 is attached to this reading. Among the other lectionaries which use the Isaiah reading, there is a common tradition to use Isaiah 4 (12). The Gelasian records the use of Isaiah 5 as the accompanying canticle. The Gregorian Sacramentary does not note the canticle.

In conclusion, Zeno's later use of Isaiah 5 as a reading followed by Psalm 79 as a canticle has no equivalent in early liturgies. However we do have an interesting parallel in the use of Isaiah 1 in Beroldus, and a very close parallel in *Luxeuil* for the introduction of Isaiah 5 as a reading. In *Luxeuil,* Isaiah

---

[162]For the idea of unitive celebration, see K. Stevenson, 'The Ceremonies of Light: Their Shape and Function in the Paschal Vigil Liturgy', *Ephemerides Liturgicae* 99 (1985) 170–85; summarised in M. Perham and K. Stevenson, *Waiting for the Risen Christ* (London, 1986) 3ff.

[163]In fact there are pages missing in the MS at this point, and the extant reading comprises Isaiah 1:1-7 and 5:10-24. But, presuming that the arrangement of the MS is regular, Salmon deduces that the reading would have included the rest of chapter 1 and the beginning of chapter 5: *Collectanea Biblica Latina,* 7:106-7.

5 is added to, rather than replacing, Isaiah 1. This may be evidence of Isaiah 5 having been used as a canticle and then becoming a reading, as we shall see below occurs with the song of the three children, except that the reading goes on beyond the song of the vineyard as far as verse 24. We may therefore have evidence of a conflation of traditions: on the one hand that of the reading of Isaiah 1 and on the other of Isaiah 5. In Zeno when the traditions meet the former is suppressed by the latter. In *Luxeuil* the two readings are joined together.

It may have been supposed that the use of Daniel 3 (15) as well as Psalm 41 might show a similar conflation of various lectionary traditions. In the Roman Missal, Psalm 41 is used to accompany the movement to the baptistery; the same is the case in Zeno, and no doubt underlies the use of the psalm as a reading in the Gelasian and Gregorian Rites. The use of Daniel 3 would seem to have a very similar purpose, for example in the Armenian lectionary at Jerusalem where the canticles following from the reading cover the baptisms in the same way as does the threefold litany in the Gelasian and Gregorian Rites. Since in *Luxeuil* the song of the three children, in an Old Latin version, is incorporated into the reading of Daniel 3 which is in a Vulgate translation,[164] the text of the song must have come from a different book—a liturgical text of the song as a canticle? But these sources do not mention the reading and the psalm together. We are arguing largely from silence here, but the explicit joining of the two traditions, admittedly very common in the lectionaries, might have been thought to be a late conflation were it not for our early witness.

What may we conclude about the place of Zeno in the development of the paschal Vigil?

First, the use of sermons after each of the readings, although only to be found in Zeno, may have been common in his time, and may well be linked with the *praefationes* of the later Gallican liturgy.

[164]Ibid., 7:113, note 1; 111–15.

Secondly, the various readings and psalms show connections with what, in later years at any rate, seem to have been different local traditions. The inclusion (a retention from ancient use?) of the reading of the Passover and the use of Isaiah 1 can be taken as evidence of links with the Ambrosian Rite of Beroldus and particularly with the Gallican Rite of *Luxeuil,* which in addition shows evidence of the use of Isaiah 5 as a reading rather than as a canticle, and also Daniel 3 as a reading and the song of the three children originally as a canticle. *Luxeuil* however is silent about the use of Psalm 41, where we have to look to Roman use, such as we see in the Gregorian and Gelasian Rites, and to the Mozarabic Rite. The combination of Daniel 3 and Psalm 41 in Zeno is remarkable for its early date, and would seem to indicate an ancient and long-lasting tradition.

In conclusion, Zeno is a source of the highest importance for the history of the Vigil service. There is no other contemporary source in the West, and no other source anywhere for the practice of preaching after each reading. Zeno's date makes him particularly important in that, at the end of the fourth century, he bears witness to the period before the introduction in the West of Good Friday and Holy Week and the end of the celebration of the Pasch on one night. His Vigil readings therefore include the institution of Passover as well as the Red Sea, and we can see links with Melito of Sardis in celebrating Passover as well as with the later rites reviewed above. Comparison with those rites gives us much important information. First, Baumstark's belief that the Vigil originally had twelve readings and was only later reduced cannot stand unchallenged.[165] In Jerusalem this was perhaps the case, but this our earliest source for the Latin West strongly suggests the contrary shape of a short series of readings which grew with time. Secondly, Zeno stands as an early precedent for many of the features of the Gallican Rite seen in *Luxeuil* and in the Mozarabic Rite, which suggests connections over the

---

[165]Baumstark, *Comparative Liturgy,* 167–68.

geographical area of Northern Italy, France, and Spain. Thirdly, we see the importance of the final elements of the Vigil, Daniel 3, and Psalm 41, as having a liturgical role as the ceremonies of initiation begin, and we see how the two elements are combined not just in the later rites but in this important fourth-century source. It would hardly seem an exaggeration to say that the sermons of Zeno of Verona hold the key to our understanding of the history of the paschal Vigil lectionary in the West.

20. ZENO'S RITE OF BAPTISM IN THE CONTEXT OF OTHER RITES

In describing the rite of baptism in Verona as witnessed to by Zeno we have already often referred to other rites both in Italy and beyond. Here we attempt to summarise the relation of the Veronese rites to the other rites.

It would be an immense task to go beyond the rites closest in time and place, and so we shall limit ourselves here to three other sources, all of which have been often referred to already. We must include Ambrose of Milan with his important and highly detailed descriptions in *De sacramentis* and *De mysteriis*. He is also the closest to Zeno in date. (Ambrose was bishop of Milan 372–97.) A little later (ca. 390–410), but closer geographically, is Chromatius of Aquileia. His baptismal rite is described, along with other liturgical details, by J. Lemarié. Lemarié's description, however, tends to interpret the rite of Aquileia in the light of that of Milan, for example supposing that there was a rite of *apertio*. [166] Such presumptions cannot be made, and so we limit our own description more closely to what is actually in the text of Chromatius. It will then appear that Chromatius's rite is close to that of Zeno. Our third source, a small but important one, is that of the Mai fragment for the prayer of post-baptismal anointing which has been discussed already and must be included here.

[166]SC 154:97–103.

First the sources may be compared in a synopsis of their main features.

Zeno	*Chromatius*	*Ambrose*	*Mai fragment*
(Saturday?)		'Sabbato'	
		Anoint	
		ears	
	Foot-	nostrils	
	washing	*(Effeta)*	
	(or after		
	renunciations)	'We came to	
		the baptistery'	
		Strip?	
Anoint	Anoint?	Anoint as	
breast		athlete	
Renunciation	Renunciation	Renunciation	
		Turn to	
		baptistery	
Enter	Enter	Enter	
baptistery	baptistery	baptistery	
Strip	Strip?		
Immersion	Immersion	Immersion	
Anoint	Anoint	Anoint	Anoint
& seal			& seal
	Lay on		
	hands	Foot-	
		washing	
White	White	White	
garment	garment	garment	
		Seal	

The basic shape of the rites is clear enough. We know whether particular anointings, for example, are pre- or post-baptismal. There are some doubtful details, for example as to precisely when it is that the practical measures of stripping for baptism and dressing in white garments take place. The pre-baptismal anointing in Chromatius is queried because, although there is no mention of it, it is so common in early baptismal liturgies that it would be rash to assume that it did not happen.

There is considerable agreement between the various rites. The preliminary rites do not occur in the baptistery and so must be either in the church or in some ante-room, often the day before the paschal Vigil, and the candidates enter the baptistery at the time of the actual immersion. Insofar as we can talk about a most common pattern with so few sources, it consisted of a pre-baptismal anointing of the breast, and then the renunciations. The candidates enter the baptistery, strip, and are immersed. They are anointed after baptism and there is a rite of sealing. Dressed in white garments, they return to the church for the baptism.

Ambrose is the only one to describe an earlier anointing of the ears and nostrils: the *Effeta* rite. But he says that this anointing comes on the Saturday *(sabbato)* which is when Zeno seems to have had his anointing of the breast and renunciations. Chromatius has the rite of the washing of feet before baptism,[167] and is the only writer to describe a laying on of hands afterwards. However if he had a pre-baptismal anointing he never mentions it. Ambrose has the washing of the feet after baptism, between the anointing and the spiritual seal. But now let us turn to the individual features of the rites.

(i) Pre-Baptismal Anointings

As noted above, it is so common in the rites to have an anointing and renunciations together at some point before baptism

---

[167]The footwashing certainly occurred before the immersion, as described by Lemarié (ibid., 98–99 and note 3, commenting on *Sermon* 15). However I believe that Lemarié is wrong in supposing that it happened after the renunciations, directly before the immersion. In *Sermon* 14 Chromatius describes the candidates making their renunciations and then going on to baptism, and there is no mention of the footwashing. There is nothing explicit elsewhere to place the footwashing in this sequence of events, so I suspect that it must have happened earlier, perhaps on the Saturday.

that we have included that anointing as a possibility in Chromatius, though he does not in fact mention it. Ambrose has the anointing of the candidate as an athlete, preparing the candidate for the contest ahead.[168] This explanation has no parallel in Zeno.

It is in the context of these rites that we saw evidence in Zeno for the anointing of the breast. Zeno declares that the anointing is for the end of the winter of sin, and for expelling from the breast all crimes and protecting the candidate against their return.

Ambrose connects his earlier anointing of the ears and nostrils with the healing by Christ of the deaf-mute, when he touched the man's mouth and ears. Ambrose then has to devise a reason why the nostrils are touched in the rite, and not the mouth! He does not make any issue of the use of oil, but speaks of Christians being the 'good odour of Christ', which points to the use of oil. Later rites, e.g., the Gelasian rite, have the ears and nostrils touched with spittle,[169] but I think that Ambrose did not do this. The basic interpretation of the rite is shaped by the story of the healing: it is the opening *(apertio)* to the divine words, not a sealing or defence against what is harmful such as we find in Zeno.[170]

Chromatius nowhere mentions a pre-baptismal anointing. Whether or not it was part of the rite, it evidently had little or no part in his understanding of baptism. It is interesting that he connects the idea of the forgiveness of sins to the foot-washing which comes before baptism, just as Zeno does to the pre-baptismal anointing. Ambrose too connects the foot-washing with forgiveness, not of one's own sins but of inherited sin,[171] or with washing off the 'serpent's poison'.[172]

---

[168]*De sac.* 1.4. There are Eastern parallels. Cf. *AIR,* 19. *De myst.* omits any mention of the anointing here.

[169]Gelasian Sacramentary, 1.43.

[170]*De sac.* 1.2–3.

[171]*De myst.* 32.

[172]*De sac.* 3.7.

(ii) The Renunciations

The renunciations are very similar in the various writers, as would be expected. There was very little variety in the forms to be found in early Christian rites. Common to Zeno, Chromatius, and Ambrose is the tendency to have a somewhat loose paraphrase of the formula of renunciation. Zeno often talks of renouncing the world ('saeculum') and mentions the assault of the devil, his angels, and the world ('mundum'), from which we have suggested that the actual formula of renunciation might have been, 'Abrenuntias diabolo? . . .pompis eius? . . .saeculo?'

Chromatius seems to describe a similar threefold formula: 'You were asked whether you renounced the world and its pomps and works'.[173] Lemarié however suggests that the actual liturgical formula may have had a twofold shape,[174] after the pattern of Ambrose who has 'Abrenuntias diabolo et operibus eius? Abrenuntias saeculo et voluptatibus eius?'[175] Whatever the actual wording, we are presented with a twofold and a threefold formula. It seems unlikely that all threefold formulae can be compressed into the twofold pattern on the strength of Ambrose, and so it is best here to suppose that there was a variety of practice, and that the threefold renunciation as reported by Chromatius is a correct description of the liturgy in his church.

As said above, there is no record of a rite of adhesion in Zeno, nor is there evidence after the renunciations of a turning round to the East to enter the baptistery such as we find in Ambrose.[176] However the invitations to the font do presuppose that the candidates are suddenly confronted by the sight of the font and the clergy around it.

---

[173]'Interrogatus es utrum renuntiares saeculo et pompis atque operibus eius': Chromatius, *Sermon* 14.
[174]SC 154:98, n. 1.
[175]*De sac.* 1.5.
[176]*De myst.* 7.

(iii) The Immersion

Immersion is of course the central and essential rite of baptism, but it is rarely described. Zeno speaks as though the candidates are immersed in running water, perhaps from a fountain. Ambrose and Chromatius give no details. But we have other sources for early Roman practice. Davies notes how in the Lateran baptistery water issued from the mouth of a golden lamb, given by Constantine, and says, 'It seems likely that the officiant either guided the candidate's head under the flow or directed the flow on to his head with a vessel.' Certainly, as Davies shows from archaeological evidence, the fonts of the early Church were nearly all too small to allow immersion in the pool of water in the font itself, and so the common method of baptism must have been similar to the method described above.[177]

Ambrose gives us a text for the interrogatory form of words for baptism,[178] but Zeno only refers to the 'sacrae interrogationes', so we have nothing here to compare with Ambrose.

(iv) Post-Baptismal Anointing

It is in the post-baptismal anointing that we find most variety between the rites. Much of the evidence has already been discussed at great length above. The Mai fragment is of great interest here, since I have quoted it as a direct parallel to the rite that I have identified in Zeno, namely an anointing that followed directly after the immersion, while the candidate was still in the font. This anointing with chrism was described as being for the gift of the Holy Spirit in Zeno and in the Mai fragment, and Zeno also has the marking of the sign of the cross on the forehead, though we cannot say what the practice was of the author of the Mai fragment.

---

[177]Davies, *The Architectural Setting of Baptism,* 23–28. For the Lateran baptistery, see C. F. Rogers, 'Baptism and Christian Archaeology', *Studia Biblica et Ecclesiastica* 5 (1903) 270. Cf. Pesci, 'De Christianarum', 37.

[178]*De sac.* 2.20.

Ambrose has a similar anointing of the candidate, but the sealing comes with a later, second anointing. Here Ambrose may be compared with the *Apostolic Tradition* and Roman practice. Chromatius is vague. He mentions an anointing with chrism,[179] and also a laying on of hands for the giving of the Holy Spirit (which we do not find in the other writers) but he does not give us the liturgical details.[180] Since he does not mention a sealing with the sign of the cross, it could well be that he knew an anointing similar to that of rites of Zeno and the Mai fragment, but where the laying on of hands replaces the sign of the cross, at any rate in Chromatius's understanding of what is important in the rite. Certainly the chrism is only mentioned once; it is then described as salvific ('salutare'), but it is of vague purpose and evidently not prominent in Chromatius's thinking.[181] There is no reason to suppose that there was a double post-baptismal anointing in Chromatius.

Between the two anointings in Ambrose there is the washing of the feet, not known by Zeno, and the dressing in the white garments. The latter is mentioned in Zeno and Chromatius but there is little or no detail. We have a hint in Zeno of the candidates carrying lights. We do not have evidence either way in the other writers.

(v) A Simple or Magnificent Rite?

Zeno throughout the ceremonies is notable for the simplicity of his liturgical practice. He has the basic shape of a pre-baptismal anointing, the renunciations, entry to the baptistery proper for the immersion, post-baptismal anointing and sealing following directly on immersion, and dressing in a white garment. Chromatius and Ambrose have the additional foot-washing. Ambrose has the additional post-baptismal anointing, known from the Roman Rite, and he alone describes the

179Chromatius, *Sermon* 14.
180Chromatius, *Sermon* 15.
181Chromatius, *Sermon* 14.

earlier pre-baptismal anointing. He also has a different, two-fold shape of the renunciations.

If we are to understand complexity in the liturgy as evidence of growth over time, then Zeno may be seen to represent an early form of baptism in Italy. Whatever our ideas about liturgical development, the rites of Zeno and Chromatius show remarkable similarity in contrast to Ambrose. Chromatius does show individual touches in his rite in the footwashing, especially in its curious position, and in the laying on of hands. He is highly reticent about anointings, but his vagueness about their purpose is similar to what we have observed in Zeno. Whether the differences between the rites of Aquileia and of Verona were ancient or the work of an inventive individual, the spirit of the two rites is the same, and very different from that of the complex and magnificent rite used and described by Ambrose.[182]

21. LIMITATIONS AND INSIGHTS

In the problem of discovering the rites of initiation as known by various writers, Zeno presents us with a task that is both formidable and rewarding. He does not give us Ambrose's wealth of detail, nor does he even give his information with clarity. He teases those in his congregation whose knowledge is limited by the *disciplina arcani,* and we too, whose knowledge is limited by the passing of years, find his allusive manner frustrating. With such limitations on us, our inquiry relies heavily on the context of similar ritual practices in other churches; thus, while we can with some assurance recognise what Zeno is referring to from parallels elsewhere, we are not necessarily able to identify practices in Verona that differed

[182]Cf. Baumstark, *Comparative Liturgy,* 20. But we may not always take a growth in complexity to be the rule; leaving aside the question of its geographical position, and even whether it describes an actual or an ideal situation, the *Apostolic Tradition* describes an early and highly complex rite. For a broader discussion of the problems of liturgical development, see P. Bradshaw, *The Search for the Origins of Christian Worship* (London, 1992).

from those witnessed to by contemporary authors. However it is not likely that the rite described by Zeno was radically different from what we know of elsewhere. There are enough clear parallels for us to be sure of the basic shape of the rite, and we have been able to make sense of the references in his sermons, both clear and obscure, in the context of the various differing rites of North Italy and the Church of the Latin West.

In fact the place where Zeno offers the most important information is where the evidence is most clear. We have no contemporary parallels in the West for the readings of the Vigil service, and no parallels anywhere for the practice of preaching after each reading. In Zeno the evidence is extremely good and detailed: we can establish the lectionary from the successive sermons, and in places we know of the accompanying psalms and canticles. Zeno sheds an important new light on the history of the paschal Vigil in the West, and offers many insights into the development of the later Vigil rites.

The baptismal rites themselves are less clear in their evidence and, although all his references can be explained satisfactorily, Zeno has to be understood in the light of contemporary rites rather than as shedding dramatic new light on them. He takes his place among the variety of authors attesting fourth-century baptismal rites. He is similar to all, and identical to none. Indeed, of the four early Italian rites compared, it would seem that none are identical. Even the Mai fragment is unusual in its form as a prayer and there is no evidence that even Zeno, who is closest to it in thought, used that liturgical form. Zeno therefore joins an ever more complex picture of the early history of the baptismal liturgy.

Chapter Six
ZENO'S THEOLOGY OF BAPTISM

1. READING THE SERMONS

The liturgy that lay behind the sermons was the result of a wide and long-standing tradition, to which Zeno himself made little or no contribution. The theology, on the other hand, while it likewise stood in a tradition, was more amenable to personal shaping by the preacher. Zeno was an able though not outstanding theologian and did not, as far as we know, contribute to the theological issues of the day. His understanding of baptism is not especially profound. But it will become clear in the following study how he demonstrates in his sermons a personal and ingenious use of baptismal imagery in which various themes are developed together to unusual lengths and with a certain sophistication. With his concrete use of images he could develop a presentation of the faith that was both integrated (we could hardly call it systematic) and personal.

This examination of Zeno's theology and imagery depends on the various references scattered through his sermons. There is no systematic presentation. The examination is conducted purely on the basis of following the use of certain images and themes that constantly recur in the sermons. Occasional references will be made to similar ideas in other writers, but it is impossible to attempt a proper comparison such as has been attempted with the liturgy, since to do so would in effect be a writing of the history of baptismal theology. Here the purpose is simply to describe what Zeno says in his sermons.

An attempt has already been made to follow such themes in Zeno by G. de Paoli, who in a short article gathers together various references under the themes of baptism as regeneration, baptism and faith, baptism and penitence, and baptism and the Holy Spirit.[1] Reference will be made to this article from time to time, but here we may note a difference of emphasis between de Paoli and the present work. The four themes used by de Paoli are ones that we would certainly find important today. Under these headings, in only a few pages, he attempts to assemble a very large variety of material, and it might be felt that in doing so he has failed to do justice to other themes that, as we shall see, are certainly prominent in the sermons. This present study, by beginning with the images used by Zeno, will give much less prominence to some of de Paoli's special concerns, particularly to the relation between baptism and faith and penitence. However it is hoped that by this means a much wider and richer understanding of Zeno's thought will be revealed and his individual genius brought to light.

We will begin with remarks on the reactions and feelings of the candidates, the general presentation of certain images, and the all-important context of Easter Day. Then the order of themes will approximately follow the candidates through the rites of initiation, at various stages of which different images come to the fore.

2. THE ATTITUDES AND REACTIONS OF CANDIDATES DURING THE CEREMONIES

In various places during the ceremonies Zeno refers to the attitudes and reactions of the candidates. Sometimes he witnesses to their evident confusion rather than to the results of their edification. Standing at the entrance to the baptistery, the candidates in their ignorance simply do not know what

[1]G. de Paoli, 'L'iniziazione cristiana nei Sermoni di S. Zeno di Verona', *Rivista Liturgica* 54 (1967) 405–17.

to do.[2] When the bishop urges them to approach the font he needs to overcome their confusion. And of course not all is revealed with the administration of baptism, for the rule of the *disciplina arcani* means that they are still ignorant of the meaning of the ceremonies they are undergoing. When they have returned to the church Zeno acknowledges their ignorance,[3] though his post-baptismal sermons are not particularly helpful with regard to explaining either what has occurred in the baptisms or what is about to happen in the Eucharist.

But for the most part the candidates' reactions to the rite are described more positively. First, the mental state of the unbaptised is seen to be wretched. Before baptism the person is haunted by fear of judgement and condemnation and, even worse, by his own conscience which never gives a moment's respite.

> My brothers, the person who remains in his first birth cannot be happy. He is burned at every moment by the flaming torch of scorching sins, he carries round with him the stench of the prison, he detects the executioner before he can see him, he is in terror of mention of the judge, from a whisper he supposes that he is being sought, that he is found out. He has no prospect of security: perhaps there is no one to accuse him, but there is always one who knows and can bear witness— himself. For conscience, more fierce than any torture, never leaves the sinner.[4]

But the rites of initiation, likened to trial and execution, in fact hold no terrors for the candidates, and the baptised are

[2]Cf. I.55: 'Why do you stand there, different in race, age, sex and rank, who soon will be one?'

[3]Cf. I.38.2.

[4]'Beatus esse non potest, fratres, in prima nativitate persistens, quem aestuantium delictorum fax incensa omnibus momentis exurit; qui paedorem sui secum carceris portat; qui carnificem sentit, antequam videat; qui nomen iudicis pertimescit; qui, sicunde susurrus ingruerit, se quaeri, se aestimat inveniri; cui securitatis profectus est nullus, etiam si contingat ei accusatore carere, teste conscio, cum se ipso carere non possit, quia violentior omni tortore conscientia numquam suum deserit peccatorem': II.10.1.

free of all that has shackled them in the past. 'Rejoice, my brothers in Christ! Guard carefully, strictly and faithfully the royal favour of mercy which you have received. For every action for which you are liable has been cancelled. Rejoice freely! Now you owe nothing to the world.'[5]

Exultation is the theme of the sermons given after the baptism. As the candidates come back into the church, the welcoming congregation would no doubt communicate the feeling that they have arrived home, they now belong, they are now part of the Church. Exultation is their natural reaction and it is vocalised by the bishop.

Earlier, in the baptistery, exultation is by no means excluded; that same word, 'Exsultate', begins two of the eight invitations to the font.[6] But there are other emotions at this point; as we have already seen Zeno tries to overcome the hesitancy of the candidates; he urges them to rush to the font. According to him the scene is inviting, the warmth and sound of the running water beckons them in.[7] The attraction of the scene is described in terms of the candidates being thirsty, with reminiscences of the longing hart of Psalm 41. They are bidden to come to the *desiderata,* to quench their thirst and to fill themselves with the water.[8] The attractiveness is also described in terms of the candidates coming to their mother—the font—who offers adoption and, indeed, a joyful and painless second birth. 'Now the saving warmth of the everlasting font invites you, now our mother adopts you so that she may give birth to you, but not in the manner in which your mothers bore you . . . but with joy and gladness'.[9]

[5]'Exsultate, fratres in Christo, acceptaeque indulgentiae regale beneficium diligenter, fortiter ac fideliter custodite. Etenim omnis actus vester contractus ablatus est. Securi gaudete: nihil saeculo iam debetis': I.42.1.

[6]It is no coincidence that one of the Daniel sermons, II.15, which begins, 'Exsulta, Christiane', is wrongly entitled *Item Invitatio fontis* in the α MSS.

[7]E.g., I.23.

[8]E.g., I.12; II.14.

[9]'Iam vos sempiterni fontis calor salutaris invitat; iam mater nostra adoptat ut pariat, sed non ea lege, qua vos matres vestrae pepererunt . . . sed laeta gaudentes': I.32.

The reaction of the candidates through their initiation is not just one of emotion. A change of behaviour is expected and described in these same sermons. Speaking of the baptised person as having died and been reborn, Zeno says,

> He is the same and yet he is not the same. The old dwelling place remains, but there is a new inhabitant with a change in his way of life who shows to the unbelievers the dignity of his birth by virtues of every kind.[10]

> How splendid it is, brothers, and how salutary, that you choose to admire the one who a short time ago you scorned, and to imitate the virtue of the one whose corruption you cursed. You were always horrified at his greed; now you are amazed at his pouring out his goods far and wide to the poor and needy. You knew him as a shrine of idolatry; now you rejoice that he is a temple of God.[11]

The moral conversion goes hand in hand with the change of beliefs. In the above quotation the rejection of idolatry and the taking on of the Christian creed just as much as the moral change is the result of baptism. We may see the same in the allegory of viticulture. In the ritual questions and answers the turning to Christ and the rejection of the devil and his works combine doctrinal and moral considerations, and the effect on the candidates is likewise combined. They reject the world, their eyes are opened to Christ.[12]

Throughout the ceremonies, Zeno presupposes the faith of the candidates.[13] The catechesis beforehand teaches them the articles of faith, in the ceremonies they profess it at the very

[10]'Ipse est et tamen ipse non est. Vetus quidem videtur domicilium, sed novus est inquilinus mutatione morum nativitatis suae nobilitatem incredulis variis virtutibus monstrans': II.24.3.

[11]'Quam speciosum est, fratres, quamque salutare, quem paulo ante ridiculo habueris, admirari; cuius exsecratus sis corruptelam, optes imitari virtutem; quem cupidum semper horrueris, stupeas passim in pauperes et egenos sua bona universa fundentem; postremo quem noveris idolatriae fanum, gaudeas dei templum': II.29.3.

[12]II.11.5.

[13]Cf. de Paoli, 'L'iniziazione cristiana', 412–13.

moment of baptism, and they experience its fruit in the Eucharist. But their faith plays more than a formal role: it is integral to their death to sin and to their rebirth. 'When the flesh has been killed by saving baptism with the unsullied faith of the one who believes, it arises anew from the holy waters of the parental font, now pure, now free'.[14]

The role of faith is elsewhere stated to be of the essence of salvation. It is what differentiates those to be saved from the rest of humankind which is under the sentence of death: 'There is no doubt in the matter. For just as the prince of evil through envy reduced by his seed the first created beings from angels to humans, so by the seed of the Holy Spirit the Lord will raise all those who believe in him from the dead to be glorious angels'.[15] Faith, or its absence, is noted in the Old Testament stories. The Jews delivered by God are condemned for unbelief,[16] but the three children are saved by their faith.[17]

In all that happens the candidates are not just spectators, nor, even if they are ignorant of the meaning of what is happening, are they merely receivers of the rites of initiation. They come with penitence for their sins and with faith in God that he will grant redemption. In the rites that redemption is communicated to them, and they receive it with joy and exultation.

3. THE COMMUNICATION OF INITIATION THROUGH ITS SENSUAL ASPECTS

The rites of initiation presented to the candidate a drama, perhaps we should say an opera, of salvation effected through

---

[14][Caro] cum mera fide credentis salutari fuerit necata baptismate, nova paterni sacro resurgit fontis ex gurgite iam pura, iam libera': I.2.25; cf. I.55; II.28.

[15]'Nec res in ambiguo est; quemadmodum etenim ille princeps iniquitatis suo semine per invidiam protoplastos ex angelis in homines derivavit, ita dominus omnes in se credentes sancti spiritus semine a mortuis rursus gloriosos in angelos excitabit': I.2.26.

[16]I.29.

[17]II.22.

entry into the Church. The experience included the panoply of all five physical senses. Other writers may refer to these in their catechetical lectures; thus Ambrose during the description of the *apertio* ceremony describes the candidates as being sensitive to the 'aroma of Christ', quite possibly a reference to the use of oil in the ceremony.[18] Zeno positively rejoices in the sensual aspect of the rites: 'Hurry, hurry for a good wash, brothers! The water, living with the Holy Spirit and warmed with the sweetest fire now invites you with its soft murmur. Now the bath attendant is girded up and waiting for you, ready to provide the necessary anointing and washing'.[19] In even this short quotation the mingling of sight, sound, and warmth brings the baptistery before us almost as clearly as it presented itself to the candidates. And likewise in similar passages: 'The sweet murmur of the stream of nectar invites you: hasten without delay to the milky water of the life-giving font',[20] and, 'Now the solemn hymn is sung, behold soon the the sweet crying of infants is heard; behold from the single womb of their parent proceeds a dazzling throng'.[21]

Thus Zeno describes the procession out of the baptistery, resplendent with white robes and carrying lights. Here the sight communicates a theological point. So often it is the diversity of the candidates that is stressed, in age, sex, race, and rank.[22] Now in the one birth of baptism, all these become the 'dazzling throng' proceeding in unity from the one font. Indeed it must be the identical white dress in which the candidates return to the church from the baptistery that allows Zeno not only to compare them to loaves of bread but to suggest that they are identical in every other respect. He acknowl-

[18]*De sac.* 1.3.

[19]'Properate, properate bene loturi, fratres! Aqua viva spiritu sancto et igne dulcissimo temperata blando murmure iam vos invitat. Iam balneator praecinctus exspectat, quod unctui, quod tersui opus est praebiturus. . .': I.23.

[20]'Quos nectarei fluenti dulce murmur invitat, lacteum genitalis fontis ad laticem convolate': I.12.

[21]'Solemnis hymnus iam canitur, ecce mox infantum dulcis vagitus auditur, ecce parientis uno de ventre clarissima turba procedit': II.28.

[22]E.g., I.55.

edges that some appear smaller than others, but still dares to claim they are really the same weight.[23] In this sermon we have a remarkable development of sensual imagery as well as rhetorical flair: 'Those whom you see with the delightful smell of this excellent baking . . . no bitter smoke has blighted. . . . Indeed they are not sooty or stale or burnt or undercooked or mouldy. Their colour is milky, their taste is milky'.[24] The sense of smell is being picked up here, with the baptistery and those who have gone through it giving off a sweet smell and leaving off all foulness.

The contrast of the spiritual and the worldly often occurs in the interpretation of smells. The new birth of baptism is said to be unlike the first natural birth. In the first there is pain and crying and filth and stink. The second birth is one of joy and freedom in the sweet-smelling mysteries of the Church.

> Now our mother adopts you so that she may give birth to you, but not in the manner in which your mothers bore you when they brought you into the world, themselves groaning with birth pains and you wailing, filthy, done up in filthy swaddling clothes and surrendered to this world, but with joy and gladness and freed from all your sins, and she feeds you not in a stinking cradle but with delight from the sweet-smelling rails of the holy altar.[25]

Much of the pleasant smell must have come from the oil and chrism which would have filled the baptistery with their

[23]I.41.3.

[24]'Hi, quos videtis, egregia coctura suave redolentes . . . non fumus amarus infecit. . . . Certe caccabacei non sunt, non vetusti non usti non crudi non mucidi. Lacteus illis color est, lacteus sapor est': I.41.2.

[25]'Iam mater nostra adoptat ut pariat, sed non ea lege, qua vos matres vestrae pepererunt, quae et ipsae partus dolore gementes et vos plorantes, sordidos, pannis sordidis alligatos huic mundo dediticios intulerunt; sed laeta gaudentes, caelestis < . . . > libera peccatis omnibus absolutos non foetidis cunis, sed suave redolentibus sacri altaris feliciter enutrit a cancellis': I.32.

strong aroma. But the Eucharist also has its smell and its taste. Zeno refers to the 'sweet-smelling rails of the holy altar', and in I.24.1 the purity of the Eucharist is contrasted with the foulness of worldly banquets.

For Zeno, dirt and foul smell are symbolic of sin. The filth of the first birth, of prison, of the worldly life and of punishment for sin are, at least in these sermons, brought together and identified one with another.[26] The sweet smell of oil, bread, and wine communicate freedom and new life in the Church, filled with the grace of the Holy Spirit.

4. THE THEOLOGY OF EASTER DAY

The theme of the astrological Easter is usually the one with which Zeno introduces the Vigil service in the Easter proclamation. In itself it is always being repeated with the cyclic passage of the calendar, but it points beyond itself to the original Easter Day.

> The same as its predecessor and as its successor, ever new in its long old age, the parent of the year and the year's offspring, it precedes the seasons which it follows and gives birth to its own beginning from its end so as to sow the ages and bring them together. This is when, similarly, but once only, out of love for his humanity, its maker, our Lord and God, died and rose again, never indeed to repeat his death.[27]

In the above passage the day undergoes a kind of cyclic existence, rather like 'Old Father Time', where the young and new succeeds the old and decaying. But while the day is a pointer to the mystery of the resurrection, the latter by

---

[26]E.g., I.49; II.10.1.

[27]'Idem sibi sucessor idemque decessor, longaeva semper aetate novellus, anni parens annique progenies; antecedit quae sequitur tempora et, ut saecula colligenda disseminat, parit sibi de fine principium. Hic est, quo similiter, verum tamen semel, amore hominis sui eius artifex deus et dominus noster occidit et exortus est rursum, numquam sane repetiturus occasum': II.19.1-2.

its very nature cannot be cyclic; it is a once-for-all event. The day is repeated, but the death and resurrection certainly cannot be. The repeated day is still the link with the original, un-repeatable, Easter Day, and is the means of access to it; through the day one appropriates the resurrection life.[28] The day not only reminds Christians to celebrate the events of Christ's resurrection; it communicates the effects and gifts of the resurrection.[29]

Thus the day provides the link with a past historical event. But it also provides a link with the future. The candidates are baptised at dawn, but the dawn is not just that of the earthly day but points to the eternal day: 'Rising from [the font], new with the new day, and, radiant with their own light, [the candidates] come with us in a safe course on the heavenly path of immortality to the time of promise where one rises for ever'.[30] So the day points to the fulness of the Christian mystery both in the resurrection and the final and eternal day. The cyclic day is one with the culmination of history in Christ, and so is one with Christ himself. Through the day he is the fulness of all times and seasons.[31]

Within the context of the day, Zeno can work out the sym-bolism of the seasons, which likewise are pointers to the sav-ing mystery. Again, like the day, the cyclic seasons point beyond themselves to the historical process and its eternal cul-mination in heaven:

> And so today for our *competentes* the winter of sin is finished; they will rejoice in the consecrated oil. Today smiling spring will make them into various kinds of flowers with their vari-ous gifts when they are immersed in the healing wave and rejoice in the harvest of cloudless summer and begin to eat

[28]E.g., I.16.2.

[29]E.g., I.6.

[30]'Surgentes inde novello novelli cum die, sua luce radiantes, nobis-cum possint inmortalitatis per aerium tramitem cursu servato ad repromis-sionis tempus, ubi in perpetuum quis oritur, pervenire': I.44.

[31]E.g., I.33.4.

the new bread. The autumn's new wine will not hinder them; they will be filled with it and happily drunk, and aglow with the warmth of the Holy Spirit. God the Father almighty will grant that no one among us will ever grow cold.[32]

Thus winter, spring, summer, and autumn all represent stages in Christian initiation, but the result is permanent and cannot be repeated.

This kind of treatment of Easter is really a patristic commonplace.[33] But Zeno develops it in a typical example of his fanciful yet concrete imagery. Chromatius of Aquileia soberly likens the newly baptised to spring lambs: 'In this season the ewes lamb in safety, for they do not fear the cold of winter. In their likeness the Church of God in this season like spiritual ewes bears the lambs of the faithful to Christ and feeds them with the milk of life and the drink of salvation'.[34] Cyril of Alexandria likens the flowers of spring to virtues.[35] But for Zeno the theme of the Easter Day as the springtime of the year and the harbinger of new life spills over into the description of the newly baptised as the flowers.

Spring we must understand as the sacred font, from whose rich vessel our infants are brought forth, the dazzling sweet flowers of the Church which are engendered not by the Zephyr

[32]'Competentibus nostris finitur hiems peccatorum. Oleo confecto laetabuntur. Hodie eos etiam ver arridens diversos in flores diverso charismate redditurum, cum salubri unda perfusi, limpidae aestatis messe gaudentes panem novum coeperint manducare. Quos autumnale quoque non morabitur mustum, quo repleti inebriatique feliciter spiritus sancti calore fervebunt, qui ut numquam refrigescat in omnibus nobis praestabit deus pater omnipotens': II.13.

[33]Cf J. Daniélou, *The Bible and the Liturgy* (Notre Dame, Ind., 1956), 287–92.

[34]'Nam hoc tempore et oves secure iam pariunt, quia nullum frigus hyemis pertimescunt. Ad quarum similitudinem hoc tempore Ecclesia Dei velut oves spiritales greges fidelium tamquam agnos procreat Christo, nutriens eos lacte vitae et potu salutis': Chromatius, *Sermon* 17.3.

[35]Daniélou, *The Bible and the Liturgy,* 291; Cyril, *Second Paschal Homily,* PG 77: 429D–432B.

wind but by the Holy Spirit and which in their blessed faith exhale the divine perfume of various gifts but the one birth.[36]

Today smiling spring will make them into various kinds of flowers with their various gifts when they are immersed in the healing wave.[37]

One curious feature of Zeno's treatment of the theme of Easter Day is that, while there is much about the created order, no actual mention is made of the belief that Easter Day was the anniversary of the creation of the world and of the Passover deliverance of Israel.[38] Both events are described in the readings during the Vigil, but Zeno seems for the most part content to leave the readings to speak for themselves. Passover and the Red Sea may look forward typologically to Christ and the Church, as does the story of the three children. But the events communicated by the return of the day are above all the day of resurrection and the last day.

5. BAPTISM AS ENTERING INTO DIVINE HISTORY

The sacrament of baptism has not to do with some timeless state of affairs but is closely bound up with a divine mystery which is revealed in history and which will be fulfilled through history. There are countless references in the sermons to past divine history, and the eschatological theme is equally strong.

Entry into divine history, as we have seen, is effected through Easter Day. (Presumably this would not have ex-

[36]'Ver sacrum fontem debemus accipere, cuius divite ex alveo Favonio non vento, sed spiritu sancto generante odorem divinum beata spirantes fide diverso charismate, sed una nativitate ecclesiae flores clarissimi ac dulces nostri funduntur infantes': I.33.2.

[37]'Hodie eos etiam ver arridens diversos in flores diverso charismate redditurum, cum salubri unda perfusi': II.13. Zeno also addresses the candidates after their baptism as 'dulcissimi flores mei': I.25.13.

[38]Cf. Gaudentius, *Tractatus I in Exodum* 1–3; Daniélou, *The Bible and the Liturgy*, 292.

cluded baptisms on other occasions in case of necessity.) The events of the Old Testament dispensation, for example the institution of the Passover and the crossing of the Red Sea, are treated as typologically looking forward to the Christian sacraments of baptism and Eucharist, though this by no means reduces their nature and importance as historical events. Each and every baptism and Eucharist derives from the supreme historical event, the first Easter Day, and looks forward to the final historical event of fulfilment in heaven.

So strong is this idea that the corporate sense of baptism in Zeno strongly influences the individual administration of the sacrament. All join into the common history of the Church. For all the baptised are children of the same mother, born from the same womb, brothers and sisters. They are incorporated into the same body of Christ. They are built into the same tower which includes all Christians and which will be completed at the end of time.[39] And of course this applies equally to all Christians, not just those baptised on the same day. For, as we have seen, each Easter Day is but the same day returned.

Besides the understanding of the Easter Day itself, the paschal Vigil gives the opportunity of presenting the history of salvation through the various readings and sermons. The proclamation explains the day; the reading of Genesis 1 invites the idea of the fulness of revelation and creation being one. Christ is seen to be the true beginning ('principium').[40] The creation of humankind in the image of God is not fulfilled in the first creation because changeable human flesh cannot represent the unchanging nature of God. The true image is the spiritual image of the heavenly man which is granted to the faithful through baptism.[41] And so it can be seen that the story of creation as told in Genesis is properly understood in terms of Christ, the 'principium' and the fulfillment into which Christians enter when they are baptised into Christ.

[39]II.6.8; cf. Hermas, *Vis.* 3.8.
[40]I.17.1.
[41]I.27.2–3.

The story of the Fall is found in Zeno as well, and salvation restores the fallen as well as perfecting the imperfect. Through the devil, the beings originally created by God had been demoted from angels to humans, and through the Holy Spirit the Lord restores all who believe in him to be angels.[42] The new spiritual creation heals the old creation. The sin of Adam and Eve at the tree in Eden is reversed by the Man hanging on the tree of the cross and the spiritual Woman, the Church.[43]

When Zeno discusses the Passover and Red Sea experiences he maintains that they really point to the Christian gospel. They are images of the Christian truth—*imagines* of the *veritas*. Now the Jews lack the Passover prescribed by the Law ('legitimum pascha') and they have lost sight of the true lamb, Christ. The historical fate of the Temple and of the Jewish nation proves that the Old Testament *imago* has totally given way to the New Testament *veritas*.[44] Each of the events of the Passover and Red Sea has its counterpart in Christian salvation, whose perfection shows up the limitations of the *imago*. Not just a generation is saved, as through the Red Sea, but all generations, through the font; Christ is the leader, not Moses; the people enter the water voluntarily, not in flight from the enemy; Israel goes into the desert, and Christians into heaven.[45]

In all these sermons, the eschatological element is also very strong. Zeno is quite emphatic that, just as baptism enables one to share in the divine history and revelation which finds its fulfillment in Christ, so the grace of baptism also finds its fulfillment in the kingdom of heaven which is to come. The eschatological dimension is integral to the understanding of the day. And so the baptisms lead not just to a particular spring morning, but to a day which points to the final eternal day:

[42]I.2.26; cf. II.10.2.

[43]I.3.20.

[44]E.g., I.28. See below.

[45]I.46B. See Hillier's perceptive remarks on this sermon, *Arator on the Acts*, 162–63.

It gives birth to its own beginning from its end, and today it will also grant this to our *competentes* whom now the happy sunset invites so that, immersed in the milky depth of the sacred ocean, and rising from there, new with the new day, and, radiant with their own light, they may come with us in a safe course on the heavenly path of immortality to the time of promise where one rises for ever.[46]

The safe path to heaven is a theme we find in the sermons on the crossing of the Red Sea. There the Jews went on into the desert. But the Church (represented in Exodus by Miriam) leads her people whom she has borne with hymns not to the desert but to heaven.[47] The festal procession of the newborn here is the one that goes in triumph from the baptistery to the church, where they share in the heavenly banquet.

In the allegory of the four seasons as the rites of initiation (II.13) the Eucharist is the culmination, not just of the day but of the Christian life. The bread of the Eucharist comes with the summer, and the wine is the autumn's new wine: 'God the Father almighty will grant that no one among us will ever grow cold'.

The allegory of the vineyard (II.11) is most interesting here. Zeno in describing viticulture keeps approximately to the order of the rites of initiation. The water of the font comes early on, then follows the sign of the cross, and ceremonies of renunciations and anointings. But then the allegory points to the whole of the Christian life, and the fruit on the vine and its leaves represent not the Eucharist but the divine law by which the Christian is defended and nourished.[48] The Eucharist is delayed in the allegory. For after temptations, culminating

[46]'Parit sibi de fine principium, hoc nostris quoque hodie competentibus praestaturus, quos iam nunc felix invitat occasus, ut sacri oceani lacteo profundo dimersi, surgentes inde novello novelli cum die, sua luce radiantes nobiscum possint inmortalitatis per aerium tramitem cursu servato ad repromissionis tempus, ubi in perpetuum quis oritur, pervenire': I.44.2; cf. I.57.

[47]II.26.3.

[48]II.11.5.

in martyrdom (the vintage), the new wine is transferred to the owner's cellar to mature and the Christian ascends to heaven. But the persecutors also drink the wine—of judgement.[49] In the light of the earlier sermon, the new wine would seem to represent the Eucharist. Zeno does not forget the Eucharist in his allegory; he portrays it in its proper context of the end of time, as the goal of the earthly pilgrimage.[50]

The reception of the denarius, signifying the chrismation in the name of the Trinity, also has its eschatological fulfillment: 'one denarius; whoever receives it freely and does not scorn what he has received, but persists in his work right to the end, will dwell in the tower when it is completed and possess inestimable riches'.[51] This must refer to the parable of the labourers in the vineyard in Matthew 20:1-16. Of course there they receive their denarius at the end of the day, but the mood in which they receive it is important. The baptismal denarius is paid in advance, and glad reception and faithful work lead to even greater gifts.

Evidently Zeno cannot think of Christian life in this world except in the context of its future fulfillment. Baptism, Eucharist, and the Christian life all have their true meaning only in the light of the final eternal day.

Even the image of God borne by the baptised (discussed below), which Zeno seems to claim is the true image of God, has a new fulness in heaven: 'Those who bear it in holiness, as did the apostles and all the just, will bear not only the image, but even God himself, as it is written, "You are the temple of God, and the Spirit of God dwells in you"'.[52]

To conclude, while it would be strange to discuss the sacraments of initiation without any mention of their fulfillment

[49]II.11.6.

[50]Doignon, 'Refrigerium et catéchèse à Vérone', notes how Zeno's description of the Eucharist, using terms such as *refrigerium, dulcis, mustum,* owes much to contemporary ideas of Paradise.

[51]II.6.8.

[52]'Quam qui sancte portaverint, sicut apostoli omnesque iusti, non tantum imaginem, sed ipsum deum quoque portabunt, sicut et scriptum est: Vos estis templum dei, et spiritus dei habitat in vobis': II.30.4.

in heaven, whether in the spiritual sphere or at the end of time, the sheer dominance of the eschatological in Zeno's thought is most remarkable. The Easter Day of the resurrection is the one that knows no sunset. It is the final eternal day. Each annual Easter Day shares in it and communicates it. Baptism is access to the eternal day. But the paschal Eucharist of the initiation would seem to belong more to the end of time than to the earthly sphere. In Zeno's allegories it does not provide food for the journey but is the feast at the end of the journey.

6. THE THEME OF *IMAGO/VERITAS*

A theme that runs right through Zeno's sermons can be summarised as the contrast between *imago* and *veritas* (image and truth). It is nowhere developed in detail, and often we find the contrast described in slightly different ways (e.g., *umbra* [shadow] for *imago*). But it still has a remarkable frequency and consistency, where the partial and worldly *imago* is contrasted with the spiritual *veritas*, the full and eternal revelation of God.[53]

The contrast between *imago* and *veritas* is seen first of all in typology, when the Old Testament is taken to prefigure the New Testament dispensation. 'Job, when understood, dearly beloved brothers, bore the image of Christ. And so comparison indicates the truth'.[54] The Church, like Christ, may be described as the *veritas* of the OT *imago*. 'Nineveh bears the image of the Church'.[55] And the Church's sacraments likewise constitute the *veritas*: 'Tamar produced the necklace, ring and staff, and delivered herself from imminent punishment

[53]Truzzi, 267–69 picks up the relationship of Old and New Testament in the use of *imago/veritas* in Zeno and also in Chromatius (e.g., *Sermon* 17A.1) and Gaudentius (*Tract. in Exod.* 2.9–11; CSEL 68:25f.).

[54]'Iob, quantum intellegi datur, fratres carissimi, Christi imaginem praeferebat. Denique comparatio indicat veritatem': I.15.7; cf. I.37.1: 'Iacob habet imaginem Christi'.

[55]'At vero Nineve imaginem portat ecclesiae': I.34.9.

by the mystery of their number: the Church herself in truth, in the name of the Father and of the Son and of the Holy Spirit, not only extinguishes the present fires of the devil but also will overcome the fires of the day which is coming'.[56]

The mystery *(sacramentum)* of the number, the three objects, is what saves Tamar, by virtue of pointing to the threefold naming of the Trinity in baptism. So here *sacramentum* is close in sense to the idea of *imago*. Is there a different sense, though, namely that in *sacramentum* (but not in *imago*) a benefit or grace is imputed? For Tamar, as for the three children, the *sacramentum* provides protection.[57]

Elsewhere Zeno does not describe the *imago/veritas* contrast in detail: 'Time does not permit me, brothers, to give the truth for the image'.[58] But even in these cases the contrast can be clear enough. In I.9 Zeno is commenting on the reading of the crossing of the Red Sea, and as he describes the crossing, and the subsequent drinking from the rock and eating the manna, he is following in the New Testament tradition of see-ing all these events as types of Christian initiation.[59] The lim-ited nature of the *imago* may be contrasted with the full and perfect *veritas*. The *imago* passes away before the *veritas*, and the Jews are condemned for clinging to what has passed away.[60]

So far the instances of *imago/veritas* have been all in the con-text of Old Testament typology. But there is also a very im-portant group of places where this kind of contrast is used when Zeno is discussing human nature.[61] In baptism the ini-

[56]'Thamar protulit monile, anulum, virgam seque liberavit sacramento numeri ab imminenti supplicio; ecclesia ipsa veritate, in nomine patris et filii et spiritus sancti, non tantum diaboli praesentes ignes exstinguit, sed etiam futuri diei iudicii incendia superabit': I.13.13.

[57]E.g., I.53.1.

[58]'Tempus non sinit, fratres, imagini reddere veritatem': I.9.

[59]1 Corinthians 10:1-5.

[60]I.18.2; I.46B.1; I.52; II.25.

[61]Cf. Gaudentius, *Tract. in Exod.* 2.9-11, who uses the idea of humanity being in the image of God, though he does not apply the theme to human nature in the same way as does Zeno. Gaudentius contrasts the many *imagi-*

tiands are said to become their true selves: 'Our water receives the dead and casts them up alive, from natural beings made into true human beings, and ones who will proceed from humans into angels, if the advance of years does not disfigure their infancy'.[62]

This might not of itself seem to be connected with the idea of *imago/veritas*, but it and other similar passages provide the context for Zeno's description of the phoenix in his sermon I.2, on the resurrection: 'Its tomb is its nest, its embers are its nurses, ash is the seed for the body to be procreated, its death is its birthday. And so after a moment it rejoices in its grave, not a shade, but the truth, not an image, but the phoenix, not another, but as it were a better other yet its former self'.[63] Zeno is following the traditional story of the phoenix which is always born again from the ashes of its dead parent, and 'not another but a better other yet its former self' might sound appropriate. But this is reminiscent of a description of the initiand after the new birth of baptism: 'He is the same and yet he is not the same. The old dwelling place remains, but a new inhabitant rejoices in the change in his way of life and will prove to the unbelieving the dignity of his birth by virtues of every kind'.[64] And while 'better' could refer to the new though passing youth, the description 'non umbra sed veritas, non imago sed Phoenix', is a theological description of the appropriation through baptism of redeemed human nature. Zeno explains this in the sermon on the resurrection:

---

nes of God (humans) with the one God. He does not integrate the *imago/ veritas* of humanity with that of history as Zeno does. Truzzi, 267–68.

[62]'Aqua nostra suscipit mortuos et evomit vivos, ex animalibus veros homines factos, ex hominibus in angelos transituros, si provectus aetatis eorum infantiam non mutaverit': II.10.2.

[63]'Sepulcrum nidus est illi, favillae nutrices, cinis propagandi corporis semen, mors natalicius dies. Denique post momentum festo exsultat in tumulo, non umbra sed veritas, non imago sed Phoenix, non alia, sed quamvis melior alia tamen prior ipsa': I.2.21.

[64]'Ipse est et tamen non est ipse. Vetus quidem videtur domicilium, sed novus inquilinus exsultat mutatione morum nativitatis suae nobilitatem incredulis variis virtutibus probaturus': I.42.2.

Since all flesh has long been assailed by the shameful temptations of this world and the darkness of the dead, it is brutish and condemned to a wretched, frail and detestable position. But when it is killed by the saving baptism with the unsullied faith of the one who believes, it rises anew from the holy waters of the parental font, now pure, now free, now beyond the ways of this world, now above death. Now it seeks heavenly things, now it disdains, I do not say this world's mockeries, but, what is more honourable, its very self. Now it seeks the truth not an image, now it desires not its own but the things of the spirit.[65]

The old mortal 'flesh', then, is the *imago*, and the new spiritual 'flesh' is the *veritas* and is appropriated through baptism.

So we must believe that the image of God is not this fleshly garment but the spiritual image of the heavenly person which of his abundance he lavishes on us from the sacred font. Paul clearly shows forth this matter when he says, 'Just as we have borne the image of the man of dust, so we shall bear the image of the man of heaven'. Those who bear it in holiness, as did the apostles and all the just, will bear not only the image, but even God himself, as it is written, 'You are the temple of God, and the Spirit of God dwells in you'.[66]

---

[65]'Omnis caro quam diu flagitiosis illecebris huius mundi ac tenebris feralibus agitatur, profecto pecuina est ac misero, fragili detestabilique versatur in iure. At cum mera fide credentis salutari fuerit necata baptismate, nova paterni sacro resurgit fontis ex gurgite iam pura, iam libera, iam a conversatione mundi huius extranea, iam morte superior, iam caelestia aspirans, iam, non dicam saeculi ludibria, sed, ut sit honoratior, se ipsam contemnens, iam veritatem non imaginem quaerens, iam spiritalia non sua desiderans': I.2.25.

[66]'Non ergo carnale hoc indumentum imaginem dei debemus accipere, sed caelestis hominis spiritalem, quam nobis plenitudinis suae pio de fonte largitur. Quam rationem Paulus evidenter prodidit dicens: Quemadmodum portavimus imaginem eius, qui de limo est, portemus et eius imaginem, qui de caelo est. Quam qui sancte portaverint, sicut apostoli omnesque iusti, non tantum imaginem, sed ipsum deum quoque portabunt, sicut et scriptum est: Vos estis templum dei, et spiritus dei habitat in vobis': II.30.3-4.

And so we see that the spiritual body is itself the image of God. Or, to put it in Zeno's terms, the *veritas* of the human being is the *imago* of God, and finds the reality of God in the fulfillment of heaven.

It is remarkable how Zeno has managed to integrate the two different uses of the *imago/veritas* imagery. First there is the temporal or typological relationship of the Old Testament *imago* to the New Testament *veritas*. The idea of humanity as the *imago* of God would not seem normally to have a temporal aspect. However, Zeno manages to incorporate it into the Old Testament scheme. The spiritual *veritas,* which is the *imago* of God, is achieved when the individual enters into the New Testament *veritas* through baptism. Zeno does not tell us how being the temple of God and having the Holy Spirit in the heavenly fulfillment differs from being the *imago* and possessing the Spirit on earth, but he looks to fulfillment for every individual in the fulfillment of history.

7. THE DEVIL AND THE BAPTISMAL LITURGY

> But our keys bring out everything, whatever they find, and they allow nothing to remain, but they open the innermost regions of the breast; carefully they drive out crimes of every kind and again carefully they shut the breast again to prevent the return of anything worthless that has been removed.[67]

This passage would seem to describe ceremonies of exorcism and sealing as understood by Zeno. The description of the exclusion of sin and locking up the breast against its return harks back to the parable of Jesus (Matt 12:43–45) about the return of a demon with companions to an exorcised person. This is taken up by Optatus of Milevis:

[67]'At vero nostrae [claves aureae] acervatim absolvunt quicquid invenerint nec aliquid subsicivi esse patiuntur, sed pectorum aperiunt cuncta penetralia, diligenter universa crimina expellunt ac rursus diligenter accludunt, ne quid illo vel frivolum, inde quod excluditur, revertatur': II.24.1.

No one who is born, even if born of Christian parents, can be without an unclean spirit, which must be removed and separated from the person before the saving bath. This is done by exorcism, by which the unclean spirit is cast out and flees to the desert. The house within the believer's breast is emptied, it is made clean. God enters and lives there, as the apostle says, 'You are the temple of God, and God dwells in you'.[68]

But Optatus is not necessarily representative of his age in believing in the possession by demons of all the unbaptised. Augustine says that people are not literally possessed by the devil but are subject to him.[69] Theodore of Mopsuestia describes the exorcists as advocates—συνήγοροι—in a court case against Satan, asking God to remove the devil's authority over the candidates.[70] The emphasis of these bishops' sermons even when Satan is mentioned in the liturgy is on freedom from the world. Thus in the renunciations in *De sacramentis* Ambrose quotes, 'When the question was put to you, 'Do you renounce the devil and his works?'' what was your reply? "I do renounce them". And, "Do you renounce the world and its pleasure?" What was your reply? "I do renounce them"'.[71] And he comments, 'So you have renounced the world, you have renounced this age'.[72] And Augustine, in the passage referred to above, likewise emphasises the impor-

[68]Omnis homo qui nascitur, quamvis de parentibus Christianis nascatur, sine spiritu inmundo esse non possit, quem necesse sit ante salutare lavacrum ab homine excludi et separari. Hoc exorcismus operatur, per quem spiritus inmundus depellitur et in loca deserta fugatur. Fit domus vacua in pectore credentis, fit domus munda; intrat Deus et habitat apostolo dicente: vos estis templum Dei, et in vobis Deus habitat': Optatus, *De schismate Donatistorum* 4.6.

[69]Augustine, *De nuptiis* 1.20.22.

[70]See below. Cf. Kelly, *The Devil at Baptism,* 149ff. Kelly believes that Theodore in fact amended his liturgy to fit his understanding.

[71]*De sac.* 1.5; *AIR,* 101: 'Quando te interrogavit: Abrenuntias Diabolo et operibus eius, quid respondisti? Abrenuntio. Abrenuntias saeculo et voluptatibus eius? Quid respondisti? Abrenuntio'.

[72]Ibid., 1.6; *AIR,* 102: 'Ergo abrenuntiasti mundo, abrenuntiasti saeculo'.

tance of sin: 'Then what is in them, by which they are held in the devil's power until they are rescued from it by the mystery of the baptism of Christ? What is there except sin?'[73] This is all similar to Zeno's comment, which must refer to the renunciations: 'Rejoice freely! Now you owe nothing to the world',[74] and, 'The one who renounces the world by his bond is spiritually bound by the sacred questions'.[75]

And just as the devil would seem to disappear from the commentaries on the renunciations, to be replaced by the world, so in his reference to the exorcisms Zeno talks about the removal of sin and the breast being sealed against the return of sin, even when, in all likelihood, the liturgical formulae would have talked about removing the devil.

Apotropaic rites are likewise not explicitly or necessarily anti-demonic. The twelve gates of the spiritual temple are defended from enemy attack by a cross.[76] But in the allegory of viticulture it is the commandments of religion that defend the Christian. The cross is said simply to enable the Christian to live and acquire immortality.[77]

Although exorcism evidently took a low profile in the initiatory rites, it was by no means unknown to the bishop and people of Verona. There is a description of exorcism in sermon I.2.6 (on the resurrection), where Zeno seeks to prove the survival of the soul after death by describing the identification and casting out of the souls of dead people who have possessed the bodies of the living. A few features of the argument are compared by Löfstedt with passages in Lactantius and Cyprian.[78] However the visual description is not based

---

[73]'Quid ergo in eis est, per quod in potestate diaboli teneantur, donec eruantur inde per sacramentum baptismatis Christi? Quid est nisi peccatum?': Augustine, *De nuptiis* 1.20.22.

[74]'Securi gaudete; nihil saeculo iam debetis': I.42.1.

[75]'Ligaturis adstringitur, cum renuntians saeculo sponsione facta sacris interrogationibus obligatur': II.11.5.

[76]II.6.7.

[77]II.11.4-5.

[78]CCL 22:16, note on lines 49/51; Lactantius, *Div. inst.* 2.15.3; 5.21.4. Cyprian, *Ad Demetrianum* 15; *Quod idola dii non sunt* 7.

on them, and there is a notable difference in the argument, namely that in Zeno it is the spirits of dead humans—idolators or those who had died violent deaths—that possess the bodies while in Cyprian and Lactantius they are demons. The idea that the possession is the agency not of demons but of dead humans is almost but not entirely without parallel in early Christian literature. Justin Martyr among examples of survival of the soul mentions those who are possessed by the souls of humans, and who are described as demon-possessed.[79]

Justin like Zeno was seeking to establish the survival of the human soul. But other writers, for dogmatic reasons, were keen to deny that the dead were responsible for possession. Tatian finds the idea inconsistent with his theory of the soul.[80] Tertullian and John Chrysostom both cite instances of possessed people claiming to be inhabited by souls of the deceased, but they ascribe it to demonic fraud. In Tertullian the demons claim to be relatives of the possessed or gladiators or *bestiarii,* in order to upset the Christian belief that such souls are sent to hell.[81] Chrysostom is keen to deny that people who die violent deaths become demons (though wicked people can become like demons) and says that the demons put the story about in order to discredit martyrdom.[82] But under pressure from the exorcist, Tertullian reassures us, the demon is forced to admit its true identity. One is led to speculate how the theories of possession are shaped by those of the fate of the soul, and how, even if under protest, the symptoms of the possessed are eventually made to fit the contrasting diagnoses of various theologies.

[79]*Apologia* 1.18.4.

[80]Tatian, *Oratio ad Graecos* 16; 13.

[81]Tertullian, *De anima* 57.5.

[82]John Chrysostom, *Sermon 2 on Lazarus* 1–2; Zeno also mentions possession by those who die violently.

8. THE FIRST ANOINTING—FOR FORGIVENESS

> Today for our *competentes* the winter of sin is finished; they
> will rejoice in the consecrated oil.[83]

Attributing the action of the forgiveness of sins to a point
before the immersion in the font is typical of Zeno. As we
shall see below, he sees the font as a source of 'positive' virtues (e.g., new birth), and wants to attribute 'negative' aspects
(e.g., the death of the old self) to the preliminary rites. The
description of the use of oil and the role of the Holy Spirit
in the forgiveness of sin is unusual, but we can find a scatter-
ing of parallels throughout the early Church, beginning with
Eastern Christianity.

The *Apostolic Constitutions* have three accounts of baptism.
The first two are very similar to one another, but the third
and fullest account has some distinctive features, among them
the description of the blessing of the oil for the pre-baptismal
anointing as being 'for the forgiveness of sins and preparation for baptism'.[84] In Cyril of Jerusalem the first anointing
with the exorcised oil is said to have several purposes: to make
the initiates sharers in Jesus Christ, the cultivated olive tree
(cf. Rom 11:24); to symbolise partaking of Christ's richness;
to drive away every trace of the enemy's power, including
cleansing all traces of sin.[85]

In the Egyptian tradition we find the same remission of sins
ascribed to the pre-baptismal anointing in a prayer of Sarapion
'in regard to the anointing oil of those who are being baptised', even invoking the words of Jesus, 'Whosesoever sins

---

[83]'Competentibus nostris finitur hiems hodie peccatorum. Oleo confecto laetabuntur': II.13.

[84]*Ap. Const.* 7.42.2; *DBL*, 33.

[85]Cyril, *Mystagogical catecheses* 2.3; *AIR*, 75. Cyril is unusual in the Syrian
tradition also for identifying the post-baptismal anointing with the gift of
the Holy Spirit, but he is not unique in this. Theodore of Mopsuestia's
Baptismal Homily 3.27 also has a post-baptismal anointing with a pneumatological significance. See *AIR*, 207–8, and note 65.

ye forgive, they are forgiven them' (John 20:23).[86] Sarapion also, again like Cyril, identifies the post-baptismal anointing with the gift of the Holy Spirit, but this is very common in the East outside the Syrian tradition.[87]

Among Western rites, the Gelasian Sacramentary has in its blessing of the oil for pre-baptismal anointing (the 'exorcised oil') the prayer, 'that this unction, being purified by divine sacraments, may be for the adoption of body and spirit to all who shall be anointed with it, unto the remission of all their sins'.[88] Pseudo-Germanus (ca. 700) describes the pre-baptismal anointing as being for healing the wound of sin.[88a]

There is a further parallel for attributing the remission of sins to a preliminary rite (albeit a different one), in Chromatius. In *Sermon* 15 he teaches his candidates about the meaning of the washing of feet, which in Aquileia came at some point before the baptism. Several times in this sermon he identifies this ceremony with the forgiveness of sins; indeed, it would seem to be the dominant idea in his sermon. Abraham, says Chromatius, washed the Lord's feet in order to gain forgiveness. When Gideon washes the Lord's feet, the fire which consumes the sacrifice is the Holy Spirit who burns away sins. Of Christ's practice, Chromatius says that the disciples washed his feet for the forgiveness of their sins and he washed theirs to cleanse them from the filth of sin.[89]

All this by no means removes from baptism itself the role of the forgiveness of sins. The grace of the font simply extends back, as it were, into this preliminary rite. Chromatius elsewhere talks of baptism bringing about the remission of sins.[90] Indeed, he concludes the sermon on the washing of feet with a summary of the entire initiatory rite.

---

[86]Prayer 15; *DBL,* 85.

[87]Ibid., Prayer 16.

[88]'ut fiat haec unctio divinis sacramentis purificata in adoptionem carnis et spiritus eis qui ex eo ungueri habent in remissionem omnium peccatorum': 1.40.

[88a]*DBL,* 164; *BA,* 116–18.

[89]Chromatius, *Sermon* 15.2-3.

[90]Chromatius, *Sermon* 14.1.

We wash the bodily feet; he washes the feet of the soul. We baptise the body; he forgives sins. We baptise; he sanctifies. On earth we lay on hands; he gives the Holy Spirit from heaven. And so, catechumens, my children, you must hasten to the grace of baptism so as to put aside the filth of your sins and be made clean throughout by our Lord and Saviour Jesus Christ.[91]

The comparison between Chromatius and Zeno is instructive. Both are evidence of the same tendency to attribute aspects of the effects of baptism (the forgiveness of sins and the gift of the Holy Spirit) to ceremonies that accompany the actual immersion. However the ceremonies to which they attribute these effects differ. Zeno attributes them both to anointings of oil or chrism. Chromatius, while he certainly has at least a post-baptismal anointing, applies the gift of the Holy Spirit to the laying on of hands. In all likelihood he knew of a pre-baptismal anointing as well, but he nowhere mentions it, and he has (to my knowledge) a unique ascription of the forgiveness of sins to the washing of feet instead.[92]

9. BAPTISM AND MARTYRDOM

The subject of martyrdom occurs often in the sermons on the readings of the Vigil. The readings on Daniel naturally raise the subject, but we find it also for example in II.11.6–7, on Isaiah 5:2. With these sermons it might be supposed that the idea is an isolated one which does not enter into the other images in Zeno's explanations of baptism. However we find

[91]Nos pedes corporis lavamus; ille autem lavat gressus animorum. Nos aqua corpus tingimus; ille peccata remittit. Nos tingimus; ille sanctificat. Nos in terra manus imponimus; ille de caelo Sanctum Spiritum donat. Quapropter, filii catechumeni, festinare debetis ad gratiam baptismi, ut depositis sordibus peccatorum, mundi per omnia efficiamini apud dominum et Salvatorem nostrum, Iesum Christum': Chromatius, *Sermon* 15.6.

[92]Ambrose attributes to the post-baptismal washing of feet the forgiveness of hereditary or original sin, but our own sins, he says, are forgiven in baptism; *De myst.* 32.

that there was a widespread connection between baptism and martyrdom in the Church from the fourth century onwards.[93]

We have the most explicit link between baptism and martyrdom in Gennadius of Marseilles. Gennadius compares catechumens who receive initiation with martyrs: in each the sacrament of baptism is fulfilled. The former confess their faith before a priest, the latter before their persecutor; the former are sprinkled or dipped in water, the latter are sprinkled with their blood or consumed by fire; the former receive the Holy Spirit through the laying on of a bishop's hand, the latter become a dwelling place of the Holy Spirit, because it is not the martyrs who speak but the Holy Spirit who speaks through them.[94] Gennadius is a late writer (fl. 470), but we may begin with him because he is so explicit.

A century earlier, Zeno presents the paschal baptism as a courtroom scene, in which the initiand is tried and then executed.[95] For us, the courtroom motif, the sinner before God condemned and sentenced to death, sounds like modern popular evangelicalism. But for Zeno and his contemporaries the courtroom was the same as for Gennadius a century later, a confrontation between the gospel and the world, between the martyr and the judge.

Two passages stand out in Zeno; both seem to be loosely based on Tertullian. Tertullian tells the imprisoned Christians that they have already left the prison of the world, the *saeculum*. The world has worse darkness, chains, and dirt than can any physical prison, and they have left the world.[96] Zeno also presents the world as the prison when he tells the newly

---

[93]See my article, 'Baptism Portrayed as Martyrdom in the Early Church', *Studia Liturgica* 23 (1993) 158–76, from which this discussion is taken, for a wider treatment of the question. P. Cramer tries to establish a link between the *Passio* of Perpetua and Felicity and contemporary, early third-century baptism (*Baptism and Change*, 73–86) but his case seems to be far less sure.

[94]Gennadius, *De eccles. dogmat.* 74; see Fisher, *Christian Initiation*, 54–55.

[95]E.g., I.42.

[96]Tertullian, *Ad martyres* 2.1–2.

baptised, 'Rejoice, you now owe nothing to the world. You are freed of earthly chains and bonds. Terror and filth are past'.[97] And, in the second passage, as far as Tertullian is concerned, the pagan sinner fears the court, but the Christian does not: 'If pointed out, they pride themselves on it; if accused, they do not defend themselves; when examined they confess of their own accord; when condemned they give thanks'.[98] And Zeno likewise says of baptism: 'It is a new kind of judgement, in which the guilty, if they deny the crime, are condemned; if they acknowledge it, they are acquitted'.[99]

The contradiction between the judgement of the world and of God was and is a Christian commonplace. Father Pierre-Marie Gy has explored the ambivalence of the Christian term *confessio* in the language of penance in the Middle Ages. Part of the ambivalence is rooted in the Hebrew *hôdâ(h)*, 'confession of sin' and 'glorification of God'.[100] But Gy puts the force of the ambivalence in the language of the pagan courtroom:

> The pagan governor summons me before him and questions me: 'Are you a Christian?' I reply, 'Confiteor'. He understands this to mean, 'I confess I am guilty', and decides my head should be cut off. But when I say 'Confiteor', I am conscious of having confessed my faith, borne witness to the faith. Other Christians will say I am a confessor of the faith, perhaps a martyr.[101]

Upside-down judgement is found in all sorts of ways in the divine courtroom. 'You will judge the judges', Tertullian tells

[97]II.24.1.

[98]Tertullian, *Apologeticum* 1.12.

[99]II.10.2. For the connection with Tertullian, cf. Löfstedt's note on the text.

[100]Cf. Christine Mohrmann, 'Linguistic Problems in the Early Christian Church', *Etudes sur le Latin des Chrétiens,* vol. 3 (Rome, 1965) 185 (= *Vigiliae Christianae* 11 [1957] 11–36). 'This double meaning finds its fullest literary exploitation in St Augustine's Confessions'.

[101]Pierre-Marie Gy, 'The Inculturation of the Christian Liturgy in the West', *Studia Liturgica* 20 (1990) 12.

the martyrs,[102] and, 'The world will endure the judgement, not of the proconsul but of God'.[103] The martyrs in the *Passio* of Perpetua and Felicity shout, 'You judge us, and God judges you'.[104] Cyprian has the same motif of the courtroom. Here is total concentration on the judgement by Christ of the confessor. 'Let it be before your eyes, dearly beloved, that he, who alone received all judgement from the Father and who will come to judge, has already brought forth the sentence of his judgement and of his future trial, pronouncing and attesting that he will confess before his Father those who confess and that he will deny those who deny'.[105]

There is a hint of a reaction against the proconsul in the claim that Christ alone received the power of judgement. Very different is the treatment by Theodore of Mopsuestia of the courtroom motif in his *Baptismal Homilies,* where the preliminary rites are portrayed as a court case against the devil who appears to be the real villain, and at first the candidate appears to be more weak than evil, and more sinned against than sinning: 'When you present yourselves to give in your names, in the hope of finding a dwelling-place in heaven, the exorcisms are, so to say, a law-suit with the devil; you are freed from slavery to him by God's judgement'. However attention reverts to the candidates and their own condemnation:

> You stretch out your hands to God in the attitude of one at prayer. For we have fallen into sin and the sentence of death has thrown us to the ground. . . . The rest of your body should remain upright, looking up to heaven. By this attitude you present, so to speak, a request to God, asking him like a petitioner for liberation from your ancient fall and a share in the joys of heaven.[106]

[102]Tertullian, *Ad martyres* 2.4.

[103]Ibid., 2.3.

[104]*Passio Sanctarum Perpetuae et Felicitatis* 18.

[105]Cyprian, *Ep.* 58.3; trans. Sister Rose Bernard Donna, *Fathers of the Church,* vol. 51 (New York, 1964) 165.

[106]Theodore of Mopsuestia, *Baptismal Homily* 2.1–4; *AIR,* 176–78.

The courtroom motif links martyrdom and baptism, as is most clearly seen in the writings of Gennadius. However the interpretation of the motif varies according to its context. When applied to the martyrs, they are innocent, the faithful witnesses to Christ the only true judge. At the Last Judgement God will vindicate them, and the world will recognise that by condemning the martyrs it has invited judgement on itself. In the context of baptism in Zeno and Theodore, and in the later tradition of penance as outlined by Gy, the candidate accepts the verdict and judgement of God, and only by doing so receives his gracious love and forgiveness. The basic motif remains the same—the perfect judgement of God. But whereas the martyr is the faithful confessor of Christ, the candidate preparing for baptism comes in from the world and still shares in its guilt until that guilt is confessed and forgiveness is received.

10. GUILT AND JUDGEMENT

According to the novel logic described above, the effects of baptism are described in terms of forgiveness gained for the candidates with the imagery of a court of law and with criminal proceedings being taken against them.

Zeno begins with the state of the pagan sinner before coming to the court, which is the most miserable conceivable. He imagines the prison, the officers, the judge, and all terrify him. Worst of all, he has to live with his own conscience:

> My brothers, the person who remains in his first birth cannot be happy. He is burned at every moment by the flaming torch of scorching sins, he carries round with him the stench of the prison, he detects the executioner before he can see him, he is in terror of mention of the judge, from a whisper he supposes that he is being sought, that he is found out. He has no prospect of security: perhaps there is no one to accuse him, but there is always one who knows and can bear witness—himself. For conscience, more fierce than any torture, never

leaves the sinner. Until now, my brothers, you were in this guilty state.[107]

But then the sinner comes to the pre-baptismal scrutinies, which are pictured as pleading in a court. The procedure of the court of law is, of course, novel. It forgives the one who confesses the fault and condemns the one who denies guilt. Much therefore seems to depend on the attitude of the sinner. The candidates hurry to be punished. And this perception of God and his justice is gained as the sinner becomes a Christian through conversion, teaching, and initiation:

> Until now, my brothers, you were indeed in great guilt. But you have been examined strictly and you have prayed well for yourselves in vigil in order to receive mercy. You have been most favourably heard. It is a new kind of judgement, in which the guilty person, if he denies the crime, is condemned, but if he confesses, he is forgiven. What logic, what power, what graciousness has our judge! Sinners of every kind rush to be punished by him so that they may live happy.[108]

The initiands rush to be punished, and the punishment for the one who confesses is still carried out. For just as the preliminary rites are taken to be the examination in court of the sinner, he or she is executed and baptism is the burial

[107] 'Beatus esse non potest, fratres, in prima nativitate persistens, quem aestuantium delictorum fax incensa omnibus momentis exurit; qui paedorem sui secum carceris portat; qui carnificem sentit, antequam videat; qui nomen iudicis pertimescit; qui, sicunde susurrus ingruerit, se quaeri, se aestimat inveniri; cui securitatis profectus est nullus, etiam si contingat ei accusatore carere, teste conscio, cum se ipso carere non possit, quia violentior omni tortore conscientia numquam suum deserit peccatorem. In hoc reatu, fratres, usque nunc fuistis': II.10.1-2.

[108] 'In magno quidem reatu nunc usque fuistis, sed fortiter examinati estis et, ut indulgentiam perciperetis, pro vobis ipsis bene vigilastis; optime estis auditi. Novum iudicii genus est, in quo reus, si excusaverit crimen, damnatur, absolvitur, si fatetur. Magna ratio, magna potestas, magna pietas iudicis nostri, a quo universi generis peccatores, ut possint beate vivere, puniri festinant': I.42.1.

of the body and its new birth.[109] 'The gracious sword descends into the sinner's entrails, and in one and the same blow, the physical body remaining unharmed, kills the old self and creates a new one, and buries it in the element of the sacred stream'.[110]

In II.29 the idea of the death sentence is joined with that of release from the prison, which is associated with the world:

> Rejoice freely! Now you owe nothing to the world. Behold, there is no weight or rattling of earthly chains on your necks. Your hands are not bound in any manacles, your feet are not burdened with any fetters. No terror distracts you; no squalor degrades you. You feared the one who knows your crimes: now you do not fear your conscience. For your old self has been happily condemned so that he may be forgiven, buried in the wave of the sacred waters so that he may be quickened in the nest of the tomb and taste the privileges of the resurrection.[111]

In either case the penalty is paid, and the sinner walks free through the grace of God.

11. ZENO'S TREATMENT OF THE THEME OF WATER

Zeno elaborates on the water of the baptismal font in various ways, notably with the themes of refreshing one's thirst,

---

[109]The idea of a sentence being carried out is also to be found in Ambrose, where it is the sentence given in Genesis 3:19: 'You are dust and to dust you shall return'. Immersion or burial in the font carries out the sentence. *De sac.* 2.16–19.

[110]'Descendit quippe gladius pius in viscera peccatoris et . . . interficit hominem veterem, creat novum, sacri gurgitis elemento sepelit': II.10.2.

[111]'Securi gaudete; nihil saeculo iam debetis. Ecce nullum pondus, stridor nullus est mundanarum vestris in cervicibus catenarum. Vinculis nullis impeditae sunt manus, nullis pedes onerati compedibus. Non vos ullos terror exagitat, non ullae sordes obfuscant. Qui conscium timebatis, conscientiam non timetis. Vetus enim homo vester feliciter condemnatus est, ut absolveretur, sacri gurgitis unda sepultus, ut sepulchri nido vivificatus resurrectionis iura gustaret': II.29.1.

washing, and burial, but not normally the death of the old self.

The idea of refreshment has at its base not only the nature of water in itself but also the psalm sung on moving to the baptistery, speaking of the desire of the deer for the waters. Similarly the candidates are bidden to hurry to what they desire and to fill their very beings with it.[112] It can hardly be meant that the candidates were expected to drink the baptismal water, but that is the language that Zeno uses. Nothing restrains his imagery.

The theme of washing is connected to the idea of sin as dirt, and also contrasts with the first, natural birth with its filthiness. We have already examined this theme of dirt and cleanliness, but here the most relevant illustration is when Zeno, in his typically realistic style, compares the font to the public baths.[113] And after the washing in the font, the white garments are of course the symbol of cleanliness and innocence: 'Steadfastly and faithfully throw off that old self of yours with his filthy garments; soon you come forth all new, all robed in white'. 'Rejoice, heavenly peoples, new children in Christ, and guard with perpetual care against staining in any way the whiteness of your flowering spiritual birth today. What is given cannot be repeated'.[114]

The death of the old self in the font would naturally suggest the theme of drowning, but for Zeno the death sentence passed on the candidate by God is carried out by the sword in the manner of a secular execution. The water therefore receives a person who is already dead; it has the role of the grave or tomb:[115]

[112]Ps. 41.1; *Sermons* I.12; II.28. The Ballerini commentary (PL 11: col. 477–78, no. 3) gives a different, or at least supplementary, meaning to *desiderata,* as referring to the sacrament, from the preparation involved which excited the desire of the candidates. Cf. Ambrose, *De sac.* 4.2.7.

[113]I.23.

[114]'Constanter igitur ac fideliter hominem istum vestrum veterem foeterosis suis cum pannis abicite, novelli omnes, omnes candidati': I.49.

'Aetheriae gentes, exsultate, novella pignora in Christo, florentissimique hodierni spiritalis ortus vestri candorem, ne quo pacto maculetis, perpeti diligentia custodite, quia nescit iterare quod praestat': I.38.1.

[115]Cf. Ambrose, *De sac.* 2.19; Daniélou, *The Bible and the Liturgy,* 46–47.

The gracious sword descends into the sinner's entrails, and in one and the same blow, the physical body remaining unharmed, kills the old self, and creates a new one, and buries it in the element of the sacred stream. And while it is the nature of all water to take living people into its depths and to cast them up dead, our water receives the dead and casts them up alive, from natural beings made into true human beings, and ones who will proceed from humans into angels.[116]

So the nature of water is reversed; in the font it is lifegiving rather than destructive of life. This fits very well with the image of water as giving life to plants (as we see in the allegory of viticulture in II.11). The image of the font is overwhelmingly positive, and all that is negative—the killing of the old self—has been completed before baptism. The font is the agent of birth to new life. Whereas we might think of the font as death and life together, drowning and resurrection, dying as we go down into the water, rising as we come up, Zeno normally thinks of the candidate as already 'dead' when entering the font. The font is the place of burial, but it is lifegiving, not death dealing.[117]

Redemption is still intimately linked with the water, and Zeno does not explicitly name some earlier point when the candidate 'dies'. If he did have one in mind it might have

[116]'Descendit quippe gladius pius in viscera peccatoris et uno eodemque ictu, incolumi corporis manente materia, interficit hominem veterem, creat novum, sacri gurgitis elemento sepelit. Et cum omnium aquarum natura sit talis, ut, cum in profundum homines susceperit vivos, evomat mortuos, aqua nostra suscipit mortuos et evomit vivos, ex animalibus veros homines factos, ex hominibus in angelos transituros': II.10.2; cf. II.29.1.

[117]There are a number of exceptions to this. There is a suggestion in the invitations to the font (e.g., II.23) that Zeno can be thinking of death taking place in the font. We also find the same idea in II.29.2, where the font, pictured as mother Church, like a wicked stepmother kills the people she receives and then as a loving mother brings them to life. But, *pace* de Paoli ('L'iniziazione cristiana, 413f.) the theme of the death of the old person is a minor one, and there is far greater emphasis on birth and new life. Elsewhere the imagery used is closer to what we have seen associated with *imago/veritas*; in baptism the candidates become 'true human beings from natural beings' (II.10, above).

been the renunciations, when the old self is, as it were, put
away, but this kind of specific timing is an inappropriate reading of his sermons. Rather we have again the principle we
have already seen in the pre-baptismal anointing for forgiveness, namely that aspects of redemption which properly belong to baptism itself are extended to preliminary or
subsequent ceremonies. Before baptism the rites deal with sin
through the imagery of renunciation, anointing for forgiveness, and the courtroom motif. The candidate dies. The rites
after baptism talk of the gift of the Holy Spirit and sharing
in the path to heaven through the anointing, sealing, and the
procession into the church. But all these ideas, negative and
positive, properly belong to the central rite of baptism, and
would be affirmed as such by Zeno and all the Church Fathers
we have here examined.[118]

12. THE HOLY SPIRIT IN BAPTISM

The central role of the Holy Spirit in baptism is so much to
be expected that it would be remarkable had it not occupied
a like place in Zeno's expositions.[119] Baptism is administered,
as he says, in truth, in the name of the Father and of the Son
and of the Holy Spirit,[120] and each person is reborn 'by water
and the Holy Spirit'.[121]

The presence of the Holy Spirit may be communicated
through the baptismal water itself.[122] De Paoli also attributes
to the idea of the working of the Spirit such phrases as 'saving warmth' ('calor salutaris'),[123] 'gracious font' ('pius

[118]This approach to liturgy is more fully discussed in my essay 'Liturgy
and Ceremonial,' in *Liturgy in Dialogue,* ed. P. Bradshaw and B. D. Spinks
(London, 1994) 9–27.

[119]Cf. de Paoli, 'L'iniziazione cristiana', 414–17.

[120]I.13.3. For the actual form of words used, see above.

[121]I.13.12; cf. I.2.26.

[122]I.23; I.33.2.

[123]I.32. De Paoli, 'L'iniziazione cristiana', 416.

fons'),[124] 'sweet murmur' ('dulce murmur'),[125] and 'sacred ocean' ('sacri oceani')[126] and, in the comparison of the initiands to wheat cooked in the oven, 'they have been cooked not in an oven but a font, not with human but with divine fire' ('excocti sunt non furno, sed fonte, non humano, sed igni divino').[127]

We have seen the role of the forgiveness of sins in the prebaptismal anointing and the activity of the Holy Spirit in that anointing. But the Holy Spirit is also seen in the post-baptismal anointing: 'Oil signifies the gift of the Holy Spirit'.[128] And it is likewise present in the sign of the cross which would be given at the same time: 'We are marked not with the scar [of circumcision] but with this sign of the Holy Spirit'.[129]

We have already included the grace and gift of the Holy Spirit in the principle discussed above of the extension of images and effects from baptism proper to the accompanying ceremonies. The Holy Spirit is imparted throughout the rite of initiation, which is, theologically, a single complete action. As was seen above in the description of the liturgy, the action of baptism and anointing was certainly described as one event and may indeed have been just that. We are not dealing with 'post-baptismal' anointing in Zeno but 'cum-baptismal' anointing.

13. BAPTISM AS REGENERATION

If we were to look for any particular theme as being the dominant one in Zeno's exposition of baptism, de Paoli is surely right in saying that it is regeneration.[130] The brevity of this

[124]II.23.

[125]I.12.

[126]I.44.2.

[127]I.41.2.

[128]'Oleum donum spiritus sancti significat': I.13.10.

[129]'Hoc spiritus sancti non signaculo sed signo censemur': I.3.21.

[130]De Paoli, 'L'iniziazione cristiana', 408–12. For the treatment of the theme in other Church Fathers, cf. Daniélou, *The Bible and the Liturgy*, 47ff.

present description of the theme would seem to belie its importance in the sermons and the frequency with which it occurs. I hope that in the sermons in themselves, in the investigation of the liturgy, and above all in nearly every section of this survey of Zeno's theology, the idea of regeneration is already quite apparent to the reader, and so here will concentrate on the way in which Zeno describes regeneration in terms of a second birth.

The new birth is described very often in terms of a natural human birth, with the baptised as newborn babies.[131] In the baptistery the font is the womb of the mother, the Church, from which the newborn issue forth.[132] They are then clothed like babes—in the white garments[133]—and fed like babes—from the altar rails.[134]

The new birth, as we have already seen, is contrasted with the first carnal birth, to the detriment of the latter whose unpleasant aspects are dwelt on with some relish. And, of course, the new birth admits no final death.[135]

A common figure for the newborn baptised at Easter is that of flowers. The symbolism of the new Easter Day at the beginning of the year with its promise of growth and life carries over into those who are baptised.[136]

14. IMAGES OF UNITY

The unity of the newly baptised is frequently emphasised by Zeno. All races, ages, and sexes are united in the Church. While we might think of the unity being expressed predominantly as 'one body in Christ', for Zeno this takes second place to the dominant theme of 'one birth', shared

---

[131]Cf. e.g., II.29.1.
[132]I.55; II.28.
[133]I.38.3.
[134]I.32.
[135]I.16.2.
[136]I.33.2.

in by all, from the one mother Church.[137] This theme of *mater ecclesia* is of course by no means unique to Zeno. It was almost a commonplace in many early writers, notably in Cyprian.[138] Unity is in what the baptised share: 'one birth, one milk, one pay, one honour of the Holy Spirit'.[139] But the individuality of the people is not lost. Rather their strangeness to one another is abolished. It is more as if they are now of one family, full brothers and sisters together.[140]

Less frequently we find the theme of the one body:

> This is renewal, this is resurrection, this is eternal life, this is the mother of all, who has united us, brought us together from every race and nation and straightway made us one body.[141]

> The day of salvation has come, lavish with every kind of gifts for all who attend on the Lord's mystery. . . . Thus it gathers all into the one grace of the body of Christ and leads them to the heavenly realms.[142]

The allegory of viticulture would invite the idea of the candidates as shoots grafted into the vine, but Zeno interprets the allegory with the individual vine shoots, planted in the soil, as the candidates. The theme of identical and/or related individuals predominates over that of physical unity.[143]

The stress on the unity of identical individuals rather than on absorption into a single whole can be seen by comparing

[137]Cf. de Paoli, 'L'iniziazione cristiana', 409–10.

[138]Daniélou, *The Bible and the Liturgy*, 47–49. K. Delahaye, *Ecclesia Mater* (Paris, 1964).

[139]'unam nativitatem, unum lac, unum stipendium, unam spiritus sancti dignitatem': II.29.2.

[140]I.24.1; I.38.2.

[141]'Haec renovatio, haec resurrectio, haec vita aeterna, haec est mater omnium, quae nos adunatos, ex omni gente et natione collectos unum postmodum efficit corpus': I.55.

[142]'dies salutaris advenit, officiis sacramenti dominici omnibus omni genre munerum largus . . . sicque cunctos in unam Christi corporis gratiam congregatos ad caelestia regna perducit': I.6.

[143]II.11.2.

Zeno's illustration of the rites of initiation as the preparation of bread with the treatment of the same idea by other writers. The most famous instance is to be found in Augustine, who represents the various individuals as being made into one loaf:

> Remember, you did not exist, and you were created: you were carried to the Lord's threshing floor, you were threshed by the labour of cattle, that is, of those who proclaim the gospel. When you were set aside as catechumens you were stored in his barn. You gave in your names: you began to be ground with fasting and exorcism. After that you came to water, were moistened and made one. You were cooked then, when the ardour of the Holy Spirit came near, and now have been made the Lord's bread.[144]

Gaudentius uses the idea in a manner similar to Augustine:

> And so just as many grains of wheat have been ground into flour and it is made by water and perfected by fire into bread, spiritually here is understood an image of the body of Christ, which we know is made one body out of the multitude of the whole human race and is perfected by the fire of the Holy Spirit.[145]

In Zeno there is a similar process, but the *competentes* are likened to individual loaves of unleavened bread ('panes azymos'). Some may seem bigger or smaller than others, but

---

[144]Recordamini et vos: non fuistis, et creati estis, ad aream dominicam conportati estis, laboribus boum, id est, annuntiantium evangelium triturati estis. Quando catechumeni differebamini, in horreo servabamini. Nomina vestra dedistis; coepistis moli ieiuniis et exorcismis. Postea ad aquam venistis, et consparsi estis, et unum facti estis. Accendente fervore Spiritus sancti cocti estis, et panis dominicus facti estis. Denis 6.1; *Miscellanea Agostiniana*, vol. 1 (Rome, 1940) 30; trans. *DBL*, 106.

[145]'Deinde quoniam panem de multis tritici grani in pollinem redactis per aquam confici et per ignem necesse est consummari, rationabiliter in eo figura accipitur corporis Christi, quem novimus ex multitudine totius humani generis unum esse corpus effectum, [et] per ignem sancti spiritus consummatum': Gaudentius, *Tract. II in Exodum.*

really they are all identical.[146] The idea of the candidates as individual loaves is not used by Zeno alone. Chromatius does not use the image of the bread-making for the rites of initiation, but when stressing the moral duties of the neophytes, he talks of them as individual 'azimi': 'And so the Apostle says, "Cleanse out the old leaven that you may be a new dough, as you really are unleavened loaves [*azimi*])". We are *azimi* if we remain without the leaven of wickedness. We are *azimi* if we are uninfected by any dough of sin'.[147]

We see demonstrated here both the use of common imagery among Church Fathers, and the subtle variations which it may undergo. Zeno stood within a rich and varied tradition of baptismal catechesis of which we have only tiny fragments, and the variety of presentation and interpretation we have seen here can only be a hint of what is lost forever.

15. TWO THEOLOGIES OF BAPTISM?

This survey of themes in the sermons has revealed a wide, balanced, and sophisticated use of imagery by Zeno. The sensual imagery of smell and light communicates the symbols used by the the baptismal liturgy. Zeno expects that the candidates will experience the liturgy and God's gift of new life through sight, smell, and sound. Other images and symbols are presented through comments by the preacher and through the liturgical spoken formulae. When the candidates enter the baptistery the idea of the Church giving birth through the font, if they do not already know it, is suggested by the bishop in his invitation. Their visual similarity, all dressed in white garments, is used to suggest the image of their being brothers

---

[146]I.41. It has been noted above how the uniform appearance of the newly baptised in their white robes is used by Zeno to talk of their unity.

[147]'Et ideo apostolus ait: "Expurgate vetus fermentum ut sitis nova conspersio, sicut estis azimi." (I Cor 5:7) Azimi sumus si sine fermento malitiae manemus. Azimi sumus si alieni sumus ab omni conspersione peccati': Chromatius, *Sermon* 17A.2.

and sisters, identical together. The work of the Holy Spirit is constantly brought to mind through formula and comment.

In all this the theology and symbolism of baptism was probably traditional. But the imagery of martyrdom and the motif of the courtroom introduce into the baptistery elements which we now know to have been new ones in the late fourth century, when dying with Christ was for the first time applied to baptism. Cyril of Jerusalem used Pauline imagery from Romans.[148] Zeno uses the martyr literature as does Gennadius later. Death to the old self and to the world and condemnation of sin are presented in the liturgical formulae of renunciations. Their meaning and emphasis are amplified by the sermons. But Zeno does not integrate Romans 6 with this imagery, nor does he manage to integrate fully the two ideas of the font as the life-giving womb of Mother Church and as the place of dying and rising. For him the font is still essentially the life-giver and the death dealing is normally restricted to the preparatory rites.[149]

In this clash of images Zeno is sharing fully in the new challenges confronting the Church in the fourth century. Confronted with establishment and magnificence when once there had been persecution, swelled with converts rather than derided by the mob, feted by emperors who were now ranked with the apostles rather than with Satan, the Church needed a new self-understanding and had to negotiate a different relationship with the age. Once the contrast between the Church and the world was all too obvious. In the Church of the second and third centuries baptism was about being born of water and the Spirit, about cleansing and enlightenment. Dying with Christ was not to the fore, even in the West where the custom of baptism at Easter might easily have suggested it. That motif was taken up by the martyr literature, and only when martyrs belonged to the past was it freed for the liturgy and

[148]Cyril, *Mystagogical Catecheses* 2.5.

[149]See my article, 'Paschal Baptism and Rebirth: A Clash of Images?' *Studia Patristica* 26 (1994) 41–46, for a fuller discussion of this shift of emphasis in Zeno and also in his contemporary, Pacian of Barcelona.

became part of the Church's new definition of itself over against the world. Now there was all the magnificence of establishment, but also converts to be tested in new ways, there were princely bishops but also monks and nuns and ascetics. One contrast between Church and world had gone; another was coming into place. Zeno lived just at the time when this change of understanding was happening, and we see in his sermons the two theologies sitting, slightly uncomfortably, side by side.[150]

But embracing even these disparate theologies is Easter Day which is the context of all that happens. Whether baptism is new birth or death and resurrection, it is conferred through the day that communicates the victory of Christ. Everything that is personal in the rites or shared with a small crowd of fellow candidates is lifted to the plane of history and the plan of salvation from the Creation through all God's works. These are recited in the Vigil readings, but most of all the Easter Day communicates the resurrection and the achievement of the last eternal day. Easter Day is cyclic, but points to the unrepeatable work of God in Christ and to the eternal culmination in him. History is eschatological, working towards its final goal. By being made members of the Church, the candidates enter into the reality of which Old Testament history and their own personal lives are but a pale image or shadow. The reality they enter is likewise a shadow of the reality of the final day, but even this is theirs by foretaste through baptism.

Such is the theology to be seen in the sermons. None of the themes or images is totally unique to Zeno, but they are nearly all developed in particular ways according to his own character and outlook. All the diverse symbolism is welded together by an idiosyncratic but forceful and capable personality, presenting the mystery of salvation in a way both traditional and personal. Zeno's achievement is remarkable.

[150]For a fuller discussion of this change of understanding in the ancient Church see my article, 'Baptism Portrayed as Martyrdom in the Early Church', *Studia Liturgica* 23 (1993) 158–76.

CONCLUSION

Petronius said that Zeno multiplied the joys of salvation. His effervescent spirit melted the medieval sculptor, and whether we look on his image, read about him, or read his own words, that bright enthusiasm shines through.

As a witness for historical liturgical practice, Zeno is of immense importance. He is a unique source for the paschal Vigil in the Western Church of the fourth century. Of course, with no other contemporary sources we cannot tell whether he represents the exception or the rule. In many ways Zeno might be seen as a representative of a liturgical world that was passing away. The life of his congregation seems to show a simplicity that was already out of date. In Ambrose all the various aspects of the baptismal ceremonies are distinct in liturgical practice and in theological meaning. In Zeno neither is the case. Here we have similarities with the time of Tertullian who himself knows a rite with ceremonies in search of meaning, but is less happy with that vagueness than is Zeno. The latter never appeals to detail; he describes but he never analyses, and we have to go to great efforts to establish the rite he uses, and its similarities with and differences from other rites. As a result we have clear evidence of the considerable variety of liturgical practice of the fourth century. There was no one norm, either ancient or newly developed. Each bishop and see followed its own practices, broadly in line with other churches and, at times, open to influence and novelty. But there is no evidence of a desire for detailed conformity.

In the theological imagery he uses in his sermons more than anywhere else Zeno can be seen as an individual. He takes themes old and new, develops, reshapes, and knits them together, and presents them in a refreshing, distinctive, and sometimes delightful, sometimes bizarre fashion. As a theologian he never acquired greatness, but neither does he deserve neglect. Recent studies have discovered something of his originality and his creative handling of Scripture. No doubt there is much more to be discovered. As an orator his sermons contain a classical rhetorical style of the highest order, a unique expression of theological teaching mediated through a blending together of concrete images, a lively sense of humour, and a warm love of his congregation and his God.

Zeno appears to us as a remarkable man; purely for himself he would be worthy of study, and across the centuries he wins our affection as he jokes with his congregation, chides the widow who contemplates remarriage, bitterly attacks the enemies of Catholic Christianity, teases the catechumen, and sings a solemn hymn of praise to Easter Day. As our only representative of the life of Italian Christianity in the period before Ambrose, he is immensely important and sadly neglected. This study goes some way to redressing that neglect.

Appendix

TABLE OF SERMONS
IN THEIR VARIOUS GROUPS,
SHOWING THEIR ROLE AND CONTENT

Numbered groups are of sermons from the Easter Vigil, the 'paschal groups'. Lettered groups are of non-Vigil material, the 'non-paschal groups'. *Item* (underlined) signifies where the use of the word shows the beginning of a new group.

no. and title	liturgical role	comments
BOOK I		
GROUP A		
1 De pudicitia		
2 De resurrectione		
3 De circumcisione		
4 De patientia		
5 De avaritia		
GROUP I		
6 <u>Item</u> praefatio	paschal Vigil	
7 Genesi	paschal Vigil	
8 Tr Exodi	paschal Vigil	
9 Tr sequentiae Exodi	paschal Vigil	
10 Tr Esaiae	paschal Vigil	recto/verso
(10B)	paschal Vigil	recto/verso
11 Tr Danielis	paschal Vigil	
12 Tr psalmi xli	paschal Vigil	
GROUP B		
13 Tr de Iuda	catechetical (Easter Week)	
14 Tr de avaritia	Sunday sermon	
15 Tr de Iob	catechetical (Lenten)	

GROUP II

16	<u>Item</u> praefatio paschalis	paschal Vigil
17	De Genesi	paschal Vigil
18	De Exodo	paschal Vigil
19	De sequentia Exodi	paschal Vigil
20	De Esaia	paschal Vigil
21	De avaritia	verso
22	Tr Danielis	paschal Vigil
23	De psalmo xli	paschal Vigil
24	Post traditum baptisma	paschal Vigil

'STRAY'

25	<u>Item</u> tractatus	catechetical (Easter Week)

GROUP III

26	<u>Item</u> praefatio	paschal Vigil
27	De Genesi	paschal Vigil
28	De Exodo	paschal Vigil
29	<u>Item</u> Exodi secunda	paschal Vigil
30	Tr Esaiae	paschal Vigil
31	Tr Danielis	paschal Vigil
32	Invitatio fontis	paschal Vigil

GROUP C

33	<u>Item</u> tr diei dominici	paschal Vigil X-series
34	Tr Ionae prophetae	catechetical (Lenten)
35	Tr Psalmi centesimi	catechetical (Lenten)
36	Tr de spe, fide et caritate	
37	Tr de somnio Iacob	catechetical (Easter Week)
38	Tr de xii signis ad neophytos	paschal Vigil X-series
39	Tr de Archadio martyre	Passio
40	Tr de Susanna	
41	Tr diei dominici de comparatione tritici	paschal Vigil X-series
42	Tr ad neophytos alio die paschae	paschal Vigil X-series

43	Tr de Abraham patriarcha	catechetical? (Easter Week)

GROUP IV

44	Praefatio paschalis	paschal Vigil
45	De Genesi	paschal Vigil
46A	De Exodo	paschal Vigil
46B	De sequentia Exodi	paschal Vigil
47	Tr Esaiae	paschal Vigil
48	Tr Danielis	paschal Vigil
49	Invitatio fontis	paschal Vigil

GROUP V

50	De Genesi	paschal Vigil	
51	De Exodo	paschal Vigil	
52	Sequentia Exodi	paschal Vigil	
53	Tr Danielis	paschal Vigil	
54	De nativitate Christi	Christmas?	stray
55	Ad neophytos	paschal Vigil	

GROUP D

56	Tr fidei	paschal Vigil X-series	
57	Tr paschae	paschal Vigil X-series	
58	Item tr Paschae	paschal Vigil X-series	verso
59	De Abraham	catechetical (Lenten)	
60	De Esaia	fragment	verso
61	Item de Esaia	?paschal Vigil X-series	
62	Item de Abraham		

BOOK II

GROUP E

1	De iustitia	
2	De timore	
3	Tr fidei	
4	De spiritu et corpore	
5	De eo quod scriptum est: Cum tradiderit regnum deo et patri.	Christmas?

6	De aedificatione domus dei a Salomone	consecration of church	
7	De continentia		
8	De nativitate domini	Christmas?	
9	De humilitate		

GROUP VI

10	De baptismo	paschal Vigil	
11	Tr de Esaia	paschal Vigil	
12	De nativitate domini et maiestate	paschal Vigil	
13	Tr paschae	paschal Vigil	
14	Tr paschae vel invitatio fontis	paschal Vigil	
15	Item invitatio fontis	paschal Vigil	wrong title really De Dan
16	Tr Exodi	paschal Vigil	
17	De die paschae	paschal Vigil	
18	Tr Danielis in pascha	fragment?	stray? verso? wrong title

GROUP VII

19	Item in die paschae	paschal Vigil	
20	Item de die paschae	paschal Vigil	
21	Tr de Esaia	paschal Vigil	
22	Tr Danielis	paschal Vigil	
23	De baptismo	paschal Vigil	
24	Item tr de baptismo	paschal Vigil	

GROUP VIII

25	Tr paschae	paschal Vigil	recto
26	Item tr paschae cuius supra	paschal Vigil	verso
27	Tr Danielis in pascha	paschal Vigil	recto
28	Invitatio fontis cuius supra	paschal Vigil	verso
29	Tr paschalis	paschal Vigil	recto
30	De Genesi cuius supra	paschal Vigil	verso

BIBLIOGRAPHY

(i) Texts

Zeno

Sancti Zenonis episcopi Veronensis sermones. Ed. P. and G. Ballerini
(Verona, 1739). Reprinted in Migne, *Patrologia Latina*
11:9–760.

S. Zenonis episcopi Veronensis sermones. Ed. G.B.C. Giuliari. Verona,
1883.

Zenonis Veronensis tractatus. Ed. B. Löfstedt. Corpus Christianorum,
22. Turnholt, 1971.

Other Sources

Ambrose. *De excessu Satyri.* CSEL 73:207–325.

_____. *De officiis ministrorum.* PL 16:25–194.

_____. *De paenitentia.* CSEL 73:117–206.

_____. *De sacramentis, de mysteriis.* Ed. Dom B. Botte, SC 25 bis.

_____. *Epistulae.* CSEL 82.

_____. *Expositio Psalmi CXVIII.* CSEL 62.

_____. *Letters.* Trans. Sister Mary Melchior Beyenka. Fathers
of the Church 26. New York, 1954.

Ps.-Ambrose. *De lapsu virginis.* PL 16:383–400.

Ambrosiaster. *Quaestiones Veteris ac Novi Testamenti.* CSEL 50.

Ammianus Marcellinus. *Res gestae.* Ed. W. Seyfarth, 2 vols. Leipzig,
1975.

Apostolic Constitutions. Ed. M. Metzger. SC 320, 329, 336.

Apuleius. *Metamorphoses.* Ed. D. S. Robertson, 3 vols. Paris,
1940–45.

Athanasius. *Apologeticum ad Constantium.* SC 56.

Augustine. *Confessions.* CSEL 33.

————. *De Genesi adversus Manichaeos.* PL 34: col. 173–220.

————. *De nuptiis.* CSEL 42.

————. *Enarratio in psalmos.* CCL 38–40.

————. *Epistulae.* CSEL 34, 44, 57, 58.

————. *Miscellanea Agostiniana.* 2 vols. Rome, 1930.

————. *Sermones.* PL 38–40.

Basil the Great. *Letters.* Ed. Y. Courtonne, 3 vols. Paris, 1905.

Beroldus sive Ecclesiae Ambrosianae Mediolanensis kalendarium et ordines saec xii. Ed. M. Magistretti. Milan, 1894.

Bobbio Missal. Ed. E. A. Lowe. London, 1920. (HBS 58).

Canones Apostolorum et conciliorum. Ed. H. T. Bruns. Berlin, 1839.

Chromatius of Aquileia. *Sermons.* Ed. J. Lemarié. SC 154, 164.

Coronatus. 'Prologus in vitam Sancti Zenonis Episcopi'. PL 11: col. 199–204.

Cyprian. *Opera.,* Ed. G. Hartel. CSEL 3.

Cyril of Alexandria. *Paschal Homilies.* PG 77: col. 401–981.

Cyril of Jerusalem. *Catechetical Lectures.* SC 126.

Egeria's Travels to the Holy Land. Ed. J. Wilkinson, 2d ed. Warminster, England, 1981.

Eusebius Gallicanus. CCL 101.

Gaudentius. *Tractatus.* CSEL 68.

Gelasian Sacramentary. Ed. L. C. Mohlberg, O.S.B., Rome, 1958.

Gregorian Sacramentary. Ed. J. Deshusses. Fribourg, 1971.

Gregory of Elvira. *Tractatus Origenis.* CCL 69.

Gregory the Great. *Dialogues.* PL 77: col. 149–430.

Hermas. *The Shepherd.* Ed. Kirsopp Lake, *The Apostolic Fathers,* 2 vols. London and Cambridge, Mass. (Loeb Classical Library) 1959.

Hilary of Poitiers. *In psalmos.* CSEL 22.

Hippolytus. *The Apostolic Tradition.* Ed. B. Botte, *La Tradition Apostolique de Saint Hippolyte.* Münster Westfalen, 1963.

G. Iulius Victor. *Ars rhetorica.* Eds. R. Giomini and M. S. Celentano. Leipzig, 1980.

Innocent I. Ed. R. Cabié, *La lettre du Pape Innocent ler à Décentius de Gubbio.* Louvain, 1973.

Jerome. *Epistulae.* CSEL 54.

————. *Tractatus de psalmis.* CCL 79.

John Chrysostom. *Sermons on Lazarus.* PG 48.

John the Deacon. *Ad Senarium.* Ed Dom A. Wilmart. *Studi e Testi,* 59; 170–79. Rome, 1933.

Justin Martyr. *Apology.* Ed. A. W. F. Blunt. Cambridge, 1911.

Lactantius. *Divine Institutes.* CSEL 22.

Lectionary of Luxeuil. Ed. P. Salmon. *Collectanea Biblica Latina,* vols. 7, 9. Rome, 1944–53.

Liber comicus. Ed. G. Morin. Maredsous, 1893.

Le Liber Mozarabicus Sacramentorum. Ed. M. Férotin. Paris, 1912.

Liber ordinum. Ed. M. Férotin. Paris, 1904.

Mai, A., ed. *Scriptorum veterum nova collectio,* 10 vols. 1830–38.

Manuale Ambrosianum. Ed. M. Magistretti. Milan, 1905.

Ps.-Maximus of Turin. *Anonimo Veronese: Omelie mistagogiche e catechetiche.* Ed. G. Sobrero Bibliotheca 'Ephemerides Liturgicae' Subsidia 66. Rome, 1992.

Melito of Sardis. *On Pascha.* Ed. S. G. Hall. Oxford, 1979.

Missale Gothicum. Ed. H. M. Bannister, 2 vols. London, 1917–19. (HBS 52/54).

North Italian Services of the Eleventh Century. Ed. C. Lambot. London, 1931. (HBS 67)

Optatus. *De schismate donatistorum.* CSEL 26.

Les 'Ordines Romani' du haut moyen age. Ed. M. Andrieu, 5 vols. Louvain, 1948–61.

Passio sanctarum Perpetuae et Felicitatis. Ed. H. Musurillo, *The Acts of the Christian Martyrs.* Oxford, 1972.

Quintilian. *Institutio oratorica.* Ed. and trans. H. E. Butler, 4 vols. London and New York (Loeb Classical Library) 1921–22.

Roman Canon. Ed. B. Botte, *Le canon de la messe Romaine.* Louvain, 1935.

Sarapion. 'The Sacramentary of Serapion of Thmuis'. Ed. F. E. Brightman. *Journal of Theological Studies* 1 (1899–1900) 88–113, 247–77.

Siricius. *Epistulae.* PL 13: cols. 1131–78.

Tatian. *Oratio ad Graecos.* Ed. M. Whittaker. Oxford, 1982.

Tertullian. *Opera.* CCL 1–2.

Theodore of Mopsuestia. *Baptismal Homilies.* Eds. R. Tonneau and R. Devreesse. *Studi e Testi* 145. Vatican City, 1949.

Versus de Verona. Ed. G. B. Pighi. Bologna, 1960.

Virgil. *Opera.* Ed. R. A. B. Mynors. Oxford, 1972.

(ii) Studies

Arns, R. P. Evaristo. *La technique du livre d'après Saint Jéôme.* Paris, 1953.

Baumstark, A. *Comparative Liturgy.* Trans. F. L. Cross. London, 1958.

Beatrice, P. F. *La lavanda dei piedi.* Rome, 1983.

Bigelmair, A. *Des heiligen Bischofs Zeno von Verona Traktate (Predigten und Aussprachen).* Munich, 1934.

————. *Zeno von Verona.* Aschendorff, 1904.

Bovini, G. *Ravenna Mosaics.* London and New York, 1978.

Bradshaw, P. *The Search for the Origins of Christian Worship.* London, 1992.

Brightman, F. E. *Liturgies Eastern and Western,* vol. 1. Oxford, 1896.

Brown, P. *Augustine of Hippo.* London, 1967.

Busch, B. 'De initiatione christiana secundum Sanctum Augustinum'. *Ephemerides Liturgicae,* 52 (1938) 159–78, 385–481.

Chaffin, C. E. 'Maximus of Turin and the Church in North Italy,' (unpublished thesis). Oxford, 1970.

Chavasse, A. 'Les deux rituels romain et gaulois de l'admission au catéchumenat que renferme le Sacramentaire Gélasien'. In *Etudes de critique et d'histoire religieuses,* 79–98. Lyons, 1948.

Cipolla, C. 'Il Velo di Classe'. In *Le Gallerie Nazionali Italiane,* vol. 3. Rome, 1897.

Cramer, P. *Baptism and Change in the Early Middle Ages, c.200–c.1150.* Cambridge, 1993.

Daniélou, J. *The Bible and the Liturgy.* Notre Dame, Ind., 1956.

Davies, J. G. *The Architectural Setting of Baptism.* London, 1962.

Delahaye, K. *Ecclesia Mater.* Paris, 1964.

De Paoli, G. 'L'iniziazione cristiana nei Sermoni di S. Zeno di Verona'. *Rivista Liturgica* 54 (1967) 407–17.

Di Berardino, A., ed. *Patrology,* vol. 4. ET P. Solari. Westminster, Md., 1991.

Doignon, J. 'Myriam et son tamburin dans la prédication et l'archéologie occidentale au IVe siècle'. *Studia Patristica* 4 (1961) (*Texte und Untersuchengen* 79) 71–77.

————. 'Refrigerium et catéchèse à Vérone'. In *Hommages à M. Rénard,* vol. 2 (Collection Latomus 102) 220–39. Brussels, 1969.

Dolbeau, F. 'Zenoniana: Recherches sur le texte et sur la tradition de Zénon de Vérone'. *Recherches Augustiniennes* 20 (1985) 3–34.

Dudden, H. *The Life and Times of Saint Ambrose,* 2 vols. Oxford, 1935.

Evans, E. *Tertullian's Homily on Baptism.* London, 1964.

Fainelli, V. *Codice diplomatice Veronese.* Venice, 1940ff.

Finn, T. M. *Early Christian Baptism and the Catechumenate: Italy, North Africa, and Egypt.* Message of the Fathers of the Church, vol. 6. Collegeville, Minn., 1992.

Fisher, J. D. C. *Christian Initiation.* London, 1965.

Galli, A. 'Zénon de Vérone dans l'antiphonaire de Bangor'. *Revue Bénédictine* 93 (1983) 293-301.

Grazioli, A. 'San Zenone di Verona', *La Scuola Cattolica* 68 (1940) 174-99.

Gy, P.-M. 'The Inculturation of the Christian Liturgy in the West'. *Studia Liturgica* 20 (1990) 8-18.

Håkanson, L. 'Textkritisches zu Zeno Veronensis'. *Classica et Mediaevalia* 31 (1970) 223-38.

Hillier, R., *Arator on the Acts of the Apostles.* Oxford, 1993.

Hübner, W. 'Das Horoskop der Christen (Zeno I,38L.)'. *Vigiliae Christianae* 29 (1975) 120-37.

Jasper, R. C. D., and Cuming, G. J. *Prayers of the Eucharist, Early and Reformed,* 3d ed., New York, 1987.

Jeanes, G. P. 'Baptism Portrayed as Martyrdom in the Early Church.' *Studia Liturgica* 23 (1993) 158-76.

_____. 'Early Latin Parallels to the Roman Canon? Possible References to a Eucharistic Prayer in Zeno of Verona'. *Journal of Theological Studies,* n.s. 37 (1986) 427-31.

_____. 'Liturgy and Ceremonial.' In *Liturgy in Dialogue,* ed. P. Bradshaw and B. D. Spinks, 9-27. London, 1994.

_____. 'Paschal Baptism and Rebirth: A Clash of Images?' *Studia Patristica* 26 (1994) 41-46.

_____. *The Origins of the Roman Rite.* Alcuin/GROW Liturgical Study 20. Bramcote, England, 1991.

_____. 'The Paschal and Baptismal Sermons of Zeno of Verona' (B.D. Thesis). Oxford, 1989.

Jones, C., G. Wainwright and E. Yarnold. *The Study of Liturgy,* 2d ed., London, 1992.

Kavanagh, A. *The Shape of Baptism.* New York, 1978.

Kelly, H. A. *The Devil at Baptism.* Ithaca and London, 1985.

Lampe, G. W. H. *The Seal of the Spirit,* 2d ed. London, 1967.

Lehmann, H. J. *On Some Round Numbers in Some Patristic Texts.* Aarhus, 1974 (private publication).

Löfstedt, B. M. and D. W. Packard. *A Concordance to the Sermons of Bishop Zeno of Verona.* New York, 1975.

Löfstedt, B. 'Zwei Patristica'. *Arctos* 9 (1975) 57-60.

MacGregor, A. J. *Fire and Light in the Western Triduum.* Collegeville, Minn., 1992.

Martimort, A. G. *The Church at Prayer,* 4 vols. London, 1988.

Mitchell, L. L. *Baptismal Anointing.* London, 1966.

Mohrmann, C. *Etudes sur le Latin des Chrétiens,* 3 vols. Rome, 1965.

Morin, G. 'Deux petits discours d'un evêque Petronius'. *Revue Bénédictine* 14 (1897) 3ff.

Olivar, A. 'Preparacion e improvisacion en la predicacion patristica'. In *Kyriakon.* Eds. P. Granfield and J. A. Jungmann, vol. 2: 736–67. Aschendorff, 1970.

Palanca, L. 'The Prose Rhythm and Gorgianic Figures in the Sermons of St Zeno of Verona' (Dissertation: Catholic University of America). Washington, D.C., 1970.

Pesci, B. 'De Christianarum antiquitatum institutionibus in S. Zenonis Veronensis Episcopi sermonibus'. *Antonianum* 23 (1948) 33–42.

Philippart, G. 'La fête de S. Zénon de Vérone le 8 décembre'. *Analecta Bollandiana* 92 (1974) 347–48.

Pighi, G. B. 'Scrittori latini di Verona Romana'. In *Verona e il suo territorio,* vol. 1: 353ff. Verona, 1960.

Rice, D. Talbot. *Byzantine Art,* 4th ed. Harmondsworth, England, 1968.

Righetti, M. *Manuale di storia liturgica,* 4 vols. Milan, 1950–53.

Roberts C. H., and T. C. Skeat. *The Birth of the Codex.* London, 1987.

Robinson, J. Armitage, *The Passion of St Perpetua.* Cambridge, 1891.

Rogers, C. F.. 'Baptism and Christian Archaeology'. *Studia Biblica et Ecclesiastica* 5 (1903) 239–362.

Spinks, B. D. *The Sanctus in the Eucharistic Prayer.* Cambridge, 1991.

Stepanich, M. F. *The Christology of Zeno of Verona.* Washington, D.C., 1948.

Stevenson, K. 'The Ceremonies of Light: Their Shape and Function in the Paschal Vigil Liturgy'. *Ephemerides Liturgicae* 99 (1985) 170–85.

Talley, T. J. *The Origins of the Liturgical Year,* 2d ed. Collegeville, Minn., 1991.

Tillemann. 'Zeno Veronensis: en zijn leer over de christelijke initiatie' (Unpublished thesis). Louvain, 1975.

Truzzi, C. *Zeno, Gaudenzio e Cromazio.* Brescia, 1985.

Tyrer, J. W. *Historical Survey of Holy Week.* Oxford, 1932.

Van Der Meer, F. *Augustine the Bishop.* Trans. B. Battershaw and G. R. Lamb. London and New York, 1961.

Vokes, F. E. 'Zeno of Verona, Apuleius and Africa', *Studia Patristica* 8/2 (1966) 130–34.

Whitaker, E. C. *Documents of the Baptismal Liturgy,* 2d ed. London, 1970.

Wistrand, E. 'Textkritisches zu Zeno Veronensis'. In *Classica et Mediaevalia Francisco Blatt septuagenario dedicata,* 363–70. Copenhagen, 1973.

Yarnold, E. *The Awe-Inspiring Rites of Initiation.* Slough, 1972.

————. 'Did St Ambrose know the Mystagogic Catecheses?' *Studia Patristica* 12 (1975) 184–89.

INDEX OF PROPER NAMES

Ambrose : 1-3, 8, 9, 12-14, 17, 18, 44-5, 102-4, 113, 138-40, 142, 149, 152, 154, 158-9, 160-4, 166, 167, 170-4, 177-8, 180, 184, 186, 191, 192, 195, 196, 197, 206-13, 221, 236, 241, 247, 248, 259-60

Ps-Ambrose : 190

Ambrosiaster : 193, 196

Apostolic Constitutions : 239

Apuleius of Madaura : 16, 129, 180-1

Archadius (martyr) : 16, 23

Arles (First Council of) : 160

Armenian Lectionary of Jerusalem : 175-6, 200-2, 204, 205

J. Armitage Robinson : 129

Arns, R. P. Evaristo : 47

Athanasius : 8, 13

Augustine : 1, 3, 13, 18, 35, 44, 133, 135-7, 156, 160, 169, 185, 188, 236-7, 243, 254

Bagata, R. : 5

Ballerini, P. and G. : 5, 6, 10-12, 22, 29, 47, 48, 103, 105-7, 112, 125, 156, 183-5, 194, 197-8, 248

Bangor Antiphonary : 19

Basil the Great : 102

Basil, Liturgy of : 195-6

Baumstark, A. : 161, 205, 213

Beatrice, P. F. : 165

Beroldus : 174, 184, 202-3, 205

Beyenka, M. M. : 9

Bigelmair, A. : 6, 10, 11, 34, 37, 107, 112

Bobbio Missal : 187

Botte, B. : 119
Bovini, G. : 164
Bradshaw, P. : 213
Brown, P. : 137
Busch, B. : 185
Canones ad Gallos : 157
Castellanus, P. A. : 5
Chaffin, C. E. : 45
Chromatius of Aquileia : 6, 12, 13, 19, 131, 133, 160, 163,
    166, 169, 172-3, 198, 206-13, 225, 231, 240-1, 255
Cicero : 32, 44
Cipolla, C. : 8
Coena Cypriani : 19, 136
Coronatus : 14-5
Cramer, P. : 117, 242
Cyprian : 16, 17, 37, 141, 160, 169, 172, 193, 237-8, 244, 253
Cyril of Alexandria : 225
Cyril of Jerusalem : 13, 140, 158, 239-40, 256
Damasus, Pope : 12
Daniélou, J. : 225, 226, 248, 251, 253
Davies, J. G. : 179, 211
Delahaye, K. : 253
de Leuco, J. : 5
de Paoli, G. : 7, 138, 216, 219, 249, 250-1, 253
De solstitiis : 115
di Berardino, A. : 9, 17, 19, 29
Dionisi, G. I., : 14
Doignon, J. : 135-6, 141, 194, 230
Dolbeau, F. : 5, 19, 22, 54, 59, 61, 66, 69, 96
Dudden, H. : 9, 16
Egeria : 13, 16, 176
Eusebius Gallicanus : 19
Eusebius of Vercelli : 13
Evans, E. : 159
Fainelli, V. : 11
Finn, T. M. : 42
Fisher, J.D.C. : 166, 242

Galli, A. : 19
Gaudentius of Brescia : 6, 12, 16, 131, 133, 140-1, 198, 226, 231, 232, 254
Gelasian Sacramentary : 160, 162, 166-7, 168, 170-1, 174-6, 197, 202-5, 209, 240
Gennadius of Marseilles : 17, 242, 245, 256
Ps. Germanus of Paris : 160, 169, 240
Grazioli, A. : 6, 14-19
Gregorian Sacramentary : 174, 176, 202-5
Gregory the Great : 15, 18
Gregory of Elvira : 193
Gregory of Tours : 160
Gy, P.-M. : 243, 245
Håkanson, L. : 54, 68, 69, 84
Hermas : 227
Hilary of Poitiers : 8, 10, 12, 13, 32, 37, 50, 53, 60, 114, 138, 160-1
Hillier, R. : 120-1, 228
Hippolytus, *Apostolic Tradition* : 160, 181, 184, 186-7, 212, 213
Hübner, W. : 133-5
G. Iulius Victor : 44
Innocent I : 181
Jeanes, G. P. : 9, 162, 191, 242, 250, 256, 257
Jerome : 1, 3, 13, 16, 17, 30, 32, 34, 44, 47, 102, 181
John Chrysostom : 103, 188, 238
John the Deacon : 166, 170-1, 180
Jounel, P. : 197
Justin Martyr : 238
Kelly, H. A. : 165, 236
Lactantius : 16, 37, 55, 88, 89, 237-8
Lampe, G.W.H. : 158-60
Lehmann, H. J. : 12
Lemarié, J. : 206, 208
Leo the Great : 13, 45, 195
Leonine (Verona) Sacramentary : 47, 119, 191
Liber Comicus : 202

Le Liber Mozarabicus Sacramentorum : 192
Liber Pontificalis : 197
Löfstedt, B. : 5, 16, 20, 22, 23, 30–43, 46, 50, 54, 63, 103, 107, 108, 112, 117, 125, 130, 131, 139, 155–6, 185, 237, 243
Luxeuil, Lectionary : 176, 202–5
MacGregor, A. J. : 176, 190
Mai Fragment : 161–3, 180, 184, 206–7, 211–12, 214
Maximus of Turin : 45
Ps. Maximus of Turin : 161
Melito of Sardis : 202, 205
Missale Gallicanum Vetus : 198–201
Missale Gothicum : 198–201
Missale Mixtum : 202, 205
Mitchell, L. L. : 160–2, 180–1
Mohrmann, C. : 109, 243
Morin, G. : 17–18
Nicetas of Remesiana : 190
'*North Italian Services of the Eleventh Century*' : 160–1
Olivar, A. : 30, 35, 44–5
Optatus of Milevis : 160, 170, 235–6
Ordines Romani : 175–6
Ovid : 55
Palanca, L. : 5, 6, 32–4, 46
Perpetua and Felicity, martyrs : 17, 29, 244
Perretti, B. : 5
Pesci, B. : 7, 165, 174, 178–9, 184, 211
Peter Chrysologus : 19, 45
Petronius of Bologna : 11, 14, 17–8, 259
Philaster of Brescia : 12, 115
Philippart, G. : 11
Pighi, G.B. : 47
Pliny : 32
Potamius : 50, 53
Quintilian : 30, 43–5
Ravenna, S. Apollinare in Classe : 136
Ravenna, Arian Baptistery : 164

Ravenna, Baptistery of Orthodox (Neonian Baptistery) : 164, 177

Refoulé, R. F. : 159

Rice, D. Talbot : 164

Righetti, M. : 184

Roberts C. H. : 47

Rogers, C. F. : 211

Rome, S. Mary Major : 136

Rome, Lateran Baptistery : 211

Roman Canon : 2

Roman Missal : 204

Rufinus : 16, 50, 53

Salmon, P. : 203

Sarapion, prayers of : 239–40

Siricius : 165

Skeat, T. C. : 47

Sparaver, F. : 123, 125, 194

Spinks, B. D. : 163

Stevenson, K. : 203

Symmachus : 32

Talley, T. J : 115

Tatian : 238

Tertullian : 16, 17, 37, 101, 117, 135, 159, 160, 167, 171–3, 193, 238, 242–4, 259

Theodore of Mopsuestia : 188, 236, 239, 244–5

Truzzi, C. : 6–12, 17, 23, 29, 39, 47, 107–8, 112, 114, 137–8, 140, 142, 146, 165, 166, 183, 197, 231, 233

Tyrer, J. W. : 174, 200–1

Van Der Meer, F. : 188

Velo di Classe : 8

Versus de Verona : 8, 14

Virgil : 73

Vokes, F. E. : 17

Yarnold, E. : ix, 101, 172, 179, 188, 239

INDEX OF SERMONS

(excluding Appendix, pages 261-3)

I

1   23, 26, 140

2   23, 26, 139, 220, 228, 233-4, 237-8, 250

3   23, 26, 138-9, 182, 191-4, 228, 251

4   23, 26, 140, 194

5   23, 26, 140

6   25, 41, 51, 54, 106, 108-11, 124, 166, 197, 224, 253

7   25, 54-6, 112-7

8   25, 56-7, 106, 117-9

9   25, 35, 36, 39, 57, 106, 119-21, 232

10A 25, 39, 50, 57, 106, 123-7

10B 25, 39, 50, 58, 106, 123-7

11   25, 58-9, 106, 127-8

12   25, 59, 106, 128-30, 178-9, 218, 221, 248, 251

13   23, 26, 105, 138, 142-3, 146, 166, 179-80, 231-2, 250-1

14   23, 26

15   23, 26; 138-40, 231

16   25, 41, 51, 59, 106, 108-11, 224, 252

17   25, 36, 59-60, 112-7, 227

18   25, 60-1, 106, 119-21, 232

19   25, 45, 61, 117-9

20   25, 50, 61-2, 106, 121-2

21   23, 28, 50, 165

22   25, 50, 62, 106, 127-8, 178

23   25, 62, 106, 128-30, 157-8, 165, 177, 179, 180, 183-6, 188, 218, 221, 248, 250

24   25, 28-9, 63-4, 106, 130-7, 165, 181, 190, 223,
           253
25   23, 28, 51, 141, 146, 226
26   25, 41, 51, 64, 106, 108-11
27   25, 36, 39, 64-5, 112-7, 138, 227
28   25, 45, 65-6, 106, 117-9, 228
29   25, 51, 66-7, 106, 119-21, 220
30   25, 67, 106, 121-2
31   25, 67, 106, 127-8
32   25, 68, 106, 128-30, 178, 190, 218, 222, 250, 252
33   25, 26, 41, 51, 68-9, 106, 108-11, 224-6, 250, 252
34   23, 26, 138-40, 165, 231
35   23, 26, 138-40
36   23, 26, 139-40
37   23, 26, 137, 138, 143-6, 171-3, 231
38   25, 26, 28, 39-41, 69-71, 104, 106, 130-7, 140,
           182, 188, 217, 248, 252, 253
39   23, 26, 28, 46
40   23, 27, 138-9
41   25, 27, 28, 39-40, 71-2, 106, 124, 130-7, 154-5,
           183-6, 222, 251, 254-5
42   25, 27, 28, 36, 39-40, 72-3, 106, 130-7, 218, 233,
           237, 242, 246, 251
43   23, 27, 138, 145-6, 194-5
44   25, 36, 39, 41, 73, 106, 108-11, 178, 189, 224,
           229
45   25, 74-5, 112-7
46A   22, 25, 75, 106, 117-9
46B   22, 25, 75-6, 106, 119-21, 189, 190-1, 228, 232
47   25, 76-7, 106, 121-2
48   25, 77, 106, 127-8
49   25, 77, 106, 128-30, 157-8, 178, 181, 188, 223,
           248
50   25, 78, 112-7
51   25, 78, 106, 117-9
52   25, 78-9, 106, 119-21, 232
53   25, 79, 106, 127-8, 232

54   23, 28
55   25, 79–80, 106, 128–30, 217, 220, 221, 252, 253
56   25, 27, 29, 36, 80–1, 112–7
57   25, 27, 29, 36, 39, 50, 81, 106, 108–11, 178, 229
58   25, 27, 29, 36, 39, 50, 51, 81–2, 106, 108–11
59   23, 27, 138–40, 194–6
60   23, 27, 49–51, 106, 172
61   25, 27, 51, 82–4, 106, 121–2, 177
62   23, 27, 138–9, 194

II

1   23, 27, 140
2   23, 27
3   23, 27, 28, 103, 140
4   23, 27, 140
5   23, 27
6   23, 27, 28, 46, 103, 104, 155–6, 177, 183–6, 188,
          190, 227, 230, 237
7   23, 27, 34, 101–2, 140, 191
8   23, 27
9   23, 27, 37
10   25, 36, 39, 84–5, 106, 130–7, 217, 223, 228, 233,
          243, 245–7, 249
11   25, 29, 85–7, 106, 123–7, 146, 153–4, 156, 171,
          173, 174, 179, 186, 219, 229–30, 237, 249,
          253
12   25, 88–9, 112–7
13   25, 89, 106, 108–11, 152–3, 167–9, 178, 224–6,
          229, 239
14   25, 90, 106, 128–30, 157, 218
15   25, 90, 106, 127–8, 218
16   25, 33, 35, 36, 39, 90–1, 106, 119–21
17   25, 91, 106, 117–9
18   23, 28, 50, 106, 127
19   25, 50, 91–2, 106, 108–11, 223

20   25, 92, 106, 117–9
21   25, 92–3, 106, 121–2
22   19, 25, 93, 106, 127–8, 220
23   25, 93, 106, 128–30, 178–9, 249, 251
24   25, 36, 39, 93–4, 106, 130–7, 170, 219, 235, 243
25   25, 95, 106, 117–9, 232
26   19, 25, 50–51, 95–6, 106, 119–21, 189, 229
27   25, 51, 96, 106, 127–8
28   25, 50–1, 97, 106, 128–30, 158, 189, 220, 221,
         248, 252
29   25, 36, 39, 97–8, 106, 130–7, 183, 219, 247, 249,
         252, 253
30   25, 36, 39, 50–1, 98–9, 112–7, 138, 230, 234